Researching IT in Education

Theory, practice and future directions

Edited by Anne McDougall
with John Murnane, Anthony Jones
and Nick Reynolds

Routledge
Taylor & Francis Group

LONDON AND NEW YORK

First published 2010
by Routledge
2 Park Square, Milton Park, Abingdon, Oxon OX14 4RN

Simultaneously published in the USA and Canada
by Routledge
270 Madison Avenue, New York, NY 10016

Routledge is an imprint of the Taylor & Francis Group, an informa business

Typeset in Garamond by GreenGate Publishing Services
Printed and bound in Great Britain by TJ International Ltd, Padstow, Cornwall

British Library Cataloguing in Publication Data
A catalogue record for this book is available from the British Library

Library of Congress Cataloging in Publication Data
Researching IT in education: theory, practice and future directions / edited by Anne McDougall,
with John Murnane, Anthony Jones and Nick Reynolds.
p. cm.
Includes index.
1. Educational technology. I. McDougall, Anne, 1945–
LB1028.3.R464 2010
371.33'4–dc22
2009025529

ISBN10: 0-415-56000-4 (hbk)
ISBN10: 0-415-56001-2 (pbk)
ISBN10: 0-203-86327-5 (ebk)

ISBN13: 978-0-415-56000-9 (hbk)
ISBN13: 978-0-415-56001-6 (pbk)
ISBN13: 978-0-203-86327-5 (ebk)

Contents

Editor's preface

This book is intended for everyone interested in, or undertaking research on, IT in education: academics, research students, teachers, policy makers and others. Our aim is to provoke thought and discussion among practising researchers, to suggest ways for research funding bodies to think about priorities in this area, and to assist novice researchers in this relatively new but already diverse and very complex area.

Serious criticisms of research on IT in education have been published in both the UK and the USA (see for example Underwood 2004). Based on these criticisms, Tony Jones and I prepared a discussion paper, 'Theory and history, questions and methodology: current and future issues in research into ICT in education' for a conference held by the International Federation for Information Processing (IFIP) in 2006. Some very lively discussion ensued, and the paper was published (McDougall and Jones 2006). This paper, a slightly modified version of which appears as Chapter 1, provided the stimulus for the writing of the book. The chapter contributors are members of the Education Working Groups of IFIP; most are from Working Group 3.3 (Research on Education Applications of Information Technology).

Although the writing project was undertaken under the auspices of the IFIP Working Group, the chapters are independent contributions by the individual authors and co-authors. No attempt is made to present an IFIP 'position' on research in this area. On the contrary, the chapters describe different approaches and perspectives, some of them contrasting markedly with one another. This is intended; there is no single 'correct' way to approach research in this area, and awareness of the range of possible methods and strategies is important for researchers.

The thirty-one contributors to the book come from ten countries: the UK, Germany, Italy, Greece, Switzerland, Iceland, Argentina, Botswana, New Zealand and Australia. Although the text does not represent a comprehensive international survey, the international nature of the material presented is evident in the illustrations and examples of research projects and findings from their own countries provided by many of the authors.

In this rapidly changing area, terminology fashions change almost as quickly as the technology does. The authors agreed that we would use the term 'information technology' (and the abbreviation IT) in education, to include the many terms that have been used to describe the use of computers and related technologies in educational contexts.

The book is organised into three sections. Following the introductory chapter is a section focused on Research Directions, beginning with a look at the history of IT in education and research findings to date. Margaret Cox reviews the development of research on IT in education, emphasising research on the impact on learning and teaching. Vince Ham illustrates the 20 years of change in IT applications in schools, and reviews research on policies and related issues. Deirdre Cook provides a brief outline of developments in theories of learning, examines roles and challenges for IT in the closely related area of assessment of learning, and raises some ethical issues and tensions within the area, suggesting some directions for research.

The next three chapters in this section present broad approaches to developing valuable research questions in this area. Based on his recent co-authorship of a major review of literature and the clear finding that providing resources is not enough to enhance learning and teaching, Bob Munro argues for a new research focus that identifies best practice and specifies how IT can best support learning. Geoff Romeo and Glenn Russell reject the notion that only scientific or evidence-based research involving randomised controlled trials will uncover 'what works'; they argue for research that both recognises the complex and contested nature of the use of IT in education, and better communicates research findings to practitioners. Andrew Fluck examines transformative uses of IT in schools, advocating research on the implications for redesign of curriculum.

This section is completed by two chapters looking at worthwhile directions for research in two more specific topic areas, and illustrating approaches to the refinement of research questions within a topic area. Anna Kristjánsdóttir notes that research on IT in mathematical learning has not been integrated with mainstream mathematics education research, and she outlines a learner-focused perspective for research in this area. Franziska Spring-Keller, acknowledging the importance of enjoyment in learning, criticises the lack of research on computer games and learning, and presents some research questions considered worthy of investigation in this area.

The second section of the book focuses on Theoretical Underpinnings to inform research design in IT in education. Mary Webb reviews models for studying pedagogy to develop our understanding of learning and teaching opportunities provided by technological developments. Steve Kennewell presents a perspective on activity and learning that extends cultural–historical activity theory (CHAT), arguing for analysis of the effect of IT in education in terms of the orchestration of its affordances and constraints by learners and teachers. Paul Nleya also discusses use of CHAT, this time in the context of work within developing countries, and complementing its use with Developmental Work Research and Change Laboratory conceptual frameworks. Bridget Somekh emphasises the importance of theory underpinning research design, and argues that research in IT in education should be grounded in theoretical knowledge about the process of innovation. Niki Davis looks at IT innovation in education from an ecological perspective, considering the classroom as an ecosystem nested within school and regional ecosystems, and advocates the development of research approaches based on interdisciplinary ecological theory.

The third section of the book explores Methodological Approaches and Applications for research on IT in education. Peter Twining examines key methodological trends in the IT in education literature, with a view to providing a better understanding of existing research findings and informing design of future research. Tony Jones outlines a multiple camera video-based methodology for data collection and analysis that addresses the complexity and multiplicity of variables in classroom-based research. In an environment where international collaboration for research is increasingly common, Rosa Maria Bottino and Michele Cerulli describe a methodological strategy for solving some of the problems of differences in theoretical frameworks and approaches among collaborating participants. Kleopatra Nikolopoulou outlines methods for studying young children's learning and development with IT, and considers some associated ethical issues. John Vincent and colleagues argue for students to be able to work in visual modes, demonstrating the benefits for some students by describing a project showing roles for IT in both the substance and the methodology of study in this area. The final two chapters are concerned with development of IT-based learning environments. Christine Bescherer and colleagues describe work on the development of intelligent computer-aided assessment systems, and suggest questions for future research in this area. Sigrid Schubert and colleagues describe a methodology for the development of IT systems to support learning of concepts in informatics.

I wish to acknowledge Dr Paul Nicholson of Deakin University, Australia, Chair of IFIP Working Group 3.3 at the time, for initiating and establishing this project. Thanks are also due to Professor Andrea Karpati of Eötvös Loránd University, Hungary, Vice-Chair of the Group at the time, for hosting a very productive authors' meeting in Budapest.

My co-editors, John, Tony and Nick, have been most generous with their time and expertise, working on chapter drafts concurrently with their heavy university teaching and research commitments. Thanks also to Mary Reynolds for checking parts of the text.

My early work on this book was done during a Visiting Fellowship at Lucy Cavendish College, Cambridge, in 2006. I thank the College for a most congenial academic environment for the work, as well as its support for the project during that time.

Anne McDougall
Melbourne, May 2009

McDougall, A. and Jones, A. (2006) 'Theory and history, questions and methodology: current and future issues in research into ICT in education', *Technology, Pedagogy and Education*, 15: 353–360.

Underwood, J. (2004) 'Research into information and communications technologies: where now?', *Technology, Pedagogy and Education*, 13: 135–145.

Contributors

Herminia Azinian, formerly Professor at the University of Buenos Aires, has focused her work on learning with ICT. She has designed and developed teacher training plans, courses and materials for the Argentinian Ministry of Education, and other government and private institutions.

Christine Bescherer is Professor of Mathematics Education at the University of Education Ludwigsburg, Institute for Mathematics and Computer Science. Her research interests include computers in mathematics classrooms, computer literacy for teachers, and semi-automatic assessment in mathematics.

Rosa Maria Bottino is Director of the Institute for Educational Technology of the Italian National Research Council (ITD-CNR). She has been active in IFIP for many years, receiving the IFIP Outstanding Service and Silver Core awards.

Michele Cerulli holds a research grant at the Institute of Educational Technology of the Italian National Research Council (ITD-CNR) of Genoa. His research concerns technology enhanced learning in mathematics and research teams' networking.

Deirdre Cook has worked as a classroom practitioner, a teacher educator with student and serving teachers and as a researcher, with a special interest in how various new technologies support and enhance learning. She currently works as a freelance researcher.

Margaret Cox is Professor of IT in Education in The Dental Institute and The Department for Education and Professional Studies, King's College London. Her 35 years' experience span many aspects of the uptake, use and implications of IT in education.

Niki Davis, Professor of E-Learning at the University of Canterbury College of Education, New Zealand, is an international leader in information and communication technologies (ICT) in teacher education, distance education, and related organisational changes. She has contributed to hundreds of publications.

Andrew E. Fluck is an education lecturer in information technology at the University of Tasmania. He prepares new teachers to be change-agents and conducts research into AlwaysOn learning, eExaminations, and the pedagogical impact of one-on-one computing in schools.

Stefan Freischlad received his diploma in Technical Informatics. He is research assistant at the Institute for Didactics of Informatics and E-learning, University of Siegen. His research interests are media competences and informatics in secondary education, focused on the Internet.

Vince Ham is a Founding Director of CORE Education, an independent, not-for-profit research centre specialising in e-learning and teacher professional development. His research interests are (practitioner) research methods, large-scale programme evaluation, and the effective integration of new educational technologies.

Anthony Jones has taught in primary and secondary schools, and now works at the University of Melbourne. Research interests include making teaching more effective through IT, and IT-enhanced learning for students absent from school for extended periods because of illness.

Steve Kennewell works at Swansea Metropolitan University, UK. His background is in teaching ICT and mathematics in secondary school, and he has worked as a teacher educator and researcher in ICT Education for twenty years.

Ulrich Kortenkamp is Professor of Computer Science and Media Education at the University of Education Karlsruhe, Germany. His research interests are computer-assisted teaching and learning of mathematics and sciences, computational and combinatorial geometry.

Anna Kristjánsdóttir is Professor of Mathematics Education at University of Iceland and Agder University in Norway. Engaged in research on ICT in learning since the 1970s, she initiated ICT as a compulsory part of teacher education in the early 1980s.

Anne McDougall is Principal Fellow at the University of Melbourne. Her publications include early school textbooks on computer studies, computer science and programming, and research books on learning programming, technology-rich school environments and selection and use of educational software.

Wolfgang Müller is Professor in the Media Education and Visualization Group at the University of Education Weingarten, Germany. His research interests include media education and e-learning, interactive storytelling and serious games, human-computer interaction, and information visualisation.

Robert K. Munro is Reader at the University of Strathclyde in Scotland and has been involved in educational research and teacher training in IT for over twenty years. A major interest is the creation of software/courseware for use in geography and history teaching.

Kleopatra Nikolopoulou works as adjunct lecturer in the Department of Early Childhood Education, University of Athens. Her research interests include uses of IT in education and their effects on learning. She has published articles in journals and conference proceedings.

Paul T. Nleya is Senior Lecturer and Head of the Educational Technology Department at the University of Botswana. He has published in local and international refereed journals. He serves as vice co-Chairperson of the Education Commission of The World Technology Forum (WITFOR).

Geoff Romeo is Associate Dean (Teaching) in the Faculty of Education at Monash University. His research focuses on design of technology-rich learning environments. In 2004 he was awarded state and national prizes for his leadership in IT in education.

Glenn Russell is Senior Lecturer in Education at Monash University. His research focus is on the ways in which IT can transform teaching and learning. Recently he jointly authored a book entitled *Transforming Learning with ICT: Making it Happen*.

Sigrid Schubert has been Professor of Didactics of Informatics and E-learning since 1998 at the University of Siegen. She received her doctoral degree in informatics in 1988. Her research interests are informatics and ICT in education, lifelong learning and e-learning.

Bridget Somekh is Emeritus Professor of Education, Manchester Metropolitan University. Her books include *Pedagogy and Learning with ICT: Researching the Art of Innovation* (Routledge 2007), *Research Methods in the Social Sciences* (with C. Lewin, Sage 2005) and *Action Research* (OU Press 2006).

Christian Spannagel is Assistant Professor for Computer Science and Mathematics Education, University of Education Ludwigsburg, Germany. Research interests are process-oriented computer science education, experimental computer science education, Web 2.0 in the classroom, computer-assisted teaching and learning of mathematics.

Franziska Spring-Keller was a doctoral student of the Educational Engineering Lab, University of Zurich, and graduated in May 2009. She is also a visiting scholar with Professor Kurt Squire and the Games, Learning and Society group, University of Wisconsin-Madison.

Peer Stechert is a researcher at the Institute for Didactics of Informatics and E-learning, University of Siegen. A member of IFIP Working Group 3.1 Informatics and ICT in Secondary Education, his research interest is understanding of informatics systems in education.

Peter Twining is Co-Director of the Centre for Research in Education and Educational Technology (CREET). His research is focused on the development of schome (not school, not home, schome – the education system for the information age). See http://www.schome.ac.uk/.

John Vincent is a Clinical Specialist in the Master of Teaching programme, Melbourne Graduate School of Education. His research highlights roles played by cognitive style in computer-generated multimodal text production, and recent work investigated effective pedagogies with interactive technologies.

Mary Webb is Senior Lecturer in Information Technology in Education at King's College London. She has researched the use of IT in learning and teaching since computers first appeared in schools, and is co-author of *ICT Inside the Black Box*.

Chapter 1

Theory and history, questions and methodology

Issues in research into information technology in education[1]

Anne McDougall and Anthony Jones
The University of Melbourne, Australia

Introduction

In 2004 the journal *Technology, Pedagogy and Education* published a special issue in response to criticisms of Information Technology research in education. The editorial for that issue referred to the 'perceived weakness in ICT research . . . firstly to identify some of the key questions that need to be answered in this area, and secondly to increase awareness of existing and new research techniques available to support the [ICT research] community in its work.' (Underwood 2004: 139). This book aims to make a contribution in this regard, examining the issues of theoretical underpinnings to research in IT in education, the problem of neglect of the history of this endeavour, the importance of theory and the history in the development of research questions, and the selection of appropriate methodologies for attempting to answer these questions.

Theory

In her editorial Underwood writes:

> Whilst it can clearly be demonstrated that there is excellent research in this sub-domain, concerns about the lack of theoretical grounding and the individual, often idiosyncratic, nature of much of the activity have been cited as weaknesses of our research. Education research in general does not always value the significance of work in ICT, and whether the criticism is valid or not, we need to address this perception. . . . The challenge is to find an integrative theoretical framework across an area of

1 Adapted from McDougall, A. and Jones, A. (2006) 'Theory and history, questions and methodology: current and future issues in research into ICT in education', *Technology, Pedagogy and Education*, 15: 353–360.

research that is fragmented by specialist concerns, in order to build intellectual bridges both with colleagues within education itself and also within other disciplines.

(Underwood 2004: 135)

The most important and fundamental role for the use of IT in education research is the provision of a huge increase in our power to study the processes of learning, and as a consequence to improve approaches to and strategies for teaching. For this endeavour there are extensive theoretical frameworks that already underpin much of the activity in IT use in education, if not our research. Learning theorists have provided an extensive literature attempting to elucidate the processes of learning, in individuals and in group and social settings. Moreover, since these theories are just those on which mainstream educational research is based, a focus on learning in IT educational research would immediately address the 'failure of the IT educational community to make contact with the central body of educational research' (Underwood 2004: 139).

The contribution that IT education research can make here is substantial. The broader educational research community has undertaken much work to substantiate, modify and develop theoretical work, but with the research tools and methods available thus far it could be argued that we still understand less about learning processes than physicists do about an equally fundamental research challenge – the workings of the nucleus. But just as improvements in technology, particularly in techniques and methods of measurement, have empowered nuclear physicists' research, so can IT provide a marked increase in our power to study learning. This is so in many ways. Where with pencil and paper technologies we could generally study only the finished version of student-developed artefacts – essays, art work, musical compositions, and so on – the capacity of software to enable recording and saving of stages in the development of an artefact enables collection of data, providing much greater insight into the process of its development. And subsequent data-focused discussions of this process with the student can reveal additional information for the researcher concerning the processes of cognitive development in individuals. Further, the development of online learning communities affords rich environments for studying some of the more social aspects of learning, and classroom use of interactive whiteboards for collaborative work opens up new possibilities for investigating in far greater detail than previously practicable the highly complex processes of learning through classroom interactions. Thus there is immense potential for research work in the sub-discipline of IT in education to make a substantial contribution to the refinement of currently accepted theories about learning, and perhaps to develop new theoretical understandings of these highly complex processes.

History

The sub-discipline of IT in education is not itself devoid of theoretical work; however, our area, more than any other the authors can think of, seems determined to neglect or deliberately ignore its own history. '[S]ome ICT research reported in the journals lacks a sense of history. . . . [I]n the excitement of the new we appear not to want to look back and learn from the lessons of the past.' (Underwood 2004: 140). The experience of one of the authors, who recently showed a draft paper to a senior colleague for comment, supports this; the colleague turned straight to the end of the paper and immediately commented, 'But you've got some references from the 1980s in here!'

One important example of theoretical work specific to our area is found in the writings of Seymour Papert (1980, 1993). For instance, his conjecture that learners in computer-rich environments with powerful learning software might develop understanding of abstract ideas in ways that cause significant questioning of some of Piaget's work is one that warrants further rigorous investigation (McDougall 1990), as is his theory of constructionist learning (Harel and Papert 1991). Another example, also from the Massachusetts Institute of Technology, is the computationally influenced model of mind and learning presented by Marvin Minsky (1987); although almost purely theoretical at the time it was developed, more recent technologies can make investigation of this work possible.

Our argument that using IT empowers research into learning is not new. Sylvia Weir (1984, 1987) referred to the 'mind-mirroring' nature of the computer, and described its power as an 'empirical window' in research on individual differences in styles and approaches to learning.

In the UK during the 1980s, major government projects supported work in universities and other centres to collaborate with teachers in the design and development of software specifically for schools, and to provide teacher professional development in the curriculum integration and use of these materials. Software developed by groups such as those at King's College Chelsea, the Shell Centre at Nottingham University, and the Advisory Unit for Computer Based Education at Hatfield, and by individuals such as Mike Matson, incorporated ingenious ways of exploiting the technology to offer learning experiences that would be difficult or impossible otherwise. Some examples are simulation programs designed to enable students to actively investigate dangerous or complex scientific, mathematical or social processes, computer-based games of many kinds that provided bases for class discussion and role play, and data bases used to focus students' development of investigative skills in history and social studies. Many of these were supplemented with sophisticated print materials stimulating valuable on- and off-computer activities. Early work in Australia also included the development of innovative and powerful educational software; examples are the suite of genetics programs developed by Judith Kinnear, and Sandra Wills's *First Fleet* (Wills *et al.* 2002).

Because of developments in technology this software has in most cases been discarded (*First Fleet* is one exception). With it has gone much of the knowledge about educational software design and the computer's potential to support and enhance learning. Readers will note that most of the software used in schools today is free of curriculum content and comprises tools designed for non-educational contexts. Much of the teaching skill and educational wisdom in the design of these earlier programs would still be relevant for learners today. But instead of studying the early work in this area and investigating ways in which more sophisticated technologies can be used to build on this thinking, we disdain the history of our discipline because early computers were inferior to our present technologies. As a result, we lose valuable findings from research and development work, findings on which we should be building current knowledge about the educational uses of IT and the potential of new technologies to enhance the processes of learning and teaching.

Research questions

In a paper titled 'If technology is the answer, what's the question? Research to help make the case for why we use technology in teaching', Roblyer (2004) states that 'We know that technology uses offer unique benefits and could have even more impact under the right circumstances.' She continues by asking, 'Why have we not provided research that captures this impact and helps justify the expense and difficulty of using technology?' (Roblyer 2004: 1), and states similarly elsewhere that 'Future research must address squarely the question of why teachers should use technology-based methods' (Roblyer and Knezek 2003: 63). Herein, we would argue, lie two problems. First, research that 'helps justify the expense and difficulty of using technology' must pre-empt its own findings; second, such research inevitably asks technocentric (Papert 1987) questions.

Roblyer's claim that we know that we can justify the expense and difficulty of using technology in teaching is not necessarily justified. We agree with Underwood, who writes that 'The strength of opinion expressed by the pro and anti research groups, each citing evidence to support their position, presents a confused picture of the value of ICT to education' (Underwood 2004: 137).

'The process of integrating technology effectively into education comes with a high price tag. Educators and policy makers look to educational technology research to help supply a solid rationale for why these funds are well spent.' (Ringstaff and Kelly 2002, cited in Roblyer and Knezek 2003: 63). Again we look to Underwood for a rejoinder.

[T]oo many of the articles . . . focus on the technology rather than the impacts of technology on human endeavour. . . . What is needed here is a

shift of focus which allows that the technology should always be of secondary importance. If it is of primary importance, then it could be argued the research should sit in computer science rather than education.
(Underwood 2004: 140)

The predominance of investigations based on research questions that make no contribution to theoretical refinement or development is, presumably, for pragmatic reasons. It is easier to undertake, and to obtain funding for research that might justify technology's expense than it is to investigate the more fundamental questions about learning and teaching processes. The former can usually be addressed using one-off survey and statistical techniques, while the latter generally require longer periods of data collection, larger quantities of data possibly with a small signal-to-noise ratio, and considerably more complex methods of analysis. Quality research in this area cannot be done with 'quick and dirty' methodologies; it requires harder work and more sophisticated data collection and analysis techniques to deal with the high levels of complexity of the processes we are investigating.

Methodology

The earliest research on learning with computers focused inevitably on the cognitive development of individuals, based on observations of individual students working in various software environments. Following the original work of Vygotsky, it is now widely acknowledged that the conversation, questioning, explanation and negotiation of meaning of an adult and a learner's peers play an important role for learning (Fosnot 1996). Vygotsky and his followers emphasise the central position of language and dialogue in human culture and cognition; they argue that learning occurs as people participate in shared endeavours with others (Duffy and Cunningham 1996). These social learning theories have been increasingly influential in education (Hall and Higgins 2005), and most teachers consider facilitation of collaborative work and discussion an important aspect of teaching (Watson 1993, cited in Cogill 2002). However, the complexity of interactions in social learning environments has meant that these theories are particularly difficult to investigate. An attempt has been made by Wegerif *et al.* (1998) who characterised three 'types of talk' as a way of understanding social thinking and the cognitive dimension of children's talk around computers. However, work of this kind has hitherto been rare, not only in educational computing but also in broader educational research.

Sophisticated approaches to collection and analysis of complex data are needed to undertake the kind of research we are advocating. Mercer *et al.* (2004) offer some valuable approaches in this regard. Chapters in a later section of the book provide a range of such methodological examples.

Conclusion

Our purpose here has been to address several of the issues raised in commentaries critical of research in IT in education. In response to concerns about a lack of theoretical grounding of research in this area we argue that, since the most important role for this research is to contribute to the understanding of the processes of learning, with a view to informing teaching strategies and approaches to developing educational software, the theoretical frameworks used in mainstream education research are appropriate underpinnings for research in the sub-discipline as well. We support criticism of the neglect of the history of IT in education and the consequent failure to build on previous theoretical work specific to the sub-discipline, research findings from early studies, and pedagogical and design knowledge that is still relevant although developed with earlier technologies. Technology-focused studies using survey techniques to evaluate or justify use of IT in educational settings, undertaken to provide information required by administrators and funding bodies, do not constitute the fundamental research needed to refine and develop theory and practice in education. Research questions investigating issues of learning and teaching are needed for quality research that will advance knowledge and inform improved practice. The types of research studies advocated here are generally more complex, difficult and time consuming to undertake than simple quantitative surveys and evaluations, and require more complex methodological approaches.

References

Cogill, J. (2002) 'How is the interactive whiteboard being used in the primary school and how does this affect teachers and teaching?' Online. Available HTTP: <http://www.virtuallearning.org.uk/whiteboards/> (accessed 11 March 2009).

Duffy, T.M. and Cunningham, D.J. (1996) 'Constructivism: implications for the design and delivery of instruction', in D.H. Jonassen (ed.) *Handbook of Research for Educational Communications and Technology*, New York: Macmillan.

Fosnot, C.T. (ed.) (1996) *Constructivism: Theory, Perspectives and Practice*, New York: Teachers College Press.

Hall, I. and Higgins, S. (2005) 'Primary school students' perceptions of interactive whiteboards', *Journal of Computer Assisted Learning*, 21: 102–117.

Harel, I. and Papert, S. (1991) *Constructionism*, Norwood, New Jersey: Ablex.

McDougall, A. (1990) 'Children, recursion and Logo programming: an investigation of Papert's conjecture about the variability of Piagetian stages in computer-rich cultures', in A. McDougall and C. Dowling (eds) *Computers in Education*, Amsterdam: Elsevier Science Publishers.

Mercer, N., Littleton, K. and Wegerif, R. (2004) 'Methods for studying the processes of interaction and collaborative activity in computer-based educational activities', *Technology, Pedagogy and Education*, 13: 195–211.

Minsky, M. (1987) *The Society of Mind*, London: Heinemann.

Papert, S. (1980) *Mindstorms: Children, Computers and Powerful Ideas*, Brighton: Harvester.

—— (1987) 'Computer criticism vs. technocentric thinking', *Educational Researcher*, 16: 22–30.

—— (1993) *The Children's Machine*, New York: Basic Books.

Roblyer, M.D. (2004) 'If technology is the answer, what's the question? Research to help make the case for why we use technology in teaching', *Technology and Teacher Education Annual, 2004*. Charlottesville, VA: Association for the Advancement of Computing.

Roblyer, M.D. and Knezek, G.A. (2003) 'New millennium research for educational technology: a call for a national research agenda', *Journal of Research on Technology in Education*, 36: 60–76.

Underwood, J. (2004) 'Research into information and communications technologies: where now?' *Technology, Pedagogy and Education*, 13: 135–145.

Wegerif, R., Mercer, N. and Dawes, L. (1998) 'Software design to support discussion in the primary curriculum', *Journal of Computer Assisted Learning*, 14: 199–211.

Weir, S. (1984) 'Logo as an empirical window', in R. Sorkin (ed.) *Pre-Proceedings of the 1984 National Logo Conference*, Cambridge, MA: Massachusetts Institute of Technology.

—— (1987) *Cultivating Minds*, New York: Harper & Row.

Wills, S., Ip, A. and Bunnett, A. (2002) 'Description of use of First Fleet Online Role Play'. Online. Available HTTP: <http://www.learningdesigns.uow.edu.au/exemplars/info/LD24/index.html> (accessed 24 January 2009).

Part I

Research directions

Reviewing the history and looking forward

Chapter 2

The changing nature of researching information technology in education

Margaret Cox
King's College, The University of London

Introduction

The initial introduction of IT in education in the 1960s was based on two main thrusts that influenced the early focus of research in this area. First, universities and national bodies recognised the need to provide a growing number of IT experts to work in the IT industry, and second, pioneering educators saw the potential for new technologies to enhance teaching and learning in other subjects (Beauchamp 2003, Cox 2005). Initially, IT resources available in education were invested in the teaching of computer science at university and later at school level (Rushby 1983). However, once computer use became of interest in other subjects, research into IT in education focused on the effects of particular computer programs on students' learning (cf. Suppes 1968, Bork 1981) rather than the effectiveness of teaching computer science. One of the main purposes in the 1960s and 1970s for using IT in education in many countries, was to enhance existing teaching and learning practices or to enhance the existing curriculum. The research and development of IT in educational settings was therefore often intertwined with the design of the IT tools themselves and provided feedback for improving the software design (Reeves 2008).

Three main strands have been shown to be important regarding the impact of IT on education and society (Cox 2005) resulting in the diversification of educational research in this area:

* *Technological developments*: The developments in IT and associated communications software and ever decreasing costs have led to the migration of IT from industry into education, from university to school, and from commerce into the classroom.
* *Educational initiatives*: Major government policies in many countries resulted in programmes to promote and support the teaching and uses of IT in education. These programmes were enhanced by local government, industrial and commercial initiatives for the education sectors and individual initiatives contributing to and influencing the growth of IT in education.

- *Applications to teaching and learning*: The growth in the IT industry itself has resulted in a relentless growth in the numbers of IT specialists needed to serve this industry, and thus in IT courses in education both at school and university level, and in the use of IT to enhance teaching and learning in other subjects in all sectors of education.

These complementary developments, alongside the expansion and diversification of the broader field of educational research, have resulted in an evolution of researching IT in education. Research foci have diversified from measuring the impact on students' learning, to measuring the effects of teachers' pedagogies on IT use and integration (Webb and Cox 2005), the impact of the institutional culture on the uptake of IT in schools (Fullan 1991, 2003), the attitudes of teachers and students towards new technologies (Katz and Offir 1994, Knezek and Christensen 2008) and comparisons across different countries (Pelgrum and Plomp 2008, Plomp *et al.* 2009). However, there are still many limitations to the research methods used, the contexts in which such research takes place and the conclusions drawn from research studies (Furr *et al.* 2005, Cox and Marshall 2007). This chapter reviews the research undertaken over the last forty years to study the impact of IT in education, drawing on evidence from many previous research studies.

The impact of IT on students' learning

The early educational computing software was either based on tutorial style drill and practice programs following Skinner's theory of programmed learning, or simulations based on Piaget's constructivist learning theories, which allowed the learner to investigate hypotheses and explore factorial relationships. These programs included simulating laboratory experiments or other scientific processes that took too long or were too difficult, dangerous or costly for students to perform (McKenzie *et al.* 1978, Cox 1993). These same educational philosophies were applied to many Computer Assisted Learning programs throughout the 1970s, 1980s and 1990s (Watson 1993), until IT educational resources enabled the development of larger and more generic applications such as computer-based modelling and online learning (Reeves 2008).

Early research into the impact of computer simulations and modelling on learning by Papert (1980), Kurland and Pea (1983), Ogborn and Wong (1984) and many others, found that this type of software enabled pupils to conduct investigations of scientific processes, that were otherwise beyond the limits of their mathematical abilities. They could also construct scientific relationships which more accurately represented the world around them, and carry out investigations taking on the role of scientists. The techniques for measuring the impact of IT on learning included developing and applying pre- and post-concept based tests, designing specific scientific paper-based tasks which were then assessed, and observing and analysing the specific strategies that students used when working with the materials.

Using these techniques, research such as that conducted by the Tools for Exploratory Learning Project in the UK (Mellar *et al*. 1994) comparing simulations with more generic modelling software, showed that pupils were able to investigate much more complex models provided in simulations than to build their own. The Impact project (Watson 1993), which studied the effects of IT on over 2,000 primary and secondary pupils using a range of paper-based tests, pre- and post-tests, specific tasks and observations, found a statistically significant positive impact of IT on children's learning in English, mathematics and geography. This impact, however, depended upon the nature of the learning tasks and the pedagogical practices of the teacher (Cox 1993).

Ten years later, the ImpaCT2 project, also in the UK (Harrison *et al*. 2002), found that there was a statistically significant relationship between the use of IT and national test results for primary pupils (aged 7–11) in English. It was also found that the highest reported use at this age level was in English, with over 61 per cent of the pupils reporting that they used IT in English for at least some weeks in a term. However, only in the case studies did the research team identify the actual types of IT being used, so it was not possible to identify the type of IT use that had the greatest impact on the pupils' results in the range of subjects investigated (Cox and Abbott 2004).

There is also a growing body of research evidence related to the motivational effects of IT, showing that IT makes learners' lessons more interesting, more enjoyable, and more important (Cox 1999) and increases self-confidence (Knezek and Christensen 2008). Additionally, there is a large body of psychological literature based on theories and empirical evidence about the attitudinal effects on people's abilities to use IT in the workplace which has implications for teachers' practices and pedagogies (see, for example, Davis *et al*. 1989, Ajzen 1988, Compeau and Higgins 1999, Koutromanos 2005, Knezek and Christensen 2008). Evidence from these studies shows that people are more likely to use new technologies if they have a positive attitude towards them and perceive them to be useful in their work and for their professional development.

Specific examples of research into the positive effects that different types of IT can have on students' learning include:

- using data-logging to develop students' thinking skills (Barton 1997, Hennessy *et al*. 2005)
- computer-based modelling to enhance students' construction, representation and interpretation of knowledge (Brna 1990, 1991, Mellar *et al*. 1994, McDougall 2002, Cox 2003, Simpson *et al*. 2005).

Qualitative studies include measuring students' learning through collaboration:

- in pairs or groups (Watson 1993, Crook 2001)
- in whole class use with an interactive whiteboard working together online (Cox and Webb 2004)
- working on projects and evaluating each others' work (Stacey 2002, McAlister *et al.* 2004).

However, the extent of these benefits to learning depend upon the level of access to IT resources as well as the types being used (Scrimshaw 2004, Pelgrum and Plomp 2008), the actual types of use, and the teachers' knowledge, beliefs and pedagogical decisions (Laurillard 1992, Wild and Braid 1996, Cox 1997, Webb and Cox 2005).

The large body of research evidence using a range of research methods now spanning more than forty years has resulted in some common understandings of the affordances which different IT types can provide for students' learning (Voogt and Knezek 2008). Using Table 2.1 derived by Webb and Cox (2005), it is clear that the potential beneficial impact of IT on individual students' learning is very dependent upon the level of access, but furthermore upon the specific types of IT use, whether in school, university or at home. In parallel with a large number of studies of the effects of specific types of IT use on students' learning in many countries (Cox 2008), since the mid-1980s there have been studies on the uptake and use of IT in many different educational settings, discussed in the next section.

Research into IT uptake and use in education

As computers and IT resources became more widespread in the 1980s, many studies of the impact of IT on learning also showed that the level of such impact and the possible benefits to learning were very dependent upon the availability of IT resources in schools and other educational settings. Since the 1960s there have been more than ten Worldwide International Statistical Comparative Educational Assessments in education (Pelgrum and Plomp 1991, Pelgrum and Plomp 2008) that have involved large-scale quantitative surveys and tests. These studies have enabled different countries to determine what their status is, regarding for example, the relative investment in school IT resources, the level of teacher training, and the use of IT in different subjects. In such studies, the instruments are developed and piloted by a large team of researchers for use in different educational settings and countries, ensuring a high level of consistency and reliability. Results from these studies enable researchers and policy makers to assess their own progress regarding IT in education and the relative effectiveness of their past policies. It is more difficult, however, to determine the effects of IT on teaching and learning in relation to other countries because of the widely varying national priorities (Cox 2005).

Table 2.1 Affordances for students' learning (Webb and Cox 2005)

Categories of affordances	Learning supported	Type of IT used
Researching information	Acquiring knowledge, consolidating understanding	Internet, web browsers, webcams, video conferencing, content-specific CD-ROMs.
Preparing presentations and producing materials	Organising ideas, reflecting, reviewing, evaluating, consolidating understanding	PowerPoint.
Presenting	Presentation skills, organising ideas, reflecting, reviewing, evaluating	PowerPoint, interactive whiteboard.
Visually representing processes / ideas	Understanding dynamic processes	Simulations, animations.
Feedback	Knowing what areas need more learning, thinking, predicting	Simulations, mind mapping software, interactive whiteboard.
Changing variable values	Understanding relationships between variables, predicting, hypothesising	Simulations, spreadsheets.
Brainstorming	Thinking, linking ideas	Interactive whiteboard, mind mapping software.
Redrafting	Organising ideas, reflecting, reviewing	Word processors, interactive whiteboard.
Recording notes	Thinking about relationships	Word processors, interactive whiteboard.
Designing	Problem solving, decision making	Control software.
Making a drawing	Thinking about what they already know about composition	Drawing package.
Taking turns	Social skills, sharing	Roamer, shared computer.
Broadening experience	Generalising from examples, extending their ideas, classifying, generating new ideas	Internet, web browsers, webcams, video conferencing.
Drawing graphs	Thinking about relationships between variables	Spreadsheets.

In the UK, biennual surveys have been done by the Department of Education and Science (now Department for Children, Schools and Families) e.g. in 1985/6, 1987/8, 1989/90, 1991/2 and 2003/4 to assess the impact of government initiatives on the uptake and level of use of computers in British schools (DES 1991), to see changes that have taken place over specific periods, and how these have affected the actual uptake and use by teachers in schools. One common finding is that the actual integrated use of IT by teachers is much lower than might have been expected from so many sustained national and international programmes (Plomp *et al*. 2009). The uptake and integration of IT is so difficult to achieve, and to research, because it is extremely complex for teachers to learn, is always changing, and depends upon so many different curriculum priorities and implementation barriers.

There have been a growing number of studies of the uses of IT by children in both formal and informal settings. Investigating twenty children's experiences using computer games in mathematical contexts, Yelland (2003) studied the ways in which they chose and evaluated computer software in the home and at school. This type of study, using qualitative methods of observation and interviews, is widely used by researchers of IT in education but has been criticised because of the limited applicability of the outcomes to the wider population of learners (Cox and Marshall 2007). A larger study on young people's home and school IT use (Kent and Facer 2004), involving a questionnaire survey of 1,800 children in England, interviews of 190 children and visits to eleven families, focused on computer use and not on the consequent impact on students' learning. Although governments are anxious to know how widely IT resources are being used, such studies do not give any information about whether such uses of IT might benefit the learner more than others which they have not chosen to use.

There are still many unanswered questions about the benefits to children of using IT outside formal educational settings. What is more widely known is that the effectiveness of IT use in formal settings such as schools and colleges is very dependent upon the teacher.

Researching the impact of the teacher

When IT was first introduced in education, it was not understood that its effectiveness would be significantly determined and in many cases restricted by the beliefs, attitudes and practices of the teachers. A large area of educational research has now evolved to investigate how IT use affects the ways in which we teach (cf. Cox and Webb 2004, Law and Plomp 2003), the pedagogical beliefs and practices of teachers (Cox and Webb 2004, McDougall and Jones 2006), the enablers and barriers to the use of IT in education (Scrimshaw 2004, Jones 2004) and the impact on practice of the professional development of teachers.

Previous research into innovation and change has shown that the adoption of new technologies in education is a complex process involving theoretical, practical and reflective engagement (Hargreaves and Fullan 1992). This includes the professional development of teachers which both changes and is changed by the organisational context in which it takes place (Desforges 1995).

Teachers' knowledge and beliefs about how students learn will significantly affect how they approach and deliver teaching (Cox and Webb 2004, Moore 2004), including when using IT (Crook 2001, Webb 2008). There is also evidence of possible discrepancies between the beliefs of teachers and the research findings regarding effective pedagogy with IT (e.g. Scrimshaw 2004). Scrimshaw identified a recurring contrast regarding IT use between teacher-centred and student-centred models of teaching. Researchers have also shown that teachers' beliefs are resistant to change, because they are deeply rooted in their own experiences and are usually unconscious (Pajares 1992, Yerrick *et al.* 1997) and changes in belief follow rather than precede changes in behaviour (Fullan 1991). These complex interrelationships between beliefs and pedagogical change in relation to IT use may explain the limited uptake of IT so far, and the limited impact of professional development to date on teachers' abilities to adopt IT in their teaching.

The effects of teachers' professional development

There are many studies that have shown that once teachers have finished their initial training they do not take the initiative to improve their practice and learn new skills. Desforges (1995), in a literature review of the shift from novice to expert teachers, found that many teachers were perfectly satisfied with their practices and a considerable effort would be necessary to create the possibilities of restructuring knowledge about teaching and learning in the face of experience. If teachers see no need to change or question their current professional practice, they may not take up the use of IT in their teaching despite receiving additional IT training. These issues are difficult to research and often overlooked when evaluating the uptake of IT in education.

The attitudes of teachers towards IT and their willingness and ability to use IT have been reported in a range of empirical studies (Knezek and Christensen 2008). An investigation into the effects of attitudes on the use of IT and its perceived value to the users revealed a significant relationship between the IT abilities of the teacher and their perceived value of IT to pupils' learning (Preston *et al.* 2000). However, empirical studies (e.g. Cox 1993, Rhodes 1999, Downes *et al.* 2001) have shown that short courses to train teachers in the uses of IT have mostly focused on technical aspects of IT. In many IT professional development courses, teachers are not taught how to revise their pedagogical practices, how to replace other traditional lessons without depleting curriculum coverage, and so on (Voogt 2008). After teachers had attended such short courses, they often still did not know how to use

IT for teaching pupils; they only knew how to run certain software packages, how to access the Internet, or how to print documents.

Much research by Fullan (1991), Scrimshaw (2004) and Cox and Webb (2004) and others has shown that the most effective way to bring about the adoption of an innovation in schools is to engage the whole school in a democratic process of planning change. This means that all the teachers are involved in the decision to adopt IT in the school and are supportive of any individual teacher going on a course and willing to learn from their new knowledge and skills when they return.

From these and many other similar results it is evident that researching the impact of IT in education requires: an understanding of the complex nature of IT itself; the development and use of theories underpinning psychological and sociological aspects relating to the teacher, the learner and the educational settings; and research methods that take account of the complexity of the variables in any specific study. Furthermore, IT is not a static technology, so researchers need to keep abreast of technological developments and how these might affect education.

The slippery technology and changing perceptions and practices

A major factor that makes researching IT in education so interesting but extremely difficult is the ever changing technology itself. Table 2.2, developed from an earlier one published in 2005 (Cox 2005), shows just how many changes have occurred in the last ten years in the field of computer technologies.

As a result of this ever-changing technology, new literacies (perceptions and understandings linked to new modes of presentation and representations) are changing the emphasis and the balance of the production, content and meaning of educational resources; this is often not understood by teachers and researchers. These changes often require a recodifying and consequent new understanding of knowledge and changes in teacher-pupil relationships caused by the autonomous nature of many IT-education environments.

These lead to conflict for the teacher regarding whether to confine oneself to simple comfortable uses, stagnating in the use of IT, or to open up the use to the wide range of technologies that arrive in society at an alarming rate.

These conflicts facing education require substantial changes in the ways in which teachers are trained to use new technologies, changes in the formal school curriculum, and a reorganisation of curriculum time, teachers' professional development, home-school links and pedagogical practices. All of these open up new research foci and many challenging research questions.

Table 2.2 The evolving IT technology (based on Cox 2005)

Dates/era	Technological developments
1822–1833	Invention of the difference engine for calculating large mathematical numbers, the forerunner of computers, by Charles Babbage
1837–1896	The introduction of the telephone, cables and communications technologies
1950–1967	Development of large-scale mainframe valve-based analogue computers
	Development of miniature electronic components (transistors and diodes) and circuitry leading to the large-scale digital computer
	Increase in memory and processing capacity
1968	The creation of the Internet – ARPANET
1970–1977	Development of real-time interactive computers
	User graphics online computer terminals available at £5,000
	Internet connections for some schools
	Remote access to computers from different locations
	International networks of computers through JANET (Joint Academic Network)
	Forerunners of desktop computers: e.g. Hewlett Packard, Horizon
1977–1980	Miniaturisation of computers and components – production of small desktop computers:
	Horizon: £5,000, Apple II: £1,000, RML 380z: £2,000,
	IBM series: £2,000
	Acorn atom computer, Acorn BBC-Model A (8k of memory)
	Acorn BBC-Model B (32k of memory): £400
	Move from tape-based storage to disk-based storage of computer programs
	Prestel/Teletext – commercial and educational information provided online
1980–1984	First Apple Macintosh produced: £1,500
	Development of fibre optics facilitating fast and large-scale communication
	Development of a range of input and output devices for education, including:
	Concept keyboard/graphics tablets
	Quinkey keyboard
	Robot turtle
	Tracker ball
	Touch screens
	Speech input and output
1985–1987	Microsoft windows launched
	More powerful cheaper personal microcomputers
	IBM PC (256k of storage memory, 32k processor memory) £1,500
	Mac II (256k of storage memory, 32k processor memory) £1,000
	Invention of the World Wide Web by Tim Berners-Lee
1987–1990	New external storage devices
	CD-ROM
	Interactive video
	Plug-in memory cards

(Continued)

Table 2.2 (Continued)

Dates/era	Technological developments

1990–1995	Introduction of laptop computers
	Major increase in storage memory devices and reduced costs (>1Gbyte for £40)
	    Spread of wireless computer technologies
	    Wireless computer networks
	    Air-mouse
	Development of video-conferencing

1996–1999	Development of the electronic whiteboard Introduction of Personal Digital Assistants (PDAs) Universal growth of the uses of the Internet in education
2000–2004	Expansion of mobile hand-held technologies: PDAs, mobile phones, MP3 players Development of molecular computing technology Development of quantum computers Further increases in processing and storage of personal computers (5G storage memory, >256 MHz processor)
2005–2009	Thin client technologies in schools and colleges Development of haptics devices for use in education Development of molecular computing technology Development of quantum computers Further increases in processing and storage of personal computers and minituarisation (10G storage memory, >256k processor) Widespread access to wireless networks Web2 technology Social software environments: e.g. Wikipedia, Second Life

Conclusions

The rapid growth of IT in society has resulted in governments prioritising IT in education and wanting rapid answers to its potential for teaching and learning. Yet one important lesson to date from the studies reviewed here is that it takes a long time to measure the impact of IT on teaching and learning, and many teachers are reticent about using IT substantially in their curriculum. This is at odds with the constant pressure from governments to obtain quick answers to what is a very complex educational environment.

Researchers of IT in education themselves come from diverse backgrounds, some with an IT strength emanating from computer science, some with an artificial intelligence background based on psychological theories, and some with a sociology background relating to the institutionalisation and cultural influences on IT in education. What is evident from this review is that, without a clear understanding of the complex nature and power of IT, it is difficult to develop the appropriate methods and theories to conduct robust research studies. These difficulties are offset to some extent by the international nature of IT in education with many common developments and a sharing of research approaches and results.

In spite of the complex nature of IT, there has been in recent years a number of studies that have included the development of educational theories that can underpin educational research. These include Ajzen's (1988) theories of reasoned action and planned behaviour, Loucks *et al.'s* (1998) level of use model and Cox and Webb's (2004) pedagogical model. There are many other theories now being used to underpin research in IT in education and which will enable more consistent and repeatable research to be achieved (Marshall and Cox 2008). The research methods have changed to embrace both quantitative and qualitative techniques, which are often used in an eclectic mix according to the research aims. What is needed now is more research into the effectiveness of different research techniques across different cohorts of learners for different types of IT in relation to these theories.

References

Ajzen, I. (1988) *Attitudes, Personality and Behavior*, Milton Keynes: Open University Press.

Barton, R. (1997) 'Does data-logging change the nature of children's thinking in experimental work in science?' in B. Somekh and N. Davis (eds) *Using Information Technology Effectively In Teaching And Learning*, London: Routledge.

Beauchamp, A.P. (2003) 'An investigation into IT in the secondary school curriculum: servant or subject?' unpublished doctoral thesis, University of London.

Bork, A. (1981) *Learning with computers*, Billerica, MA: Digital Press.

Brna, P. (1990) 'A methodology for confronting science misconceptions', *Journal of Educational Computing Research*, 6: 157–182.

—— (1991) 'Promoting creative confrontations', *Journal of Computer Assisted Learning*, 7: 114–122.

Compeau, D.R. and Higgins, C.A. (1999) 'Social cognitive theory and individual reactions to computing technology: a longitudinal study', *MIS Quarterly*, 23: 145–158.

Cox, M.J. (1993) 'Technology enriched school project: the impact of information technology on children's learning', *Computers & Education*, 21: 41–49.

—— (1997) *The effects of information technology on students' motivation*, London: NCET/King's College London.

—— (1999) 'Motivating pupils through the use of ICT', in M. Leask, and N. Pachter (eds) *Learning to Teach Using ICT in the Secondary School*, Oxford: Routledge.

—— (2003) 'How do we know that ICT is having an impact on children's learning? A review of techniques and methods to measure changes in pupils' learning promoted by the use of ICT', in G. Marshall and Y. Katz (eds) *Learning in School, Home and Community: ICT for early and elementary education*, Dordrecht: Kluwer.

—— (2005) 'Educational conflict: the problems in institutionalizing new technologies in education', in G. Kouzelis, M. Pournari, M. Stoeppler and V. Tselfes (eds) *Knowledge in the New Technologies*, Frankfurt: Peter Lang.

—— (2008) 'Researching IT in education', in J. Voogt, and G. Knezek (eds) *International Handbook of Information Technology in Primary and Secondary Education*, Berlin: Springer.

Cox, M.J. and Abbott, C. (eds) (2004) *ICT and Attainment: a review of the research literature*, London: Becta / DfES.

Cox, M.J. and Marshall, G.M. (2007) 'Effects of ICT: do we know what we should know?' *Education and Information Technologies*, 12: 59–70.

Cox, M.J. and Webb, M. (eds) (2004) *ICT and Pedagogy: a review of the research literature*, London: Becta / DfES.

Crook, C. (2001) 'The social character of knowing and learning: implications of cultural psychology for educational technology', *Journal of Information Technology in Teacher Education*, 10: 19–36.

Davis, F.D, Bagozzi, R.P. and Warshaw, P.R. (1989) 'User acceptance of computer technology: a comparison of two theoretical models', *Management Science*, 35: 982–1003.

Department for Education and Science (1991) 'Results of the survey of information and technology in schools', *Statistical Bulletin,* Issue No. 11/91, London: The Stationery Office.

Desforges, C. (1995) 'How does experience affect theoretical knowledge for teaching', *Learning and Instruction*, 5: 385–400.

Downes, T., Fluck, A., Gibbons, P., Leonard, R., Matthews, C., Oliver, R., Vickers, M. and Williams, M. (2001) *Making Better Connections: models of teacher professional development for the integration of information and communication technology into classroom practice*, Canberra, Australia: Commonwealth Department of Education, Science and Training.

Fullan, M.G. (1991) *The New Meaning of Educational Change*, London: Cassell.

—— (2003) *Change Forces with a Vengeance*, London: Routledge Falmer.

Furr, P.F., Ragsdale, R. and Horton, S.G. (2005) 'Technology's non-neutrality: past lessons can help guide today's classrooms', *Education and Information Technologies*, 10: 277–287.

Hargreaves, A. and Fullan, M.G. (1992) 'Introduction', in A. Hargreaves and M.G. Fullan (eds), *Understanding Teacher Development*, New York: Teachers College Press.

Harrison, C., Comber, C., Fisher, T., Haw, K., Lunzer, E., McFarlane, A., Mavers, D., Scrimshaw, P., Somekh, B. and Wating, R. (2002) *ImpaCT2 The impact of Information and Communication Technologies on Pupil Learning and Attainment*, London: Becta / DfES.

Hennessy, S., Ruthven, K. and Brindley, S. (2005) 'Teacher perspectives on integrating ICT into subject teaching: commitment, constraints, caution and change', *Journal of Curriculum Studies*, 37: 155–192.

Jones, A. (2004) *A Review of the Research Literature on Barriers to the Uptake of ICT by Teachers*, London: Becta / DfES.

Katz, Y.J. and Offir, B. (1994) 'Computer games as motivators for successful computer end-use', in J. Wright and D. Benzie (eds) *Exploring a New Partnership: Children, Teachers and Technology*, Amsterdam: Elsevier.

Kent, N. and Facer, K. (2004) 'Different worlds? A comparison of young people's home and school ICT use', *Journal of Computer Assisted Learning*, 20: 440–455.

Knezek, G. and Christensen, G. (2008) 'The importance of information technology attitudes and competencies in primary and secondary education', in J. Voogt, and G. Knezek (eds) *International Handbook of Information Technology in Primary and Secondary Education*, Berlin: Springer.

Koutromanos, G. (2005) 'The effects of head teachers, head officers and school counsellors' attitudes on the uptake of Information technology in Greek schools', unpublished doctoral thesis, King's College, London.

Kurland, D.M. and Pea, R.D. (1983) 'Children's mental models of recursive Logo programs', *Journal of Educational Computing Research*, 1: 235–243.

Laurillard, D. (1992) 'Phenomemographic research and the design of diagnostic strategies for adaptive tutoring systems', in M. Jones and P. Winne (eds), *Adaptive Learning Environments: foundations and frontiers*, Berlin: Springer-Verlag.

Law, N. and Plomp, T. (2003) 'Curriculum and staff development', in T. Plomp, R. Anderson, N. Law and A. Quale (eds) *Cross-national Policies and Practices on Information and Communication Technology in Education*, Charlotte, NC: Information Age Publishing.

Loucks, S.F., Newlove, B.W. and Hall, G.E. (1998) *Measuring Levels of Use of the Innovation: a manual for trainers, interviewers and raters*, Austin, Texas: Southwest Educational Development Laboratory.

Marshall, G. and Cox, M.J. (2008) 'Research methods; their design, applicability and reliability', in J. Voogt and G. Knezek (eds) *International Handbook of Information Technology in Primary and Secondary Education*, Berlin: Springer-Verlag.

McAlister, A., Ravenscroft, A. and Scanlon, E. (2004) 'Combining interaction and context design to support collaborative argumentation using a tool for synchronous CMC', *Journal of Computer Assisted Learning*, 20: 194–204.

McDougall, A. (2002) 'Technology-supported environments for learning through cognitive conflict', *Association for Learning Technologies Journal ALT-J*, 10: 83–91.

McDougall, A. and Jones, A. (2006) 'Theory and history, questions and methodology: current and future issues in research into ICT in education', *Technology, Pedagogy and Education*, 15: 353–360.

McKenzie, J., Elton, L.R.B. and Lewis, R. (eds) (1978) *Interactive Computer Graphics in Science Teaching*, Chichester: Ellis Horwood.

Mellar, H., Bliss, J., Boohan, R., Ogborn, J. and Tompsett, C. (eds) (1994) *Learning with Artificial Worlds: computer based modelling in the curriculum*, London: Falmer.

Moore, A. (2004) *The Good Teacher: dominant discourses in teaching and teacher education*, London: Routledge-Falmer.

Ogborn, J. and Wong, D. (1984) 'A microcomputer dynamic modelling system', *Physics Education*, 10: 138–142.

Pajares, F. (1992) 'Teachers' beliefs and educational research: cleaning up a messy construct', *Review of Educational Research*, 62: 307–332.

Papert, S. (1980) *Mindstorms: children, computers, and powerful idea*s, New York: Basic Books.

Pelgrum, W.J. and Plomp, T. (1991) *The Use of Computers in Education worldwide. Results from the IEA Computers in Education Survey in 19 Education Systems*, Oxford: Pergamon.

—— (2008) 'Methods for large scale assessment studies on ICT in education', in J. Voogt and G. Knezek (eds) *International Handbook of Information Technology in Primary and Secondary Education*, Berlin: Springer-Verlag.

Plomp, T, Anderson, R., Law, N. and Quale, A. (2009) *Cross-National ICT Policies and Practices in Education*, Charlotte, NC: Information Age Publishing.

Preston, C., Cox, M. and Cox, K. (2000) *Teachers as Innovators in Learning: what motivates teachers to use ICT*, London: Teacher Training Agency.

Reeves, T.C. (2008). 'Evaluation of the design and development of IT tools in education', in J. Voogt and G. Knezek (eds) *International Handbook of Information Technology in Primary and Secondary Education*', Berlin: Springer-Verlag.

Rhodes, V.J. (1999) 'IT in primary schools: the rhetoric and the reality, supporting teachers in the process of implementation', unpublished doctoral thesis, University of London.

Rushby, N.J. (ed.) (1983) *Computer Based Learning – State of the Art Report*, New York: Pergamon.

Scrimshaw, P. (2004) *Enabling Teachers to Make Successful Use of ICT*, Coventry: Becta.

Simpson, G., Hoyles, C. and Noss, R. (2005) 'Designing a programming-based approach for modelling scientific phenomena', *Journal of Computer Assisted Learning*, 21: 143–158.

Stacey, E. (2002) 'Social presence on-line: networking learners at a distance', in D. Watson and J. Andersen (eds) *Networking the Learner: computers in education*, Dordrecht: Kluwer.

Suppes, P (1968) 'Computer-assisted instruction: an overview of operations and problems', in A.J.H. Morrell (ed.) *Information Processing 68, Proceedings of IFIP Congress 1968*, Edinburgh, UK, 5–10 August, Volume 2, Paris: Unesco.

Voogt, J. (2008) 'IT and curriculum processes: dilemmas and challenges', in J. Voogt and G. Knezek (eds) *International Handbook of Information Technology in Primary and Secondary Education*, Berlin: Springer-Verlag.

Voogt, J. and Knezek, G. (eds) (2008) *International Handbook of Information Technology in Primary and Secondary Education*, Berlin: Springer-Verlag.

Watson, D.M. (ed.) (1993) *The ImpacT Report: an evauation of the impact of information technology on children's achievements in primary and secondary schools*, London: King's College.

Webb, M. (2008) 'Impact of IT on science education', in J. Voogt, and G. Knezek (eds) *International Handbook of Information Technology in Primary and Secondary Education*, Berlin: Springer-Verlag.

Webb, M. and Cox, M.J. 'Teachers' pedagogical decision making in relation to the uses of ICT for learning and teaching,' paper presented at the International Federation for Information Processing World Conference on Computers in Education (WCCE2005), Stellenbosch, South Africa, July 2005.

Wild, M. and Braid, P. (1996) 'Children's talk in co-operative groups', *Journal of Computer Assisted Learning*, 12: 216–231.

Yelland, N. (2003) 'Learning in school and out: formal and informal experiences with computer games in mathematical contexts', in G. Marshall and K. Katz (eds) *Learning in School, Home and Community: ICT for early and elementary education*, Dordrecht: Kluwer.

Yerrick, R., Parke, H. and Nugent, J. (1997) 'Struggling to promote deeply rooted change: the filtering effect of teachers' beliefs on understanding transformational views of teaching science', *Science Education*, 11, 147–159.

Chapter 3

Technology as Trojan horse

A 'generation' of information technology practice, policy and research in schools

Vince Ham
CORE Education, Christchurch, New Zealand

Introduction

> When a person goes into a store and buys a drill, she doesn't want a drill. . . . She wants a hole!
>
> (Poster on a classroom wall, 1990. Source unknown.)

In most countries, that cohort of young people who began their preschool education in the mid-1980s and are now graduating from our universities and colleges, are 'Generation 1'. They are the first generation to 'grow up digital'. They are the first generation for whom what we now call 'e-learning' has been a common, perhaps significant, part of their schooling experience. Yet much of what we do, and talk about, in relation to this first generation's use of digital technologies in education is in essence nothing to do with those technologies themselves. It is to do with what could, should, or is being done with them by teachers and by learners. It is about the outcomes of such use rather than the use itself. It is about the 'hows', and the 'whens', and even more the 'whys', and not just the 'whether'. It is a discussion not about drills, but about holes.

'It was twenty years ago today . . .'

Classrooms c.1988

At the time, you might remember it, the Apple II was the most popular computer in schools; about a quarter of children had access to a computer at home, used by parents for 'work' but by children only for games. Primary schools had on average one computer for every 60 or so students, and secondary schools had one for every 30 (Ham 1988; Nightingale and Chamberlain 1991). At the time the 'information superhighway' was not even a dirt track; few if any school computers were networked; 'multimedia' had not yet been coined as a phrase; cell phones were the ones prisoners used to call their lawyers; digital cameras were those you operated with your fingers; and the expression 'world wide web' would have evoked some sort of fantastic horror movie plot about arachnids with a global domination complex.

If you were a primary teacher, maybe one in three of you would have had one of those Apple IIs, or perhaps a BBC 'B', or a new Macintosh with its cute little 'mouse' sitting on a student desk at the back of your classroom. If you were a secondary teacher you would have had access to one, perhaps two, computers in the staff workroom, and a computer laboratory with about 15, non-networked, Apple or 'IBM compatible' machines in it, almost permanently booked out for computer studies, mathematics or senior word processing classes. You did not regularly use a computer for preparation of lesson materials, or for communication with colleagues or officials (Nightingale and Chamberlain 1991).

If you were a student finishing a year in one of those classrooms with the single computer or the school lab, you were most likely to have shared it with another student. You would have shared it to use a word processor for creative or transactional writing, and you would have done this fairly regularly during the year. You would have once or twice played a vocabulary/reading game in English, or a counting game in maths, or completed a computerised tutorial in science. If you were aged under 15 and not sitting high stakes exams, you may well have worked your way through some interactive fiction, used a city-management simulation, or hunted Carmen San Diego in social studies. Moreover, you were also far more likely to have done any of these if you were in a primary school than if you were in a secondary school. You could, in terms of available applications, have statistically analysed a survey using a spreadsheet, or analysed the social demography of early settlers using a data-base, or logged data from sensors on temperature exchange, or commanded the movements of a robotic or on-screen 'turtle'; or even automatically recorded the score of music you were playing on a keyboard linked through a MIDI interface, but you almost certainly had not (Ham 1989; Nightingale and Chamberlain 1991; Pelgrum and Plomp 1991).

If you were a random group of parents, over 90 per cent of you regarded the presence of computers in primary schools as a very good thing, but your reasons for saying this were very different from those of the teachers who taught your children. The primary educational benefit of computers in schools for most of you would have been the promise it held of your child becoming 'computer literate', gaining an 'edge' in the future job market, or being better prepared for a highly technologised 'life' beyond school. The great majority of you saw some benefit for the learning of school subjects 'across the curriculum', especially mathematics, but you would have had major worries that the time and attention given to teaching computer literacy in school would detract from that given to the 'other basics', especially reading, writing and your childrens' social development (Ham 1988).

By contrast, the teachers in the school would probably have said that the greatest benefit of computers in schools derived not from the acquisition of computing skills as such, but from their use to achieve stated curriculum objectives in a wide variety of subject areas (Ham 1989). Primary teachers would have justified the use of 'tools' like word processors for developing editing/writing skills, or interactive fiction for collaborative problem solving, graphic editors for visual expression, and so on. Their secondary colleagues would have argued that all they needed in order to realise the untapped educative potential of IT was more, and more accessible, computers, and a generation of children who had learned all the basic technical skills they needed early in their primary school careers. In other words, the force of the 'pedagogical rationale' was strong in them, and the professional will existed to integrate new communications technologies, even as the reality of using IT in classrooms was occasional and sporadic (Ham 1989).

Thus was classroom practice a 'generation' ago, when Generation 1 began their educational journey. But what of classroom practice now, as they end it?

'Yesterday . . . '

Classrooms c.2008

By contrast to 1988, digital technologies are now a ubiquitous and ever-proliferating commonplace rather than an infrequently used novelty, both in schools and in life generally. The successors to those Apple IIe, BBC and MS-DOS computers, the 'Mac' and the 'PC', have been joined in the digital pantheon by a myriad of other technologies, from iPhones to X-Boxes, from PDAs to DVDs, and from Webcams to Wifis. Literati parents no longer 'search', they 'google', while their 'clickerati' kids no longer 'call', they 'text'. While we, their digitally immigrant parents, live an increasingly technologised work life through emails, web searches, spreadsheets and databases, our digital native offspring live the 'iLife' through MSN, Skype, MySpace and YouTube. 'Windows' has replaced 'ProDOS' as the most frequently used operating system in schools; every school is linked to the Internet, 85 per cent of them via broadband, and there is a classroom computer available for every four secondary and five primary students nationwide (2020 Communications Trust 2005).

As a random group of school students today, you will use IT in your lessons a lot more often than in 1988, and you will be using an equally narrow but rather different range of IT. As in 1988, your most frequent IT-based experience will still involve using word processors for the static presentation of your work. But, unlike then, your next most common experience now will be searching for information on the Internet. Between them, these two activities could account for up to three quarters of all the IT-based activities you undertake this year. If you are a primary school student you will still use IT more often than if you are in a secondary school. You will probably play a similar proportion of maths, science or language games as your 1988 counterpart, but you will probably not work your way through interactive fiction/ decision-making simulations or hunt Carmen San Diego, as they did. You are more likely to edit digital movies or create multimedia presentations instead (Ham 2007).

If you are a random group of teachers now, the majority of you have moved from occasional experimentation to become regular 'users' of IT at school. Over 80 per cent of you have a laptop for your exclusive use provided or subsidised by your school, and some 75 per cent of you have undertaken an extended programme of professional development in integrating IT into your classroom programmes (2020 Communications Trust 2005). What is more, over 90 per cent of you routinely (i.e. average daily or weekly) now use computers to find and prepare lesson materials, or for other professional administration and communication purposes.

Around 75 per cent of you, moreover, have moved from being 'users' to become 'pushers', incorporating IT into at least some of your classroom units of work over the year; and about 16 per cent of you are 'addicts', using IT in virtually all of your classes as a matter of daily or weekly routine. For the most part, and as a matter of comparison with your 1988 counterparts, your students seem to be using IT a lot more, rather than a lot more IT (Ham 2007).

IT in classroom practice: the opportunity–uptake gap

The accumulated impression one gets from comparing the few studies that profiled student IT activities in 1988 with the more numerous studies available for the last few years, is that while the central issue confronting teachers in 1988 was justifying that use to themselves in terms of meeting specific curriculum objectives, that confronting teachers in 2008 seems to be more about coping with the vast array of possible uses. While the issue in 1988 was how to do 'something', that in 2008 seems how to do 'everything'. As our own study of IT usage in over a thousand classrooms put it:

> The range of information technologies available to teachers is massive. . . . [Thus] a study of teachers' use of ICTs is a study of use across a range of subjects and objectives of a large and apparently ever expanding range of software and hardware. In a school context this range includes: drill and practice software, interactive tutorials, educational games, interactive simulations (either fictional or modelling 'real world' situations), interactive encyclopaedias, computerised library catalogues, data logging software, mind mapping and sequencing software, content-free problem solving packages, administration databases, a wide range of generic software tools such as word processors, databases, spreadsheets, web browsers, email managers, presentation assemblers,

multimedia editing and production tools, website development tools, electronic messaging software, as well as hardware peripherals such as digital cameras, digital video, scanners, probes and sensors, palm-tops, LEGO-LOGO models, and so on.

(Ham *et al*. 2002: 87)

Not to mention, since the extract above was written in 2002, blogs, wikis, LMSs, SMSs, ILSs, 3-D modelling, Second-Life, IP voice and video-conferencing, and interactive whiteboards!

Commenting on the research implications of this, moreover, the report went on to state the importance of acknowledging the pluralist nature of the term in conducting and evaluating any study of IT in education.

There is no 'Information and Communication Technology', but there are a broad range of 'Information and Communications Technologies'. One of the major dilemmas facing the teachers . . . is the fact that in the world of schooling there can be so many different technologies used at many different levels of schools for many different educational purposes. For this reason it is neither appropriate nor useful to talk too generally about the 'effectiveness of ICT' in schools or of the 'effects of ICTs on learning'. Rather it is necessary to look closely at particular ICTs as used by particular teachers in particular teaching situations to achieve particular curriculum or learning objectives with particular students.

(Ham *et al*. 2002: 110)

From the perspective of the individual teacher, this historical proliferation of technological and pedagogical possibility seems to have proved as daunting as it might have been exciting. Faced by it, some teachers have responded by incorporating a wider range of IT-based activities occasionally in their teaching programme, but rather more seem to have responded by incorporating the comfortable few, more frequently.

From 'which ones, how?' to 'why?': policy imperatives and competing rationales

If [we] do not seize the opportunities provided by the knowledge economy we will survive as an amusement park and holiday land for the citizens of more successful developed economies.

(ITAG 1997: 427)

The market approach to education is a dead end. . . . [Rather,] e-learning has the potential to transform the way we learn. It's about exploiting technologies and using them effectively across the curriculum . . .

(Ministry of Education 2006: 3)

Thus, one of the themes that emerges from the above overview of one country's experience with IT is that the history of IT in our Generation 1 schools has been one of optimistic anticipation, but also perhaps one of unrealistic expectation; one in which the explosion in the range of things that students *could* do with such technologies may have outstripped teachers' capacity to 'keep up'.

It is also clear from international research that, in 1988 as now, teachers themselves have tended to articulate a rationale for the integration of ITs into classroom practice through pedagogically or curriculum focused lenses. As they did in 1988, teachers still describe those benefits and problems in terms of increasing 'variety' in their teaching strategies, student 'motivation' to engage with those activities, student demonstration of a range of 'cognitive abilities', opportunities for 'collaboration', the acquisition of 'content knowledge' and 'information skills', and the like (Ham and Toubat 2006).

But have these also been the rationales with the greatest currency among educational stakeholders generally? Have they been the rationales guiding educational policy on IT at the broader national and community levels? What also emerges from historical sketches like the one above is a strong sense of pluralism, not just in the range of educational activity to be evaluated by research as such uptake increased, but also in the range of perspectives, priorities, expectations and even ideologies that different stakeholders have brought to the enterprise. What emerges is a sense that, behind various stakeholders' almost universally, some would say naively, optimistic view of the potential IT holds for education, lie a number of sometimes complementary, but more often competing and incommensurate, reasons for that view. Like the parents and the teachers in the 1988 scenario above, we may have been all looking in the same direction but have been doing so for rather different reasons and with conflicting expectations of what we hoped to see. Then and now, we may have agreed about the purchase of the drills, but have had very different ambitions with respect to the holes.

Globally over the last twenty years, the various imperatives that research has isolated as the primary drivers of national and local investment in IT for teaching and learning have been numerous, though not innumerable. They reflect the often competing interests and ideologies of the broad range of those who feel they have a 'stake' in education systems worldwide. Three attempts to list and categorise these imperatives, drawn from both early on and more recently in our 'generational' timeframe, are summarised in Table 3.1. It is clear in these typologies that, although their authors may differ about the precise number of distinct rationales they detected, the specific terminology in which they are couched, or the criteria by which they are grouped, there is nevertheless more consensus than there is disagreement about what those rationales actually are.

Table 3.1 Rationales for investment in IT for teaching and learning

Pelgrum and Plomp 1991	Culp, Honey and Mandinach 2003	Twining 2005
1. A *vocational rationale* that argues that IT skills are a key source of employment options in increasingly 'knowledge-based' economies and that the job of schools is to provide technologically competent future workers. 2. An *economic rationale* that argues that each nation is part of a global economy in which a technological literate workforce is the key to a country's economic competitiveness in the world. 3. A *commercial rationale* that sees IT in schools as itself a commercial opportunity for an IT industry that both sells its products to schools and is most likely to employ the new generation of technology-literate students emerging from it. 4. A *marketing rationale*. Neo-liberal reforms in many western countries during the 1980s created an environment in which schools 'compete' for students. In such an environment access to the latest technologies in classrooms is seen as providing an 'edge' in the competition for student enrolments.	1. *Technology to address specific challenges in teaching and learning.* These rationales are about specific technologies extending teaching and learning processes, especially when they are currently problematic in some way. This includes delivering instruction to geographically distant students, helping students analyse complex data, supporting more diverse forms of writing or communication, broadening the scope and timeliness of information available to students, more efficient assessment systems, and so on. 2. *Technology as a transformative change agent.* This asserts that introducing IT into the teaching and learning process can catalyse other 'improvements' in teaching content or methods, or in schooling systems. Often the advocates of such rationales foreground the potential to use IT to change learning environments according to a particular theory held about teaching or learning. Most often mentioned among these is the agenda to use IT to trigger changes away from lecture-driven instruction and toward constructivist,	*IT category* 1. Technology use in order to learn IT skills, either through the medium of other subjects or as a subject itself. *Learning tool category* 2. As a tool to achieve traditional teaching and learning goals across the curriculum. 3. To extend and enrich learning across the curriculum. 4. To motivate learners. 5. To catalyse educational change. 6. Because of the impact of IT on the nature of knowledge. 7. To fundamentally change teaching and learning. 8. To support learners in thinking about their own learning. 9. To provide access to the curriculum for those who might otherwise be excluded from it. *Other category* 10. To increase productivity in education. 11. To reduce the cost of education.

(Continued)

Table 3.1 (Continued)

Pelgrum and Plomp 1993	Culp, Honey and Mandinach 2003	Twining 2005
5. A *cost-effectiveness rationale* that assumes that IT can improve the fiscal efficiency of schools, allow economies in budgets, rationalise staffing, teach courses to more students per 'class', or offer a broader range of subjects.	inquiry-oriented classrooms. 3. *Technology as a force for economic competitiveness.* Many rationales in this group revolve around technology skills being critical to future employment, or to the computer industry being central to economic growth. They also include more politically or socially oriented arguments around IT skills as a preparation for life, and that a more technologically literate populace will improve political decision making, increase citizen participation, increase social well-being, and so on.	12. To make education more efficient. 13. As a substitute for teachers. 14. To reward students. 15. As preparation for living in a society that is permeated with technology. 16. As preparation for work or employment. 17. To support and stimulate the country's economy. 18. To impress stakeholders (e.g. inspectors, funders, prospective parents/students). 19. To reduce inequalities e.g. between students with differential access to ICT outside formal education.
6. A *social rationale* that sees IT in schools as a preparation for 'life' in general; a life which is likely to be fundamentally affected and permeated by digital technologies.		
7. A *transformational rationale* that either assumes or requires that IT is used to change the nature of schooling as we know it, both the ways we teach and learn in classrooms and, potentially, the very way the school system is organised and structured.		
8. A *pedagogical rationale* that asserts that IT offers unprecedented opportunities to improve the way we teach, enhance learning and raise student achievement, across the curriculum.		

As a matter of historical overview, there are a number of things to note about these rationales and their significance in Generation 1's experience of IT in the world's schools.

- That educational practitioners, researchers and decision makers alike seem to draw from virtually the same list of rationales and drivers that permeate the stakeholder discourses now as permeated it twenty years ago. The actual list of possible drivers in the global policy discourse does not seem to have changed much over time.

- That different stakeholder groups tend to have *different* interests in promoting the IT agenda in schools, and thus tend to have given priority to different rationales compared to others in their thinking and decision-making around it. Teachers, for example, seem more likely to justify educational computing using pedagogical or transformative rationales, politicians using social or economic rationales, the computer industry using a commercial rationale, and so on.
- That the pedagogical and transformative rationales, in particular, break down into sub-rationales and sub-agendas over which there has been little consensus, even within the community of education professionals. As Twining's (2005) analysis in particular shows, teachers, researchers, educational administrators, and educational policy makers all bring their own particular perspectives, priorities, assumptions and ideologies to the debate. In 2008, just as much as in 1988, the apparent consensus around what teachers aim for through students' use of IT, what parents expect of it, why principals promote it, and why policy analysts put up funding cases for investment in it, is more illusory than real.
- That different rationales and imperatives have driven national policy, not just over time, but also across different jurisdictions. In the USA, for example, the economic rationale that predominated in 1983 has gradually made room for pedagogical and transformational rationales over the 1990s and 2000s (Culp *et al.* 2003), whereas exactly the opposite trend may be observed in the policy discourse in New Zealand over the same period. The result was a decade of very different funding priorities. Reflecting the predominance of the pedagogical rationale in its early policy documents, and in stark contrast to the expenditure priorities in the United States and some other western jurisdictions at the time, which were often focused on hardware provision, the predominant, indeed sole, expenditure priority in New Zealand in the 1990s was on teacher professional development. No public money was spent on hardware, software or infrastructure provision. Similarly, while economic rationales such as job creation may currently take second place to pedagogical or teaching and learning rationales in many Western countries' policy statements, those same economic imperatives often have primacy of place in the political discourse of many Asian countries (Zhang 2004).

Implications for the research agenda

The first proposition advanced in this chapter about the history of IT in education over the last twenty years has been that it has been characterised by a greater eclecticism of educational opportunity than activity in our schools;

and the second is that various stakeholders have brought to this opportunity and activity widely varied, and often competing, value propositions as to its ultimate purpose and worth. The third is that, between them, these two have combined to make it difficult, perhaps impossible, to develop a coherent research agenda for the field.

In part this difficulty may be because there is such a multiplicity of ratio-nales driving the practices we may wish to study and thus a multiplicity of questions to ask, and in part it may be because there is a myriad of effects, trends, technologies, pedagogical practices, learning outcomes, curriculum areas, and politico-cultural contexts that we can ask those questions about. In part too, it may be because we as researchers also bring to the research enterprise our own preferences around what is worth researching about IT in education, (or about education in general for that matter), our own methodological predilections about how to research it, and our own a priori assumptions about the potential positions and roles that IT might take or play within it.

The very ubiquity of possible activity and perceived benefit that has attracted many teachers to use IT with classes, also makes the study of such use particularly susceptible to a range of critiques as a research agenda. For one thing, even within the educational policy and teaching communities, people do not necessarily agree on the questions that are worth asking. A pri-mary school teacher of special needs children will be interested in the effective use of a different set of technologies from those concerning a senior physics teacher, and, even more importantly, they are likely to be interested in a different set of learning or teaching effects of those technologies. Even more important still, they are each likely to employ vastly different pedago-gical approaches to the learning activity involved. Add to that the different epistemological and methodological preferences brought by different researchers and one starts to see the problem.

A behaviourist teacher is likely to approach educational technology in a very different way from one who espouses social constructivism. But equally, a researcher interested in creativity as a learning outcome of students' use of graphics applications, is likely to ask very different questions, and to employ very different validity measures in the enterprise, from a researcher commis-sioned to investigate the use of that same graphics package in relation to improved student achievement. For the researcher in all these cases, there are significant, inherently value-laden decisions to be made about which aspects of this experience the researcher is most interested in, what questions of worth there are to be asked about it, how the IT is to be 'placed' in relation to the phenomenon of interest in developing a research strategy around those questions, and, given all of these, what methodologies are most 'fit for purpose'?

Surveying, as one national example, the history of the research conducted in New Zealand since 1988, one is struck by the same eclecticism of practice and pluralism of purpose that characterises teachers' classroom practice with IT.

The policy driven (i.e. state-commissioned) research agenda has largely consisted of programme evaluations, especially evaluations of its own teacher professional development programmes in IT, and, more recently, case studies of 'effective practice' or 'best practice' in specific classrooms. These have mostly addressed questions arising from the pedagogical and transformational rationales, and there has been little or no public investment in research specifically targeting the longer term social or economic effects of IT use in schools.

The informal (i.e. non-state-funded) research agenda has been similarly eclectic in scope and pedagogically oriented in interest. There have been researchers interested in the creativity demonstrated when students use IT, and those who are interested in mathematical concept development. There have been experimental researchers trying to isolate a 'technology effect' in individual students' use of spreadsheets, and researchers more interested in the 'pedagogy effect' of the way individual teachers approach teaching through spreadsheets. There have been survey researchers trying to correlate the frequency of students' use of IT, specifically or generically, with standardised test results as measures of student achievement, and researchers more interested in counting students' rates of access to educational websites as measures of student engagement, access or participation. There have been those looking at behaviours and those looking for cognition; those studying schools and those studying teachers; those looking at high school graduates and those looking at new-entrants, and so on. The research enterprise around IT, in short, has been as eclectic in scope as the potential for classroom practice with it has been, and, one suspects, for similar reasons.

Moreover, if there has been a significant change in the research agenda over time, other than this growing eclecticism itself, it is probably the decline in the amount of research that assumes the very presence of IT as an 'independent variable' in teaching and learning and a corresponding rise in research that is more interested in the ways students and teachers use IT, or the cultural and institutional contexts that encourage such use (Culp *et al.* 2003; Davis and Carlsen 2004). This should not be surprising. When the use of IT can be 'all things to all people', researchers investigating the worth of that enterprise cannot regard IT as a singularity any more than teachers can, cannot ask single or simple technocentric questions about it any more than teachers should, cannot confine themselves to a single set of tools or approaches any more than teachers do, and cannot assume that a single or simple rationale is driving it any more than teachers might. Like teachers, researchers have increasingly come to assume that the drill does not, in and of itself, generate the hole, and that there is a lot more to be studied about the use made of the drill, than there is about *which* drill it is.

Thus, eclecticism and proliferation in all of how IT has been studied, what it is about its presence in the classroom that has been studied, and the often implicit reasons why those particular phenomena have been deemed worthy of study in IT-mediated contexts, have meant that a coherent research agenda has not emerged, even within individual national jurisdictions. The particular rationales that practitioners, policy makers and researchers have held with regard to IT have largely determined all of the following: the kinds of IT activity a teacher is likely to value and adopt as a matter of practice in the classroom; the kinds of research questions and methodologies a researcher is likely to ask and adopt with respect of that practice; and the lenses through which either is likely to critique the activity of the other.

Conclusion

In this chapter I have argued that in the jurisdiction with which I am most familiar, and perhaps elsewhere too, the first twenty years of integrating new technology into classrooms has been characterised by a feeding frenzy of experimentation in classrooms among those teaching and learning with or through it, a disabling confusion of expectation in state policy and among those funding it, and a wondrous eclecticism of direction, method and purpose among those researching its educative value.

Whatever our pedagogical orientations or our research preferences, there has arguably been some broad agreement that the key research agenda has been about reconciling and investigating the 'value connection' between new technologies and the educative practices of teachers and learners in schools. Beneath that, however, there has been little by way of consensus or coherence. We have gone about those investigations by paying attention to a myriad of different aspects of the phenomenon, in a myriad of different ways, reflecting a myriad of different, and sometimes incommensurable, beliefs and interests. Given that this is the case, it is vitally important that any research in the field clearly declares the limitations of its scope and the ideological assumptions of its authors, just as it is important for that research then to be fairly critiqued within, and acknowledging, those same limitations and assumptions.

If I were to propose a metaphor for our experience as researchers of Generation 1's experience of IT in schools, it would be that we have been witnesses at the wedding of a precocious young technology to a tired old pedagogy, and it is timely to wonder, now, what that has meant for the couple and for their future together.

Will this marriage of new technologies to old teaching fulfil its promise as a 'love match', giving legitimacy of purpose to the one and revitalising the other, or will it prove a 'mismatch' in which they eventually find that they had little in common, and split up after a brief but passionate honeymoon? Has it been a 'shotgun wedding', forced on two unsuspecting innocents by governments socially engineering a compliant citizenry, or, worse, the moustache twirling machinations of profiteering IT corporations? Or is it just a 'marriage of convenience' – a power struggle between over-controlling partners, each of whom is trying to use the other for their own ends, presenting a falsely harmonious front to the world while taking refuge in the fiction that they're only staying together 'for the sake of the children'?

Whichever is the case, the central issue – that of determining the educational value of the use of new technologies in schools – will be resolved by a debate in respect of policies, practices and research that is not essentially about IT at all, but one that is about what constitutes quality in teaching with it and the educative benefit in students' learning about, with, or through it. Moreover, only by a clear analysis and an open declaration of the various value propositions that we all bring to the table around these 'hows', and, even more especially, these 'whys' of IT use in schools, will such debates be susceptible to resolution.

Seymour Papert closed his keynote speech to the World Conference on Computers in Education (WCCE) in Sydney in 1990, by somewhat controversially questioning why a world conference on computers was even necessary when we didn't have a world conference on pencils. Some attendees seemed to think he was predicting that, as computers became absorbed into the fabric of education, like pencils, or books, there would no longer be a need to study their presence or their impact. I like to think, though, that he was predicting what has, in the event, transpired – not that the debate around new educational technologies has become trivially irrelevant, but that it has over time shifted its focus from a debate about IT's educational relevance, to a debate about its educational *importance*. We no longer need world conferences about the drill; but we still seem to need them about the holes.

References

2020 Communications Trust (2005) *ICT in Schools Report 2005. Information and Communications Technology in New Zealand Schools 1993–2005*, Wellington, NZ: Ministry of Education.

Culp, K.M., Honey, M. and Mandinach, E. (2003) *A Retrospective on Twenty Years of Educational Policy*, Washington DC: USA Department of Education.

Davis, N. and Carlsen, R. (2004) 'A comprehensive synthesis on research into information technology in education', in T. van Weert (ed.) *World Summit on the Information Society Forum Engineering and the Knowledge Society: information technology supporting human development*, IFIP and WFEO, Geneva, December 2003, Amsterdam: Kluwer.

Ham, V. (1988) 'The other side: parents' perceptions of computers in primary schools', *Bits and Bytes*, May: 89–90.

—— (1989) 'The English classroom: putting computers in their place', *English in Aotearoa*, 8: 1–9.

—— (2007) 'National Trends in the ICTPD School Clusters Programme, 2004–2006', Unpublished research report to the Ministry of Education, Wellington, NZ: Ministry of Education.

Ham, V., Gilmore, A., Kachelhoffer, A., Morrow, D. and Wenmoth, D. (2002) *What Makes for Effective Professional Development in ICT? An Evaluation of the 23 School Clusters ICTPD Programme, 1999–2001*, Wellington, NZ: Ministry of Education.

Ham, V. and Toubat, H. (2006) *National Trends in the ICTPD School Clusters Programme, 2003–2005*. Wellington, NZ: Ministry of Education.

ITAG (1997) *ImpacT 2001. Learning With IT: the issues*, Wellington NZ: Ministry of Information Technology.

Ministry of Education (2006) *Enabling the 21st Century Learner. An e-Learning Action Plan for Schools 2006–2010*, Wellington, NZ: Ministry of Education.

Nightingale, D. and Chamberlain, M. (1991) *A Study of Computers in New Zealand Schools*, Wellington, NZ: Research and Statistics Division, Ministry of Education.

Pelgrum, W.J. and Plomp T. (1991) *The Use of Computers in Education Worldwide, Results from the IEA 'Computers in Education' Survey in 19 Education Systems*, Oxford: Pergamon Press.

Twining, P. (2005) *DICTateEd. Discussing ICT, Aspirations and Targets for Education*. Online. Available HTTP: <http://www.med8.info/dictated/rationales.htm> (accessed 3 September 2007).

Zhang, J. (2004) 'Using ICT to Prepare Learners for the 21st Century: The Perspectives of Eastern APEC Economies', paper presented to Striking Balance: Sharing Practice from East and West. A Summit on Education Reform in the APEC Region, Beijing, January 12–14. Online. Available HTTP: <http://www.apecknowledgebank.org/resources/downloads/zhang%20IT.pdf> (accessed 3 September 2007).

Chapter 4

Views of learning, assessment and the potential place of information technology

Deirdre Cook
Educational Consultant, UK

Over the last hundred years or so there have been a number of evolutions and revolutions in the theories underlying educational practices. A brief look at some of the major shifts in a few examples of learning theory reveals how ideas in this area change.

Looking at learning

A dominant model from the late 1930s and early 1940s was the behaviourist view. Here valued knowledge is held to be a reflection of a real and observable world, separate from the knower. The minds of learners are seen as spaces to be filled, their objective to accumulate knowledge of this world and the teacher's task to interpret and transmit this to the learners. 'Transmission' is a key term associated with this view; learning is seen as an observable change in behaviour, with learners largely passive and knowledge relatively stable. Teachers structure, direct and control the flow of information and the assumption is that all learners will eventually become able to replicate the content. Any difficulties are attributable to the learner. Assessment is sum-mative and aims to judge whether the learner has yet acquired the facts or concepts being taught. While this brief synopsis is necessarily somewhat superficial, it is clear that some of the features noted are to be found not only in the pedagogic practices of the past, but in present day schooling too.

Learning *with* IT, rather than about it, in this view, would see technology used in a structured and sequential way with the information or knowledge to be acquired presented in small and incremental pieces. There would possibly be some 'rewards' built in to encourage the learner to persevere towards mas-tery of the content. It is here that one finds programs focusing on presenting learners with small 'bits' of information, then opportunities to practise before moving on to the next incremental step, frequently referred to as 'skill and drill' tasks. Such an approach to learning design and assessment builds on the work of key learning theorists such as Thorndike, Skinner, Hull and Tolman.

IT offers much here in terms of increased efficiency in assessment. This view is reflected in the claims for IT as enabling a transformation in assessment practice. In the UK recently, there is increasing interest in the contribution that IT can make to speeding up the management and efficient running of tests and in minimising the assessment task itself by using electronic marking. One argument supporting this view is that it will enable 'just in time' assessment with candidates controlling when this happens: a form of 'personalisation'. Not one, however, that allows learners to adjust their curriculum or their agentive actions, or for assessment to be tailored to meet their needs. Personalisation is associated with the affordance IT provides for almost instant feedback to learners, which they are expected to use in a formative way. However, making the feedback loop truly formative is not as straightforward as the more simplistic views suggest. This requires certain conditions to be met. While the outcomes of summative assessments can be used in a formative manner, they lack the intrinsic social and dynamic potential that formative assessment really requires, focusing as they do on products rather than processes of learning.

More social views of learning

The challenges to behaviourist views came from constructivist models of learning. It is useful to focus here on three of these:

- cognitive constructivism, as in the work of Piaget where the development of an individual's cognition is fore-grounded in a world where knowledge is external, knowable and replicable;
- social constructivism, sharing some emphasis on cognition, emerging from the work of Vygotsky (Van der Veer and Valsiner 1994), who saw learning as always social and shared, existing firstly between individuals and subsequently within a person, with language use being most important;
- radical constructivism, associated with Von Glasersfeld (1995); here knowledge is also seen as an outcome of an individual's experience but of a non-objective world, a world able to be represented in multiple ways.

Generally those holding constructivist views take a more active or agentive view of learning, that is, that it has more to do with the learners' efforts in bringing about change in their understanding than in observable behaviours. The emphasis is on the processes rather than just the products of learning. Learners are actively involved in 'constructing' knowledge for themselves, in making sense of their experiential world, a world open to multiple interpretations in the radical and social views.

The teacher's goal is to organise new experiences, act as guide, facilitator and supporter of learners' sense-making actions, and to be able to make design decisions about future learning activities. Students are viewed as self regulating. Those theorists considered social constructivists acknowledge the complexities of the world, the problematic nature of knowledge and the active involvement of learners; additionally, they recognise explicitly the social and cultural nature of all the environments in which learning happens and the role played in individual learning by others. In the social constructivist view, cultural influences are seen to be of great significance; language, other tools and symbols have an important mediating role to play. At this end of the continuum there is growing interest in the influences that culture, context, interpersonal exchanges and settings have on learners and learning.

Assessment in socio-cultural perspectives considers learning as an ongoing process taking into account the learners' prior experience and their current levels of understanding. It uses this information to plan for future activity, that is assessment is formative (Black *et al.* 2002) and is ideally mutually constructed by the participants. In its more social and radical forms, constructivist assessment encourages learners to explore multiple perspectives and representations. Formative assessment is currently seen as a significant factor in raising achievement because the feedback to learners makes it possible for them to use it to close the gap between current performance and desired goals. Student engagement, motivation, participation, image and identity are all influences at work in assessment here. The teacher's role is in building an atmosphere of trust and respect, in giving feedback and dealing with misunderstandings. IT use in constructivist and social-constructivist classrooms keeps relationships central, builds in opportunities for questioning, sharing of assessment criteria and self and peer assessment, features associated with formative assessment and self-improvement. Summative assessment sits uneasily with socio-constructivist views of learning.

Emerging theories

There is increasing interest in theories of learning that are less concerned with individuals and their 'knowledge or knowing', focusing more on 'doing and belonging'. This view that cognition is situated or distributed comes from a wide and varied number of perspectives, from social anthropology, semiotics, linguistics, cognitive science and education. The shift to this view is seen by many as being as radical as the earlier shift from behaviourism to cognitivism (Kirshner and Whitson 1997). Learning here is seen as inseparable from the context in which it occurs, thus learning is situated or embedded in the discourse, culture and social interactions that accompany it. The learner's goal now is becoming a member of a group or community, being able to act in accordance with its demands, and being seen as a completely integral member from the very first activities as a novice. It is the bonds among the community members, the part-whole relationship that affects them all that is important. Individuals' identities are formed by their membership of all the social and cultural groupings to which they belong, both in everyday and educational settings. Collaboration in the collective effort of understanding is the goal, responsibility is shared and everyone contributes, no single member being responsible for the completion of any task. Teachers taking a situated approach, although more expert members, would be as much part of the learning community as anyone; the role would be to provide, indirectly or otherwise, a modelling of performance, to challenge or scaffold learning at key moments.

As with constructivist views, because of its multidisciplinary nature, there are many differences in perspectives here. Key ideas include mutual engagement, shared repertoire and joint enterprise (Wenger 1999), participation, cognitive apprenticeship, authenticity (Rogoff 1990; Lave 1991), coaching, collaboration, multiple practice, articulation of learning skills, and stories (Brown *et al.* 1989).

In a situated view of learning, assessments are needed that offer complex, authentic, real-life contexts and activities to learning communities. This allows them to work and demonstrate in integrated ways their engagement with the task, their development in the use of the tools and affordances of the context. Assessment tasks should allow them to demonstrate multiple learning perspectives, reflect on their learning and to make explicit the ways they have defined and developed a solution. This is something of a challenge, but one where the affordances of a whole range of new technologies are ideally placed to contribute to a multimodal, multimedia, many voiced and authentic record of work as it is carried out and then presented to others.

This family of theories is still emerging as influential in classrooms, so examples of assessment practices already operating and involving IT are rare. The dilemma for most educators is between what the technologies can do and what the categorising function of high stakes assessment and testing will allow. Being clear about the reasons and types of assessment practices to use is more important now than ever before.

Given the power of IT to capture both process and product and accepting that learning is collaborative as its assessment should also be, research is urgently needed to explore:

- the lifelong learning agenda, including e-portfolios
- technology's capacities for tracking the contributions of individuals and the group, and for enabling each to choose what to take forward for assessment.

Ethical considerations

Constructivist views are discernible in most current classroom practices. However, there is a tension here between the logical need within the theory for formative assessment, and the summative types of assessment or testing that currently dominate school practices. Similarly, tension exists in recognising the contribution of an individual when learning is seen as 'between persons'.

To be equitable, assessment must also bear in mind individual learners' 'opportunity to learn'; if this is unequal then the assessment would be unjust as it would only really demonstrate that discrepancy (Gee 2003). Since assessments and testing are often used to allocate resources in some way or to have some kind of 'gate-keeping' function, categorising people as skilled or less so, intelligent or less so, this is an important consideration. Since the discriminations of these processes often come to be seen as the long-term defining properties of the person and not of the assessment process, we need to be clear about the purposes of measuring learning, skills, knowledge or whatever and the ways in which we go about these activities.

There is currently concern amongst students, teachers and parents as to the appropriateness of using IT in learning in a particular discipline if when that learning comes to be assessed, the IT element is removed. This is as true about straightforward matters such as using word processing in discursive essay type assessments as it is about having access to electronically stored data in problem-solving tasks. The unresolved question is of the justification for removing from the assessment one of the tools of learning in that subject.

In the situated learning view, assessment requires us to balance out the perspectives of the individual and the group, and to keep in mind the totality of the situation including factors such as race, gender, social, class, historical and cultural contexts.

Reconciling views?

Sfard's (1998) exploration of learning suggests that we are caught between competing 'metaphors' for learning, between the metaphor of 'acquiring knowledge' and having it as a personal possession, and that of 'participation' or the more democratic idea of 'people in action'.

In the acquisition view it is not only getting knowledge that counts, but also the means of acquiring it. Consequently, some knowledge is seen as highly prized and, in a slight shift, it is often seen that the person possessing this knowledge is in some way superior to others. Like other personal possessions 'gifts' and 'potential' are seen as measurable. In Sfard's view, this allows people to be sorted into different categories. While not always an outcome of using acquisition metaphors, such attitudes can often be seen in societies where material wealth is valued and pursued. The ideas about learning considered in the earliest part of this account tend to be about 'acquisition'.

Using the participation metaphor, learning is about continual change and not about permanent labelling. Sfard considers that actions can be successful or clever but these terms do not apply to people. Participation is a more positive ideal, implying hope of success despite earlier failure. Socio and radical constructivism, communities of practice and distributed cognition can, largely, be seen as 'participatory'.

What Sfard argues is not that one metaphor is superior to the other, but rather that we need both. Noting that tensions, problems and paradoxes are everywhere in the real world and while these often seem to be contradictory and irreconcilable, it is this very tension between the two views that acts as a safeguard 'against theoretical excesses and is a source of power' (Sfard 1998: 10).

Keeping both metaphors in mind helps to clarify some of the confusion surrounding views of learning and assessment and the use of IT not only in the support of learning, but also in the processes of assessment that surround us in contemporary society. High stakes assessment has much to do with the acquisition metaphor and related learning theories and IT has a role to play here, but new technologies have much to offer more participatory models, probably for the first time in history, in showing us how to demonstrate less individualistic and more twenty-first century oriented skills.

In conclusion

IT has much to offer in supporting learning as well as assessment and testing, as these currently exist and as we might see them develop. This chapter suggests that learning and its assessment must correspond in a coherent way, and that when considering assessment involving IT, it is learning that should remain the leading idea. It suggests that we don't always get this arrangement right and, as a result, fail to recognise how successful learners are or how extensive their skills might be. New technologies and new views about learning make it increasingly important for educators to be clear about the purposes of assessment and to resolve the tensions experienced by learners and teachers. The view that keeping in mind both metaphors of learning offers us a way of balancing the differing demands of assessment is persuasive in our current situation.

Looking to the future, we need to use IT to meet the learning needs of the twenty-first century information age, and this means attending to learning, both in school and out, and to opening up opportunities for learners to demonstrate their creativity, entrepreneurship and ability to innovate.

References

Black, P., Harrison, C., Lee, C., Marshall, B. and Wiliam, D. (2002) *Working Inside the Black Box: assessment for learning in the classroom*, London: King's College.

Brown, J.S., Collins, A. and Duguid, P. (1989) 'Situated cognition and the culture of learning', *Educational Researcher*, 18: 32–41.

Gee, J.P. (2003) 'Opportunity to learn: a language-based perspective on assessment', *Assessment in Education*, 10: 27–46.

Kirshner, D. and Witson, J.A. (eds) (1997) *Situated Cognition*, London: Lawrence Erlbaum Associates.

Lave, J. (1991) 'Situating learning in communities of practice', in L.B. Resnick, J. Levine, and S. Teasley (eds) *Perspectives on Socially Shared Cognition*, Washington DC: American Psychological Society.

Rogoff, B. (1990) *Apprenticeship in Thinking: cognitive development in social context*, London: Oxford University Press.

Sfard, A. (1998) 'On two metaphors for learning and the dangers of choosing just one', *Educational Researcher*, 27: 4–13.

Van der Veer, R. and Valsiner, J. (eds) (1994) *The Vygotsky Reader*, Oxford: Blackwell.

Von Glasersfeld, E. (1995) *Radical Constructivism: a way of knowing and learning*, Oxford: Blackwell.

Wenger, E. (1999) *Communities of Practice: learning, meaning and identity*, Cambridge: Cambridge University Press.

Chapter 5

Setting a new course for research on information technology in education

Robert K. Munro
University of Strathclyde, Scotland

The alleged benefits of IT for education

For over twenty-five years IT has been touted as an invaluable, highly influential, pivotal resource capable of supporting, enhancing and ultimately transforming any area of teaching and learning. IT offers sophisticated, powerful, increasingly easy-to-use learning tools with comprehensive applicability throughout teaching and learning.

The rapid evolution and development of IT has spawned a bewildering range of previously unimagined innovative applications and processes, from word processing through to rich media-convergent technology resources with global connectivity. Integrating these applications and processes into teaching and learning contexts has never been easy and has seldom proved particularly effective in supporting learning. Technical limitations, limited software specifically designed for educational use, funding constraints and poor pedagogical training inhibited development. As users mastered one technology, they were confronted by fresh innovation.

The research dimension and the need for a fresh approach

An important research dimension developed alongside the burgeoning use of IT in education. However, research has generated limited evidence that IT has made an effective contribution to the learning process. IT has undoubtedly impacted teaching, learning, attainment and motivation, but has not exercised as powerful an impact as expected, nor has it exerted a sustained influence. The impact on the teaching process has been greater than on the learning process. Research (Condie and Munro 2007) concludes IT has enhanced presentation skills, supported basic literacy and numeracy development, contributed to the acquisition of problem solving skills and facilitated understanding of abstract and complex concepts. IT has supported and enhanced practice but has failed to transform education.

The research agenda has been imperfectly focused. Too much time, money and effort has been devoted to evaluating events, issues, activities and resources that contribute little to advancing our appreciation of how this pivotal resource develops conceptual understanding and enhances learning. Too much activity has been concerned with documenting governmental attitudes to IT and policy implementation strategies, resulting in a plethora of detailed IT-impact assessments from different countries, groups of nation states or educational institutions. Too much attention has been paid to identifying why IT initiatives have been less successful than anticipated. Becta (2001) noted that historic IT research was often on small samples, rarely controlled out the effects of things other than IT and was seldom sufficiently methodologically rigorous. There is insufficient incontrovertible, rigorous research evidence that the widespread uses and applications of IT are educationally valuable, indisputably advance teaching and learning, and exercise a positive impact on attainment and conceptual understanding. The substantial body of IT-related research activity offers no conclusive proof that the enormous investment of time, effort and finance has delivered sustainable educational benefits. Students have simply been experimental data in a global IT project. Additionally, research conclusions are not delivered effectively to educational practitioners and fail to identify how IT might best be deployed throughout education. A new research approach and more effective dissemination of research conclusions are required.

Microcomputers were introduced into educational institutions with no prior research and with no educational rationale for their use. Hardware and hastily developed educational software was delivered to schools with no guarantee of educational benefit. Teachers received minimal training in technical aspects of IT use and none in respect of pedagogical issues. Educational institutions were simply given the 'boxes' and were expected to use them in innovative and effective ways. The drive to introduce IT to education reflected governmental desire to boost the computer industry market and equip learners with tenuous work-related IT skills. However, two research strands were established and have since dominated the IT research agenda:

- documenting and describing the uptake of IT and associated policy/decision-making in specific countries (Sambuu 2005), in agglomerations of nation states such as the EU (Eurydice 2004) and even specific local authorities;
- recording (and evaluating) the introduction, dissemination and use made of IT and specific applications/technologies – usually on a national basis (Balanskat et al. 2006) or in a group of educational institutions.

The first strand reflects the drive to create an information or digital society, concern that unless IT is adopted quickly and ubiquitously nations will be marginalised socio-economically, a belief that IT can beneficially impact education, and a determination to reduce the digital divide. These themes permeate IT policy documents, reflecting a political conviction that there is no alternative to joining the IT rat race. The results of research activity, while interesting to government decision-makers, researchers and academics, offer little practical advice and support to teachers and lecturers wishing to further the learning of their pupils and students.

The strand assessing the impact of IT ranges over national snapshot studies and longitudinal surveys to detailed examinations of specific uses and applications. This research bolsters political assertions that IT resources (hardware, Internet access and teacher training) have been provided or that specific products offer undefined benefits to teaching and learning.

Numbers of computers are recorded, their distribution is described, pupil computer ratios and Internet accessibility are commented on, software product use is identified and in-service training of teachers is noted. Findings frequently mask inadequacies and inconsistencies in IT provision and seldom contain evaluation of effective IT uses.

Where is the research evidence of success of IT in education?

Condie and Munro's (2007) analysis of over 350 published literature sources on the uses and impact of IT in UK education concluded that IT development had progressed unevenly across and within schools and technologies. They confirmed a steady increase in IT availability and noted ambitious computer-pupil ratios had been achieved. However, wide variation was reported within and across schools with regard to access to reliable technologies and broadband connectivity. Simply providing resources was clearly not enough to create enhancement of learning and teaching. Unfortunately, many politicians and education decision-makers still believe that is all that is required!

The 124-page *Harnessing Technology* schools survey (Becta 2007) gathered data on key indicators of e-maturity and IT usage in schools. Only a third of these pages address IT in teaching and learning – covering lesson planning, assessment and exploration of time-saving benefits resulting from IT adoption. Just three pages deal with the impact of IT and conclude that IT could exercise a positive impact on motivation and formal attainment. There is absolutely nothing on how IT enhances learning.

In Scotland IT is considered an important, integral component of education, evidenced by its inclusion as a core component of National Educational Guidelines, a central role in the Curriculum for Excellence and the raison d'être of the National Grid for Learning. IT infrastructure provision has been considerable and Scottish teachers were fully involved in national in-service IT training schemes. Much government-sponsored research has commented on these developments (Granville *et al.* 2005). The findings are usually generalised and fail to address learning issues. A report by the Scottish Executive Education Department (SEED 2006) concluded that the primary school pupil-computer ratio was 9:1 (5:1 in secondary), more pupils had e-mail addresses, 100 per cent of schools had Internet access and that 93 per cent of teachers had participated in IT skills (not necessarily pedagogical skills) training; yet another key report obsessed with numbers, but with no mention of learning benefits.

In marked contrast, longitudinal research (Condie *et al.* 2005) found the focus of IT use in Scottish classrooms was shifting from learning about IT to learning through IT, that the use of computers to support learning was patchy, limited examples of good practice reflected the drive of enthusiasts and few pupils experienced or enjoyed regular computer access in classrooms. Indeed, access to and quality of IT provision was a major concern.

Her Majesty's Inspectorate for Education regards IT as a natural component of good teaching and learning. They noted (HMIE 2007) great progress in IT capacity building with major expenditure on hardware provision, infrastructure development and in-service teacher training. However, while they observed teachers were expected to integrate IT naturally into classroom practice they could find no widespread, consistent, best practice across the country. Despite this, they bullishly concluded that Scotland was well placed to tap the potential of IT – after twenty-five years of effort!

Years of investment, development and research has yet to convince educationalists that IT is worthwhile, cannot offer rigorous evidence of valuable uses, and seldom addresses how to effect best practice.

A new research focus

Globally, educational institutions are attempting to develop the e-confidence and e-capability of teachers and learners, capitalise on the alleged educational benefits of IT, embed IT in everyday curriculum practice and deploy a comprehensive range of IT techniques to support learning, teaching and attainment. Different institutions implement different strategies with varying degrees of success. All would benefit from guidance underpinned by research and evaluation identifying best practice, specifying how IT best supports and enhances learning, and answering questions such as:

- Can word processing transform the creative writing process?
- How do spreadsheets facilitate understanding of mathematical concepts?
- In what ways can exploration of population databases assist understanding of past socio-economic conditions?
- What strategies would help students use the Internet effectively for research?
- How might simulations be best deployed to foster understanding of social issues, e.g. global warming?

Additionally, further research should be carried out to identify whether many newer uses of IT (podcasting, blogging, digital video, PowerPoint presentations) promote and enhance, let alone transform, the learning process. If digital natives possess creative cut, rip and burn abilities, how exactly does that foster learning? Can students identify salient points in Internet text, interpret a 3-D Excel graph or focus on the key issues in a podcast any more readily than before they enjoyed access to these sophisticated IT tools? Are conclusions they reach more cogently argued than before? Is follow-up work better than that produced without IT support?

School-focused research in these areas has characteristically been concerned with identifying why IT is *not* successful (Condie and Munro 2007) and commonly concludes that:

- teachers are not fully conversant with educational uses of IT
- teachers lack vision
- teachers are not confident with new pedagogical approaches
- teachers are excluded from financial decision making regarding resources
- teachers don't have time to consolidate their learning
- teachers lack advice on best practice in their curricular or subject area
- resources are not consistently available across subjects or across schools
- many hardware resources are old and lack sophistication
- educational software is in short supply and not specifically targeted at the curriculum
- pupils do not enjoy regular access to hardware.

Such conclusions never appear to be acted upon, let alone resolved. Recommendations are noted but ignored. Research into IT use in classrooms frequently focuses on specific equipment or particular software packages. Fadel and Lemke (2006) caution that much of this is really descriptive study, not rigorous research. They conclude that descriptive studies do not provide definitive evidence of cause and effect, rather interesting results that warrant detailed research.

The Interactive Whiteboard (IWB) represents the latest breakthrough technology embraced by UK education. Entire schools have been equipped, at considerable expense, and whiteboards dominate many classrooms. As ever, descriptive studies and rigorous research has followed, rather than preceded, this widespread adoption of innovative technology. Descriptive studies (Fadel and Lemke 2006) indicate three levels of use – to increase efficiency, to extend learning through engaging materials, and to transform learning through stimulating interaction. Rigorous research, however, is inconclusive. Fadel and Lemke (2006) noted that theoretical research maintains whiteboards should contribute to learning, and Condie and Munro (2007) found qualitative studies concluded educational benefits result from their use. Higgins *et al.* (2005) identified language improvements for low-achieving primary school pupils and Somekh *et al.* (2006) found whiteboards were more widely, intensively and skilfully used in primary schools. Smith *et al.* (2005), however, concluded there was insufficient evidence to identify the actual impact on learning and that whiteboards had not transformed teaching practice.

Despite inconclusive results, this is essential research – precisely what is desperately needed to support practitioners. It needs to be wider, deeper and on an extended basis. Advanced whiteboards are already being evaluated; but while current technology engenders valuable interaction and involvement, there is currently no guarantee they enhance understanding, transform learning or will realise their technological potential!

Benefits from IT and how to achieve them

Teachers can be seduced by a limited set of attractive technologies. This can inhibit their use of a broad palette of IT options. Condie and Munro (2007) found that where IT is most effective in enhancing the learning experience, teachers integrate a range of techniques using a judicious mix of hardware, software and connectivity to develop innovative learning and teaching approaches. The most effective IT use results from a school level e-strategy addressing future developments and sustainability within a monitored and measured plan.

They concluded that IT-related investment is only worthwhile if it generates a commensurate impact on performance levels, abilities and progress of pupils. However, while research evidence on attainment was inconsistent, that on the impact of IT on motivation, engagement with and independence in learning was considerably more persuasive. Much of the literature (Condie and Munro, 2007) reported greater collaboration, greater engagement and persistence, better on-task behaviour and enhanced conceptual understanding. A growing body of evidence indicated IT could support creative thinking, promote critical thinking skills and foster problem-solving abilities, especially where specific technologies with a strong visual element were used. The impact was significant where pupil tasks had clear educational aims, were expressly designed to maximise the potential of IT and were perceived as relevant and purposeful by pupils. The evidence was strong in regard to literacy and numeracy generally, with examples of good practice and benefits in other subject areas.

Research evidence exists to confirm that IT benefits education. This is a start. The agenda should now focus on examining particular technologies and their classroom uses, and identifying exactly how IT can support creative thinking, promote critical thinking, foster problem-solving and enhance understanding. Conclusions should incorporate specific, unequivocal, reputable, reliable pedagogical advice for classroom practitioners on how to achieve best practice. Advice must be speedily and effectively communicated so practitioners, with appropriate management support, can effect implementation. Limited research findings filter down to teachers and seldom impact their pedagogy. National policy research reports and impact studies are not designed to influence the masses directly. They are primarily commissioned by politicians to illustrate how effectively they have resolved resource issues. Furthermore, many reports are so voluminous and expensive that they reach a limited audience, and with restricted access to literature and advice teachers are understandably reluctant to integrate IT in their teaching and learning strategies.

In conclusion

In every nation the uses of IT in education are being explored and assessed, and IT is being woven into the fabric of education. Developing and integrating IT in education is expensive and IT will have to prove its educational and cost effectiveness. IT integration cannot be effected satisfactorily without guidance and support from rigorous research, and this research has to be evidence-based rather than assertion led.

Let us set a fresh course for research on our IT journey across the turbulent seas of education. Governments and educational agencies must be persuaded to divert financing from data-rich resources-oriented prestige projects towards smaller scale, tightly focused evaluations of specific technologies and particular IT uses. The focus must be on what is effective, why it is effective and how it can best be integrated into curriculum and classroom practice. Claims made for the many uses of IT in our classrooms must be substantiated. The research community should be charged with communicating effectively and unambiguously with those deploying the technologies and its uses so that, supported by appropriate and adequate resources, they can effect transformation of teaching and learning to the benefit of their pupils/students.

References

Balanskat, A., Blamire, R. and Kefala, S. (2006) *The ICT Impact Report*, European Schoolnet. Online. Available HTTP: <ec.europa.eu/education/pdf/doc254_en.pdf> (accessed 16 April 2009).

Becta (2001) *The Secondary School of the Future*, Coventry: Becta, Online. Available HTTP: <http://partners.becta.org.uk/index.php?section=rh&rid=13683> (accessed 16 March 2009).

—— (2007) *Harnessing Technology Schools Survey 2007*, Coventry: Becta. Online. Available HTTP: <http://partners.becta.org.uk/upload_dir/downloads/page_documents/research/harnessing_technology_schools_survey07.pdf> (accessed 16 March 2009).

Condie, R. and Munro, R. (2007) *The Impact of ICT in Schools: a landscape review*, Coventry: Becta. Online. Available HTTP: <http://publications.becta.org.uk/download.cfm?resID=28221> (accessed 16 March 2009).

Condie, R., Munro, R., Muir, D. and Collins, R. (2005) *The Impact of ICT Initiatives in Scottish Schools: Phase 3*, Edinburgh: QiE/SEE. Online. Available HTTP: <http://www.scotland.gov.uk/Publications/2005/09/14111116/11170> (accessed 16 March 2009).

Eurydice (2004) *Key Data on ICT in Schools in Europe*, Belgium: Eurydice. Online. Available HTTP: <eacea.ec.europa.eu/portal/page/portal/Eurydice/showPresentation?pubid=048EN> (accessed 16 March 2009).

Fadel, C. and Lemke, C. (2006) *Technology in Schools. What the research says*, San Jose, CA: Cisco Systems. Online. Available HTTP: <http://www.cisco.com/web/strategy/docs/education/TechnologyinSchoolsReport.pdf> (accessed 16 March 2009).

Granville, S., Russell, K. and Bell, J. (2005) *Evaluation of the Masterclass Initiative*, Edinburgh: Scottish Executive Education Department. Online. Available HTTP: <http://www.scotland.gov.uk/Publications/2005/12/13133428/34291> (accessed 16 March 2009).

Higgins, S., Falzon, C., Hall, I., Moseley, D., Smith, H. and Wall, K. (2005) *Embedding ICT in the Literacy and Numeracy Strategies*, Newcastle, UK: University of Newcastle.

HMIE (2007) *Improving Scottish Education: ICT in learning and teaching*, UK: HM Inspectorate of Education. Online. Available HTTP: <http://www.hmie.gov.uk/documents/publication/iseictilat.pdf> (accessed 16 March 2009).

Sambuu, U. (2005) 'The usage of ICT for secondary education in Mongolia', *International Journal of Education and Development using ICT*, 1: 101–118.

SEED (2006) *The National Grid for Learning Scotland. Summary of progress report 4*, Edinburgh: Blackwell.

Smith, H.J., Higgins, S., Wall, K. and Miller, J. (2005) 'Interactive whiteboards: boon or bandwagon? A critical review of the literature', *Journal of Computer Assisted Learning*, 18: 4 91–101.

Somekh, B., Underwood, J., Convery, A., Dillon, G., Jarvis, J., Lewin, C., Mavers, D., Saxon, D., Sing, S., Steadman, S., Twining, P. and Woodrow, D. (2006) *Evaluation of the ICT Test Bed Project: annual report*, Coventry: Becta.

Chapter 6

Why 'what works' is not enough for information technology in education research

Geoff Romeo and Glenn Russell
Monash University, Australia

Introduction

Recent and ongoing criticism of educational research has led to a cry for more *evidence based practice* (EBP) built on scientifically based research (SBR) that uses *randomised controlled trials* (RCTs). This continuing criticism has been characterised by perceptions that there are serious epistemological, ontological and methodological problems which must be addressed. Whitty (2006: 161), for example, points out that there has been a whole series of reviews and criticisms indicating that educational research lacks rigour, fails to produce cumulative findings, is theoretically incoherent, ideologically biased and irrelevant to schools, lacks the involvement of teachers, and is poorly communicated and expensive. Similarly, educational research into the use of IT in education has been criticised as lacking a theoretical perspective and a sense of history, for being focused on the enabling of technology at the expense of its impact on human endeavour, and for being methodologically problematic (Underwood 2004).

The relentless criticism of educational research is not new. However, the present iteration has seen a privileging of SBR and RCTs and, a deriding (yet again) of qualitative research because it seldom looks at cause and effect. Robust debate about the very nature of science and scientific evidence has ensued. There has also been a re-focusing of attention on the purposes and nature of educational research. The debate is eclectic, problematic and complex; however, it is clear that the *what works* thesis that underpins EBP is, on the whole, refuted, and that RCT methodology is seen as too narrow.

Identifying strategies and techniques that seemingly work in practice is important, of course. However, privileging a research agenda based only on what seemingly works best in practice promotes teaching as a technical enterprise rather than an activity underpinned by value judgements, devalues professional opinion, and privileges technical research over cultural research. In contributing to the debate, St Clair (2005) challenges the notion that best practice can be defined through SBR and that educational research will lead to perfect knowledge of educational processes. He disputes the notion of induction (cause and effect) in the social sciences and argues that the existence of *superunknowns* – the infinite number of factors that could influence the interactions between humans – makes generalising from one setting to another problematic, if not impossible. The role of educational research is then to assist the teacher to reflect on what happened in setting A and determine whether it is appropriate for setting B (empirical heuristics); in such a process there is greater recognition of the value of the educator's judgement.

Biesta (2007) also challenges the notion of EBP and points to the value and importance of professional judgement. He examines three key assumptions underpinning EBP in education. The first is the model of professional action implied by EBP. He describes the model as a causal/technological model of action that has its origins in the field of medicine. The notion of an intervention is central. The effectiveness of the intervention is determined through experimental research, possibly using test scores as evidence. Biesta (2007: 8) argues that this model of professional action may be appropriate for medicine, but not for education. Being a student is not the same as being a patient; education is not a causal process but a process of symbolic or symbolically mediated interactions. Professional action in education is about making moral or value judgements – it is not so much about what appears to work in a generic sense, but what is appropriate for these learners in these circumstances. The notion that a generic, *what works* intervention can replace normative professional judgement is flawed.

Second, professional judgement is central to educational practice and is moral or value laden, rather than procedural or technical. This means that most decisions made by educators on how they will organise the learning environment (and indeed on how policy makers and administrators will organise educational systems) are ultimately value (moral) judgements rather than procedural (technical) judgements. This raises questions about the nature and purpose of educational research. Drawing on Dewey's practical epistemology, Biesta argues that research does not supply rules for action but hypotheses for intelligent problem solving. It can tell us what worked in a particular situation but not what will work in future situations. The role of the educator is to use research findings to make one's problem solving more intelligent.

Finally, Biesta makes a distinction between the technical role of research and the cultural role of research. The technical role provides strategies and techniques to solve problems; the cultural role provides different ways of understanding and imagining social reality – a theme also explored by Atkinson (2000, 2002) in her defence of postmodernism in educational research. EBP/SBR seems to be unaware that educational research can be both technical and cultural.

IT in education research

The discussion so far has been about educational research more broadly because it is important to show that it is the educational research community in general that is under siege, not just research about IT in education, and that some of the issues are non-specific. This is not to deny, however, that there are particular concerns about IT in education research. Underwood (2004), for example, raises four concerns emanating from the 2001 Research Assessment Exercise in the UK. First, Underwood suggests that the weaker research lacks theoretical perspective. She is concerned that the IT educational community tends not to connect with the central body of educational research. She argues that '. . . theoretical perspective is the communication bridge between us (the IT education community) and the rest of the education community and that a lack of a shared perspective can be damaging for ICT research' (Underwood 2004: 139). Second, Underwood suggests that some IT research lacks a sense of history. She argues that the IT community tends not to embed current knowledge on what has happened before. Perhaps the fast moving pace of technological development may be a contributing factor in the community's reluctance to look back and learn from the lessons of the past. McDougall and Jones (2006), citing the work of Papert, Harel and Papert, and Minsky agree; '. . . our area, more than any other the authors can think of, seems determined to neglect or deliberately ignore its own history' (McDougall and Jones 2006: 356).

Third, Underwood (2004) suggests that some IT research focuses on the technology rather than the impacts of technology on human endeavour. She points out that, unlike most researchers in the educational field, many researchers in IT are the designers and producers of artefacts and it is the designing and producing that becomes central to the research effort, rather than the impact of the artefact on the system, teacher or learner. Finally, Underwood suggests that IT research has methodological problems. She suggests the focus of research questions on individual context and experience and the tendency for the IT community to be unaware of the techniques and tools that are universally available and generally accepted as tried-and-tested instruments, is a form of parochialism.

Overall, Underwood suggests that if the IT research community is to improve its status then improving the research questions, methodology and analytical techniques that are used, and attempting to find an integrative theoretical framework, are vital to building intellectual bridges with the wider research community.

Future directions

It is not difficult to conclude that part of the call for SBR and EBP is a backlash against the complex and tangled world of educational theory, research, policy and practice. One only has to ask a classroom teacher, a newly enrolled research student, or a policy maker about the value, purpose and nature of educational research to discover that some of the criticism levelled at the field has resonance. Educational research is a complex and contested discipline. This, however, is not justification for the valorisation of one approach at the expense of another and is certainly not the way forward for the IT in education research community.

Before discussing what we see as the way forward there are some issues that need further exploration. In particular, the justification for theory in IT in education research per se, and the value, nature and purpose of educational research in general. Initially, it appears that the application of theory in IT in education research is characterised by confusion and even incoherence. However, there is a continuing need to consider the contested epistemological, ontological and methodological discourses of IT and that the complex labyrinth of perspectives arising from the application of a range of theories provides an opportunity to understand the world around us.

Somekh (2004) provides an example of how theory can be applied to help build new knowledge. In discussing the dissonance between student home use and school use of IT, she suggests that three bodies of theory – McLuhan's explanation of the medium as the message, Turkle's work on the impact of self and identity formation, and activity theory – enable us '. . . to reach a deeper analysis of the reasons why ICTs cannot be introduced into education as superficial additions to the existing systems, but need to be located in radical institutional and systemic change' (Somekh (2004: 175).

Most educational researchers would agree that the value, nature and purpose of their endeavours is to create

> . . . a body of theoretical knowledge and understanding that can be progressively enlarged in a systematic and disciplined way . . . [and then for] . . . practitioners to use that body of knowledge to expose and examine the taken–for–granted presuppositions implicit in the discourses and practices endemic to their own professional cultures.
>
> (Carr 2005: 333)

Conducting research to identify causal effects does have value and has a role to play in building a body of theoretical knowledge. However, narrowing methodology to RCTs and promoting a research agenda exclusively premised on *what works* in practice to achieve this aim is clearly not enough. If the aim is to create a body of theoretical knowledge, using a variety of theories and methods that helps practitioners make more intelligent decisions about how learning is organised, then we, as an educational research community, have failed to communicate this adequately and are suffering as a consequence. The role of theory, the methods of data collection and analysis, and the value and purposes of educational research are not well understood by insiders and outsiders alike. What needs to be communicated is that the contested nature of educational research is a healthy and productive phenomenon, and that the conduct of good quality research, irrespective of the methodology employed, has value, purpose and impact.

The key phrase here and the way forward as we see it, is *good quality research*. The imperative for IT in education researchers is to do good quality research and to successfully communicate its intent and value. Discussion about what constitutes good quality research is important. It is especially important when we have ontologically slippery phenomena, set in complex webs of social meanings and institutions, and a great deal of epistemological diversity among those researching such phenomena. Despite the contestation and differences of views, there are themes common to all good research that should guide us. Good quality research has '. . . purpose, rigour, imagination, care for others, and economy' (Pratt and Swann 2003: 178).

There is no single purpose that applies to all educational research. Some researchers are concerned with practice – including the design and production of artefacts in the case of IT in education – others with policy, and others with social, political or economic issues. The possible theme that combines them is that the research is of benefit to society in some way. Linked to this idea of purpose is the methodological approach that will advance knowledge. It is here that we argue, along with many others, that restricting the methodological approach to RCTs is wrong. 'There are no exclusively quantitative or qualitative ways of doing research, only quantitative and qualitative tools and procedures' (Pratt and Swann 2003: 181). It is the task of the researcher to select the tools and procedures (methods) that are appropriate to the research problem.

Researchers of IT education need to be better informed, and better use the proven tools or instruments from other disciplines and other areas of education research. However, there is also a need to develop new tools, techniques and methods to deal with new situations. For example, determining whether an asynchronous threaded discussion is on task and in-depth, is a new situation that requires new tools and techniques. It is important that these new tools, techniques and methods link with proven instruments, where appropriate, and are disseminated, shared, used, discussed, and refined. What also needs to be considered are the new opportunities that IT affords us in the collection of data. For example, McDougall and Jones (2006) argue that technology now enables a much more sophisticated and richer collection of data than ever before – we can now place three video cameras in a classroom and record activity from multiple perspectives. (See Jones's chapter in this volume.)

Good quality research also has rigour, that is, it is procedurally and logically rigorous. Procedural rigour is established by being methodical, using appropriate techniques and attending to detail. Logical rigour is established when attention is paid to the concern for argument and the soundness of evidence. Good quality research is also a creative task that requires imagination – the generation of research questions and the development of a research strategy are imaginative exercises. Good quality research is also ethical – for moral and practical reasons, and, it is economic in that it aims for economy of effort, time and resources (Pratt and Swann 2003: 182).

The Pedagogies with E-Learning Resources (PELRS) project (Somekh and Saunders 2007) is one example, among many, of good quality research. The focus of the PELRS project was the possibility of organising teaching and learning in radically different ways when we now have an array of digital and network technologies. The project employed cultural–historical activity theory (CHAT) to generate knowledge about how IT might be used to transform children's learning. The action research methodology involved working with teachers and learners by intervening in the teaching processes and changing them. One of the main outcomes of the project was the development of pedagogic frameworks that can be used by teachers and learners to think differently about learning. The frameworks underpinned by Engestrom's second generation activity theory and the learning theories of Vygotsky, provide teachers with an alternative to the traditional lesson plan. This new planning tool assists pupils to learn effectively with e-learning resources.

This project does not employ RCTs, yet it is a quality project because it has purpose, rigour, and imagination. Its purpose has been to build a knowledge base, with the help of all stakeholders – researchers, teachers, pupils and school leaders – about the implications of IT for teaching and learning, and to change IT in education pedagogy. Evidence of its rigour is reflected in its sound use of qualitative techniques to gather evidence, in its cogent linking of data, evidence and findings, and its rational use of socio-cultural theory and activity theory as a basis for the development of new instruments to assist teaching and learning. It is imaginative, innovative and creative because it recognises basic flaws with current IT in education pedagogy and develops a process for positive and innovative change (Somekh and Saunders 2007).

Conclusion

We have argued that educational research is a complex and contested discipline characterised by robust debate about the very nature of science and scientific evidence, and different epistemological, ontological and methodological perspectives. One of the consequences of this is that the nature and purposes of educational research are not well understood. This has led to criticism and a call for more SBR that uses RCTs to deliver generic classroom interventions that supposedly work universally.

While recognising that identifying strategies and techniques that work in practice is important we reject the notion that only RCTs will uncover what works and further reject the thesis that the focus on what works is enough.

A research agenda based on what works promotes a narrow and simplistic view of education. We further recognise that some see educational research as over-theoretical and theoretically incoherent, and we support the notion that as a research community we need to better communicate our nature and purpose; however, this should not be at the expense of rejecting theory. The use of theory in educational research is important and a range of theories should be available to practitioners.

In response to criticisms of IT in education research as reported by Underwood (2004), we agree on the importance of using theory to inform our work and to connect with the wider research community. Along with McDougall and Jones (2006), we agree that a considerable amount of earlier research is not being used to assist in the creation of new knowledge. Whether there is too much focus on the technology rather than the impacts of the technology on the human condition is difficult to tell. As Underwood (2004) points out, many of us are designers and producers of artefacts and much of our research is on the efficacy of technology-rich learning environments. We do not see a problem with this; however, research students often see the building of the artefact as the research project, rather than the impact of the technology on teaching and learning.

We agree with Underwood that IT in education researchers need to be better informed about, and use, the proven data collection instruments and analytical tools from other disciplines and other areas of educational research. However, we also argue that there is a need to develop new instruments, tools, techniques and methods to deal with new environments and new situations. We need also to consider the opportunities IT affords us to collect and deal with data in new and perhaps more intelligent ways. For us, the way forward as a research community is to recognise, understand and accept that our discipline (and sub-discipline) is complex and contested; to ensure that the nature and purpose of educational research is well communicated; and to make sure we engage in good quality research that has value, purpose and impact.

References

Atkinson, E. (2000) 'The promise of uncertainty: education, postmodernism and the politics of possibility', *International Studies in Sociology of Education*, 10: 81–99.
—— (2002) 'The responsible anarchist: postmodernism and social change', *British Journal of Sociology of Education*, 23: 73–87.
Biesta, G. (2007) 'Why "what works" won't work: evidence-based practice and the democratic deficit in educational research', *Educational Theory*, 57: 1–22.
Carr, W. (2005) 'The role of theory in the professional development of an educational theorist', *Pedagogy, Culture and Society*, 13: 333–345.
McDougall, A. and Jones, A. (2006) 'Theory and history, questions and methodology: current and future issues in research into ICT in education', *Technology, Pedagogy and Education*, 15: 353–360.

Pratt, J. and Swann, J. (eds) (2003) 'Doing good research', *Educational research in Practice: making sense of methodology*, London: Continuum.

Somekh, B. (2004) 'Taking the sociological imagination to school: an analysis of the (lack of) impact of information and communication technologies on education systems', *Technology, Pedagogy and Education*, 13: 163–179.

Somekh, B. and Saunders, L. (2007) 'Developing knowledge through intervention: meaning and definition of "quality" in research into change', *Research Papers in Education*, 22: 183–197.

St Clair, R. (2005) 'Similarity and superunknowns: an essay on the challenges of educational research', *Harvard Educational Review*, 75: 435–488.

Underwood, J. (2004), 'Research into information and communication technologies: where now?' *Technology, Pedagogy and Education*, 13: 135–145.

Whitty, G. (2006) 'Education(al) research and education policy making: is conflict inevitable?' *British Educational Research Journal*, 32: 159–176.

Chapter 7

From integration to transformation

Andrew E. Fluck
University of Tasmania, Australia

Introduction

This chapter examines the merits and validity of measuring the educational value of computers using conventional tests of academic achievement. I examine transformative uses of computers in schools, and how curriculum design may be reconsidered in such a context. This is illustrated by three examples of transformation through IT, in literacy practices, curriculum content and classroom pedagogy. The examples justify radical curriculum change. One way of achieving these changes is by envisioning new learning outcomes, that can only realistically be achieved through pupils using computers. The chapter concludes by considering ways forward and associated implications for research.

Assessing the effectiveness of IT integration

Downes *et al.* (2002) in *Making Better Connections* (MBC), described four types of IT use in education:

- MBC type A: encouraging the acquisition of IT skills as an end in themselves
- MBC type B: using IT to enhance students' abilities within the existing curriculum
- MBC type C: using IT to enhance students' abilities as an integral component of broader curriculum reforms that are changing not only how learning occurs, but what is learned
- MBC type D: using IT as an integral component of the reforms that alter the organisational structure of schooling itself.

Consideration of the rationales for IT and the MBC types of computer use has led to confusion about whether IT in school education is about the study of computers, or learning through and with computers. The latter has been emphasised in policy and the literature over recent years, and hence is the focus for this chapter.

IT integration (MBC type B) is the main game for many schools and educational authorities. Most current frameworks for IT in schools adopt an integrationist approach, focusing on office-like skills to support learning of traditional subjects. Frameworks such as the Australian Key Information Technology Outcomes (Fluck 1997) and the National Educational Technology Standards (ISTE 2007) from the USA use broadly similar descriptors for the main modes of computer use.

Whilst this integrationist stance has predominated we have also seen a growth in standardised testing, often at a national level. National benchmark tests of literacy and numeracy are often chosen as the indicators of educational efficacy, and many innovations are assessed by their impact on these measures. Should the value of IT be appraised this way? For many states these basic indicators of schooling success are the only reliable metrics available for comparison.

One such investigation into the alleged relationship between school IT and learning achievement in literacy and numeracy was conducted in Tasmania (Robertson *et al.* 2006). Four hundred and seventy-seven primary and high school teachers were surveyed and 50 classes observed, over three years. Most pupils only used IT for 2–4 per cent of the school week, because of limited computer availability and extra classroom activities such as music and sport. Teachers underestimated the proportion of their pupils with IT access at home by 17 per cent. According to pupil self reports, they spent 7.3 hours on a computer at home for every hour working on a school computer. Schools are indeed 'computer deserts' (Moursund and Bielefeldt 1999).

Therefore it was not surprising to find pupil use of IT accounted for only 12 ± 9.8 per cent of literacy and 6.75 ± 5 per cent of numeracy achievement variations on national benchmark tests, with a high level of statistical significance. It was not possible to distinguish these contributions from variations due to socio-economic status. Teacher IT use and school IT infrastructure had no significant relationship with the benchmark scores. It was noted that most national benchmark tests are conducted using pen on paper. The study also found that the number of computers accessed by a class of pupils largely determined the pedagogical models available to the teacher. One to three shared computers required pupils to be withdrawn on a rotational basis from the main learning programme. Four or more computers made it possible to engage in group projects.

It would seem that judging IT efficacy in schools using national benchmark testing for comparison of learning achievements is fatally flawed. Integrationist approaches are challenged by the limited success of IT in raising conventional schooling achievement test scores (Dynarski *et al.* 2007). However, Cox *et al.* (2004: 8) found 'specific uses of IT have had a positive impact on pupils' learning'.

From integration to transformation

'The symbiosis between humans and the tools they create is the basis for the creation of culture' (Bosco 2006: 2). Mind tools such as language, writing and IT are seminal. The future for IT in education is that of transformation, rather than integration into existing subject areas.

The transformative view of IT in education requires us to examine what new ways of learning (pedagogies), and what new educational outcomes (curricula) are appropriate for a new generation working with new tools. Moursund (2004) distinguishes between activities which can best be done by computers, those best done by humans and those best done by a synthesis of the two together. Moursund also identifies new fields of learning, such as computational chemistry which has emerged from this latter combination, validated by a Nobel Prize in 1998, but yet to enter most school curricula. Transformation of curriculum through the use of IT is seen as changing the content and processes of learning. This perspective moves the emphasis from learning about IT or learning through IT to learning *with* IT.

Teachers using computers in this transformative way can experience conflict. Therefore a valid opening for research will be teachers' varied responses 'to innovative ICT-curricula and how they give meaning to related new classroom practices' (Hermans *et al*. 2008: 1507). They need new epistemological tools to reconsider the curriculum supported by appropriately chosen IT.

Therefore in the remainder of this chapter I take a pragmatic approach, illustrating potential for change by reference to specific examples originating in existing curriculum areas. These examples do not presume the perpetuation of existing learning outcomes is the only way to use computers in education. They draw on MBC types C and D and suggest that entirely new ways of thinking are necessary to make effective judgements about learning transformed by IT.

Examples of transformation through IT

Transformation in literacy

Definitions of literacy have changed. UNESCO's General Conference in 1958 determined that 'a person is literate who can with understanding both read and write a short simple statement on his (her) everyday life' (UNESCO 2008:17). More recent definitions expand this to include 'speaking, listening and critical thinking with reading and writing' (DEETYA 1998: 17). The first example of transformation in literacy comes from the work of a Year 4 (age 10) pupil who created two texts. The first was handwritten and represents a typical self-reflection as shown in Figure 7.1.

This handwriting is not easy to read and therefore the text is repeated in Figure 7.2, with spelling corrected.

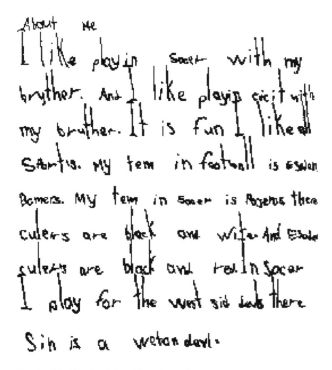

Figure 7.1 Handwriting: Year 4 student.

About Me
I like playing soccer with my brother. And I like
playing cricket with my brother. It is fun I like all
sports. My team in football is Essendon Bombers.
My team in soccer is Pajeros their colours are black
and white. And Essendon's colours are black and
red. In soccer I play for the Westside Devils. Their
sign is a Western Devil.

Figure 7.2 Interpreted text: Year 4 student.

The text has errors such as spelling, punctuation, graphology (letter shape) and grammar; fairly typical of a male pupil in this age group. The pupil created a second text (Figure 7.3) after training a voice recognition system (Microsoft Word 2003 running on Windows XP).

This text also has errors. Notably there are punctuation mistakes, and errors of grammar or style (two sentences start with the word 'and'). There is also a voice recognition error, where the computer has not rendered a surname as it

What I do at school
I don't do much at school. I work at school it is fun.
Cameron Smith is my best friend at school. And
Luke Saunders is my second best friend. And Kate
until is my third best friend. I work at school. I do
work about electricity. I do maths journals. And I
do things like I do takeaway sums. And I play with
my friends Cameron Luke and Kate in the playground.
In the playground with my friends I play chases.

Figure 7.3 Text created by voice recognition.

was uttered. These errors are unfamiliar to the classroom teacher, and the assessment of such a text must be undertaken using different conventions. Spelling and graphological errors are absent, since the computer drew words from a digital dictionary and the font approved for handwriting in this jurisdiction.

If we agree the texts are roughly equivalent in terms of standard, that the errors are similar in extent but different in type, then Table 7.1 summarises the production process for each text.

This shows a quantum leap in the rate of text production. Creating texts with voice recognition software can be ten times faster than handwriting. This example is not intended to suggest that all students should abandon their pens or pencils, but it illustrates the potential for transformation associated with a socially valued area of learning. Using voice recognition requires a set of skills which are not highlighted in most modern curricula, such as the ability to:

• speak clearly in grammatical sentences without interjection
• utter punctuation correctly for written texts
• plan a text structure beforehand and use this when speaking
• refer to supporting materials whilst speaking about them.

It may be valid to claim these skills are of value similar to, and as worthy of acquisition, as the manual dexterity needed to wield a pen or pencil. Technical

Table 7.1 Text samples compared

	Handwriting	*Voice Recognition*
Time taken	10.52 mins	1.3 mins
Words	64	85
Words/Sentence	6.2	6.6
Rate of production	6.27 words per minute	63.43 words per minute

implementation is not difficult. In pre-service teacher education, I have issued headset microphones to 25 students sharing a computer laboratory, and within an hour had them all dictating individual texts using standard Office software.

For schools to adopt voice recognition, we need the answers to research questions that arise from such a transformative use of IT. Is the increased rate of text production analogous to increased 'time on task' and hence more rapid skill acquisition? Do people have significantly different mental processes when creating texts vocally? What is the best educational mixture of hand-writing and dictation? It is a rich field for investigation.

Transformation in content

New computing technology has made a significant impact in communications media. For example, a single reporter can gather evidence and digitally record interviews which air within minutes. Hotels use LCD screens to display constantly changing visual art in their foyers. Today's youth celebrate each new music video, not just the song.

A combination of these techniques has become part of the curriculum. From 2007 Tasmanian students could enter university through study of Media Production. Media production encompasses a range of audio design, video-editing and design graphics, using advanced electronics and/or computer skills.

Media production is not the only new syllabus. Other IT-based subjects coming into schools are robotics, game-making and digital music composition. In art, old masters and pupils' own paintings can be brought to life by animating them. Science can be extended using handheld computers to record findings or as data-loggers. *Google Earth* and global positioning systems have enhanced geography studies. Research is needed into the best ways to introduce these new strands of study. Some may become options within existing curriculum areas. Others, such as game-making, are rapidly becoming the foundation for university courses and careers, but are poorly accommodated in traditional curricula.

Transformation in pedagogy

For quite some time, students taking formal examinations in mathematics have been able to use graphical calculators. Figures 7.4 and 7.5 illustrate the way in which the complexity of test questions has increased, whilst the time allowed for the examination has reduced over the course of the innovation.

Mathematics teachers may not stop here. There is interest and increasing pressure for them to adopt computer algebra system (CAS) calculators, which extend the visual capability of the device into equation solving and symbolic manipulation. CAS systems can also be implemented on general purpose computers. This can introduce the problem of collusion in examinations because the devices can communicate wirelessly.

1994 Mathematics (Stage 3) (3 hours)

On graph paper, shade the closed
half-plane represented by:
$6x + 4y = 24$.

Figure 7.4 Example of examination question to be answered without a graphics calculator.

2004 Mathematics Methods 5C (1 hour 48 minutes)
You are expected to provide a graphics calculator
approved by the Tasmanian Qualifications Authority.

The graph of the function $f(x) = 2\ln(x + 3) + 1$
intersects the axes at the points $(a, 0)$ and $(0, b)$.
(a) Find the exact values of a and b.
(b) Sketch $f(x)$. Label all relevant points
and asymptotes.

Figure 7.5 Examination question requiring use of graphics calculator.

The transformative effect of technology therefore moves academic bench-marks. Computers change what is taught, and how it is taught. There is rapidly growing use of online learning in schools to provide richer curricula in the absence of local teacher expertise, or when low pupil demand makes this approach economic. The Schome (school-home) project is an excellent example of virtual schooling in the online *Second-Life* environment, which has also allowed students to determine what is taught (Twining 2007). IT has the potential to change assessment practices, requiring new approaches that can distinguish between collaborative and individual achievements. A whole raft of research questions arise, relating to cultural adoption, teacher professional learning, societal backlash and eExaminations.

Researching transformation

The three examples merely illustrate the kinds of transformation that are possible. Others could be drawn from laptop schools, simulations, online learning objects and so on. Computers are providing a rich variety of new learnings and new ways to learn. With most personal computer operating systems being superseded in five to eight years, this rate of innovation is likely to continue in the future. Drawing analogies with Buckminster Fuller's work (1972: 289), cycles with limited design lifetimes are necessary for improvements to be made.

So what then are the most significant research questions to be addressed in the context of MBC types C and D? Transformation of learning through IT is exemplified by changes in the 'what' and 'how' of learning, changes in curriculum content and the pedagogical processes teachers employ to assist learning.

Changes in curriculum content must surely involve new assessment objectives for learners. Such changes must align with educational core values and economic training agendas: in this sense technology has an agency relationship with society. Researchers can also use familiar techniques to ascertain how pupils can best attain these new (transformed) learning objectives, and the most effective methods for learning them. Considerable theoretical effort combined with data from pragmatic trials will be required to establish the extent of IT use suitable for kindergarten children compared to older pupils.

Changes in pedagogy may depend upon new theories of learning beyond those of Vygotsky, Bruner and others. Teachers will need new skills to work with students who are studying computer-dependent content. Such skills may overlap with current classroom management expertise, but this is unlikely if the teaching is undertaken in a virtual learning environment. Cyber-bullying and plagiarism require monitoring and control, even if pupils are learning at a higher cognitive level on new learning outcomes (Harms *et al*. 2006: 14).

Conclusion

We have failed to realise the full potential of IT in school education. By using the phrase 'integrating IT into classroom practice' as a code for replicating existing learnings using computers as electric pencils, we do our pupils a disservice. We would hesitate to make flint knapping an essential prerequisite for entry into university. We should therefore be horrified by the suggestion that pupils' abilities be rated purely through their capacity to complete assessments using handwriting.

This view may cause social conflict because it shifts assessment into a new arena. Good assessment is fair and valid. Students may have grounds for complaint about the fairness if they are poor typists, or have slower computers. Yet previously some students have had fairer handwriting than others, or pens that don't blotch. We will need to revisit many of these inherent problems.

Whilst the transformation of education remains a challenge, envisioning new IT-based learning outcomes is only part of the process. Changing the nature of assessment, equipping teachers to cope with change, and engaging social approval are other parts of the equation. This is radical, systemic change, similar to the Knowsley district's closure of nine secondary schools and replacement by learning centres (Knowsley Council 2006). It needs champions, demonstrations of what works, debate, consensus if possible, and shared vision building.

How can research help in this endeavour? Research activity legitimates new thinking, and can therefore pave the way by piloting new learning outcomes in schools. Some of the research questions suggested in this chapter can guide such activities as they evaluate new curriculum content and new pedagogies. Perhaps the greatest challenge, once some of these questions have been answered, is communication of the results to the general public. Without public approval, these radical systemic changes will not take root in schools.

References

Bosco, J. (2006) *Tools, Culture, and Education: past – present – future*, Global Summit 2006 Sydney, Australia. Online. Available HTTP: <http://www.educationau.edu.au/jahia/webdav/site/myjahiasite/shared/globalsummit/JBosco_GS2006.pdf> (accessed 6 February 2009).

Cox, M., Abbot, C., Webb, M., Blakely, B., Beauchamp, T. and Rhodes, V. (2004) *A Review of the Research Literature Relating to ICT and Attainment: report to the Department for Education and Skills*, Coventry: Becta.

DEETYA (1998) *Literacy for All: the challenge for Australian schools*, M. Miers (ed.) Canberra, Australia: Department of Employment, Education, Training and Youth Affairs. Online. Available HTTP: <http://www.dest.gov.au/archive/schools/literacy&numeracy/publications/lit4all.htm> (accessed 18 March 2009).

Downes, T., Fluck, A., Gibbons, P., Leonard, R., Matthews, C., Oliver, R., Vickers, M. and Williams, M. (2002) *Making Better Connections: models of teacher professional development for the integration of information and communication technology into classroom practice*, Canberra, Australia: Department of Education, Science and Training.

Dynarski, M., Agodini, R., Heaviside, S., Novak, T., Carey, N., Campuzano, L., Means, B., Murphy, R., Penuel, W., Javitz, H., Emery, D. and Sussex, W. (2007) *Effectiveness of Reading and Mathematics Software Products: findings from the first student cohort*, National Centre for Educational Evaluation, Jessup, MD: Education Publications Center.

Fluck, A. (1997) 'Choosing and implementing a model for the cross-curriculum use of computers in schools', paper presented at Tel*Ed'97, 6th International Conference on Telecommunications and Multimedia in Education, Mexico, 13–16 November.

Fuller, R.B. (1972) *Utopia or Oblivion: the prospects for humanity*, London: Penguin.

Harms, C.M., Niederhauser, D.S., Davis, N.E. and Roblyer, M.D. (2006) 'Educating educators for virtual schooling: communicating roles and responsibilities', *The Electronic Journal of Communication*, 16. Online. Available HTTP: <http://www.public.iastate.edu/~vschool/TEGIVS/publications/JP2007%20harms&niederhauser> (accessed 18 March 2009).

Hermans, R., Tondeur, J., van Braak, J. and Valcke, M. (2008) 'The impact of primary school teachers' educational beliefs on the classroom use of computers', *Computers & Education* 51:1499–1509.

ISTE (2007) *National Educational Technology Standards for Students*, Eugene, OR: International Society for Technology Education.

Knowsley Council (2006) *Future Schooling in Knowsley: towards 21st century learning environments*, Knowsley, England: Knowsley Council. Online. Available HTTP: <http://www.knowsley.gov.uk/PDF/future_schooling.pdf> (accessed 15 February 2009).

Moursund, D. and Bielefeldt, T. (1999) *Will New Teachers Be Prepared to Teach in a Digital Age? A national survey on information technology in teacher education*, Santa Monica, USA: International Society for Technology in Education and Milken Exchange on Education Technology.

Moursund, D. (2004) *Introduction to Information and Communication Technology in Education*, Oregon, USA: University of Oregon. Online. Available HTTP: <http://darkwing.uoregon.edu/%7emoursund/Books/ICT/ICTBook.html> (accessed 15 February 2009).

Robertson, M., Fluck, A. and Webb, I. (2006) *Children, On-line Learning and Authentic Teaching Skills in Primary Education: final report*, Melbourne: Australian Council for Research.

Twining, P. (2007) *The schome-NAGTY Teen Second Life Pilot Final Report: a summary of key findings and lessons learnt*, Milton Keynes, England: Open University.

UNESCO (2008) *International Literacy Statistics: a review of concepts, methodology and current data*, Montreal: UNESCO – Institute for Statistics.

Chapter 8

Research perspectives on information technology and the learning of mathematics

Anna Kristjánsdóttir
University of Iceland and Agder University, Norway

Introduction

Complex problems in education require broad perspectives and approaches. This chapter considers some perspectives, models and directions for research on IT and mathematics learning.

Research on the learning of mathematics has increased steadily for decades (Bishop *et al.* 1996; English 2002; Lester 2007). In a review paper Nelson (1997) describes changing views of mathematics learning, arguing that teaching can be based on development of the students' own thinking and that the intellectual authority of the classroom can be based on reasoning processes where both students and teacher participate in the generation and validation of mathematical knowledge. However, many of the studies referred to do not include IT in the teaching and learning of mathematics; IT is still seen as an isolated option rather than as a natural part of mathematics learning, despite researchers criticising this for a long time.

Educational authorities worldwide have promoted IT in learning. The *Programme for Digital Competence* 2004-2008 in Norway is an example (MER 2004), but the measured effect on the subjects' learning in 2006 was minimal, although the student:computer ratio had fallen and technology was transforming the community outside school. Little attempt has been made to study how students interpret such a contradiction or how they conceptualise learning in this context. In a 2007 survey of a sample of students in grades 4–10 in Norway, an open question was: 'How do you think more students could succeed in mathematics?' Those saying that they used computers outside school every day and were familiar with IT and collaboration to find things out, hardly mentioned use of IT or collaboration in their answers. The most frequent reply was to suggest drill. Concerns arise both about conceptions of IT in learning and about learning of mathematics.

Perspectives found in presenting IT to schools

The lack of integration of IT in learning prompts the question of how IT and its affordances for learning are presented for schools. An analysis of research presentations on IT for mathematics teachers (Kristjánsdóttir 2006) reveals three quite different perspectives:

- a perspective of existence
- a perspective of integration
- a perspective of learner-focusing.

The *perspective of existence* is evident in presentations about the use of software and reports of experimental studies in classrooms. These presentations sound convincing, engaging and supportive, discussing practical issues and introducing new ideas. Such presentations can be repeated with little modification, as it is up to the audience to interpret the findings for their own circumstances. Little demand is made on the presenter to consider appropriateness to different situations, and there are few questions about wider influence. It is a one-way perspective, temporary, and in the long run rather superficial.

The *perspective of integration* is not a one-way perspective. It acknowledges the meeting of two different cultures or disciplines: mathematics, developed through millennia, with strong structural, terminological and symbolic norms, and IT, a more recent development, influenced by a variety of experts and non-experts. It explores affordances and constraints that arise when these two meet. It can be hard for a teacher to see a linkage, knowing mathematics mainly from schools, mostly without technology, and recognising IT best from social contexts. Further, IT in mathematics learning will be considered differently by teachers, based on their view of mathematics. One extreme is mathematics as a set of unconnected rules and procedures, received from a teacher or textbook and practised by drill, for use later in life. The other is mathematics constructed by each individual through collaborative and dialogical experience, undertaken in an exploring and reasoning environment. Roles for IT in these cases differ greatly.

Undertaking research and presenting with the perspective of integration is much harder than taking the perspective of existence. Not only are there the two different disciplines to consider, their relationship requires special and non-trivial attention. There are both technological and human challenges. Nevertheless, some teachers have taken this perspective early in their meeting with technology. This perspective is more mature than the other, but it too has limitations. It focuses on the disciplines of mathematics and IT, and the learner has no more influence than is the case in the first perspective.

The *perspective of learner-focusing* refers to conscious awareness of the developing characteristics of learners within a particular framework. Here mathematics and IT are not limited to school contexts. This has always been important, but now calls for a revitalised and sharpened awareness. 'Digital natives' learn much outside school, intertwined with other activities.

However, they do not always recognise learning outside school as being learning, neither are they used to reflecting over time and across borders of subjects. Such cross-reflections need advocacy. Where the perspective of existence pays most attention to the affordances of single artifacts or ideas, and the perspective of integration combines attention to subject and IT, neither of them is concerned with a transformed view of learners. In the learner-focused perspective, however, the whole is encompassed as fundamental for learning.

Lenses for research within a learner-focused perspective

Bringing learners' transformations outside school into focus within school learning is not simple, and we lack research for establishing and substantiating this. There have been different approaches to understanding learners. We present three different sets of lenses, based on context and ways to study learners. Each offers different situations and settings for observing and analysing.

The classroom is the most common setting, and often an ethnographic approach is used here. The researcher leaves the responsibility for planning and leading to a teacher. The culture is set by the school, sometimes through negotiation between teacher and students; however, most activities, sometimes even the strategies, are neither initiated nor chosen by the students. Such studies therefore do not reveal much of individual students' meaningful questioning, originating in or out of school. What is studied has been conceived, born and matured within the school-administered arena.

A second choice of lenses has been known for four decades; these comprise specially designed environments where experts in mathematics and technology have studied learners' functioning in technologically rich environments, where they may have freedom to explore and are challenged to investigate and construct. This allows researchers to closely follow the learners' interaction with the designed environment, and to react, revise, or design additional features for the learners. The lenses used by researchers are totally different from those in the school case. Through interactive design researchers communicate more actively with learners, and are engaged in learning from the students through this communication with them. Many projects are well known here, from Minsky's first ideas of microworlds, through the work of Papert, to various other studies of similar type (Noss and Hoyles 1996) and revitalisation of Euclidean geometry and holistic number learning (Bottino 2004), to name just a few. Studies have linked students with experts, opened collaboration with students at distance (Weblab 2007), or explored mobile learning and use of videogames. Human interaction with mathematical problems and the tools' mediating roles are studied, as well as learners' interactions within a community, and development of reflection as their identities as learners evolves (Lemke 2003).

A third choice of lenses: 'community learning'

Specially designed environments are important for showing how students can be inspired, challenged and scaffolded. This is, however, only reaching a limited number of students, and diffusion into schools is problematic.

Another trend is evident. Increasingly, young people know technology and are fluent at exploring it, without having learned this in school. The learning is a community learning. These efforts are inspired by curiousity and interest, and the learners do not want only to receive, but to contribute, to be heard and seen, and to share with others. We consider this to be important learning, although it is different from what most students recognise as learning from school.

Large-scale longitudional studies are needed to understand students' tacit subject learning outside school. Students today have characteristics that students have never had before. They carry a computer wherever they go, although they don't call it a computer. They don't talk about ICT, despite practising much of their C (communication) through the T (technology). They have text, 3D graphics, calculator, camera and memory for photos and short videos, as well as voice always available. It is all there on their small computer called a mobile telephone.

They do not connect their small computer or PC at home with mathematics learning or their own use of mathematics. The tools do not invite them automatically to interesting mathematical exploration of meaningful problems. Being rhetorically aware of the tools' affordances in mathematics does not help in becoming aware of mathematics' affordances in their life. Research on their conceptions of mathematics should be linked to their technological competence, applications and dependence.

Given the premise that school will survive as the main institution for educational equality, can school learn from such studies outside its own domain, understand their findings, and decide on changes to make? We contend that through well designed longitudinal research and mutual respect between researchers and teachers, it is possible to build on students' strengths in the teaching and learning of mathematics. However, sustainable models are needed.

Models for research

We are not talking here about models for politically motivated action. The research we advocate is unusual. The models should offer frameworks for identifying students' conceptions of mathematics learning in and out of school, coping with difficulties, reflecting on them and reacting to them. Further, the models need to include a collaborative element, where communities of teachers in their schools could be invited, for example, to study video data and contribute to the interpretation of the data from their perspectives, not simply be presented with the researchers' ultimate findings. The teachers could thereby improve school learning through better understanding their students and developing more engaging environments for them. Teachers' learning through this is fundamental for their capacity to change schools to meet the needs of students of today. Traditional research, where discussion occurs after the researchers have presented their results, deprives teachers of influence of this kind. The sharing of interpretation from both perspectives, teachers' and researchers', is important for deeper understanding.

There are research projects that can guide design of such studies, respecting both learners and teachers as co-researchers, identifying issues of fundamental importance for learning mathematics and creating sustainable learning environments of quality. One such is the University of Wisconsin study on children's solving of mathematical problems, begun 30 years ago, and the subsequent research on teachers' development after collaborative exploration of the data with researchers, called Cognitively Guided Instruction (CGI Math 2007). A broad systemic perspective is also important. Here we can refer to a project in Norway (Kristjánsdóttir 2009), which is illustrated in Figure 8.1. The identification processes explore texts and oral utterances for roots of different interpretations, unspoken expectations and gaps in continuity.

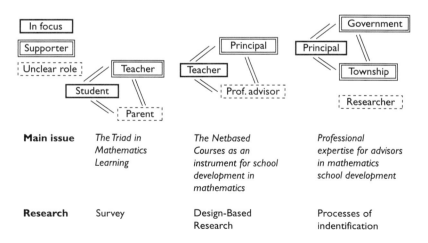

Main issue	The Triad in Mathematics Learning	The Netbased Courses as an instrument for school development in mathematics	Professional expertise for advisors in mathematics school development
Research	Survey	Design-Based Research	Processes of indentification

Figure 8.1 Multilevel holistic perspective on mathematics learning.

Final remarks

The chapter began by articulating two well-known problems: that research reported on mathematics learning with IT is not yet of much value in schools, and that studying influences of IT in learning mathematics is still somewhat excluded from mainstream research on mathematics learning. This was examined by considering three different perspectives held by presenters of research on IT for learning, and describing three different lenses that researchers can use in their choice of research settings and ways of studying learners. The text advocates use of a learner-focused perspective, approaching learners in context in and out of school, studying what they can accomplish when invited to address meaningful problems within a technological environment they know, and investigating what learning means to them. The third part of the chapter advocates use of research models involving collaboration between researchers and their subjects, including teachers and learners essentially as co-researchers, to improve relevance, communication and effectiveness of research on IT and mathematics learning.

Acknowledgement

The author acknowledges a grant from the Research Board of Norway to the project Mathematics, Learning and Teacher Competence, 2004–2009.

References

Bishop, A., Clements, K., Keitel, C., Kilpatrick, J. and Laborde, C. (eds) (1996) *International Handbook of Mathematics Education*, Dordrecht: Kluwer.

Bottino, R.M. (2004) 'The evolution of ICT-based learning environments: which perspectives for the school of the future?' *British Journal of Educational Technologies*, 35: 553–567.

CGI Math (2007) *Cognitively Guided Instruction*, Madison: University of Wisconsin. Online. Available HTTP: <http://www.wcer.wisc.edu/news/coverstories/cgi_math_encourages_ingenuity.php> (accessed 22 March 2009).

English, L. (ed.) (2002) *Handbook of International Research in Mathematics Education*, Mahwah: Lawrence Erlbaum.

Kristjánsdóttir, A. (2006) 'Different perspectives on ICT in mathematics teaching render different affordances' [in Danish], *IKT i matematikkundervisningen – muligheter og begrensninger*, Trondheim: NTNU.

—— (2009) 'Multilevel holistic perspective on mathematics learning: why it is important to explore relations and interactions widely' [in preparation].

Lemke, J.J. (2003) 'Identity, development and desire: critical questions', AERA. Online. Available HTTP: <http://www-personal.umich.edu/~jaylemke/papers/Identity/identity_aera_2003.htm> (accessed 23 March 2009).

Lester, F. (ed.) (2007) *Second Handbook of Research on Mathematics Teaching and Learning*, Charlotte, NC: Information Age.

MER (2004) *Programme for Digital Competence 2004-2008*, Oslo: Ministry of Education and Research in Norway.

Nelson, B. (1997) 'Learning about teacher change in the context of mathematics education reform: where have we come from?' in E. Fennema and B.S. Nelson (eds) *Mathematics Teachers in Transition*, Mahwah: Lawrence Erlbaum.

Noss, R. and Hoyles, C. (1996) *Windows on Mathematical Meanings: learning cultures and computers*, Dordrecht: Kluwer.

Weblab (2007) *Weblabs Project*. Online. Available HTTP: <http://www.weblabs.eu.com> (accessed 22 March 2009).

Chapter 9

The enjoyment of learning in digital environments

Franziska Spring-Keller
University of Zürich, Switzerland

Introduction

This chapter considers learning in playful digital learning environments and outlines a range of research issues needed for the design and use of games in school learning settings. Children in pre-school or kindergarten learn new things every day and enjoy learning them through play. This joy of learning is lost somehow while they are at school. Learning is perceived as an obligation and hard work. Some learning experiences may cause damage so that fear and self-doubt become linked to learning in specific subjects. What causes this change of attitude towards learning and how can it be prevented? How can the joy of learning of the early years be carried over into later childhood, youth, and even into adulthood? How can digital learning environments support this?

Several years ago, I attended a math workshop of Marie Milis, a mathematician from Belgium. Math-traumatised persons were welcome – I was one of them. We had to split into small groups and solve a real-life problem dealing with nomads and sizes for their tents. We were so involved in our discussions that the sixty minutes allowed flew by. The fear of failure was defeated by curiosity and by knowing that we were allowed to be wrong. This feeling is what is nowadays called joyful or playful learning. Learning happens through discussions, trying out different ways of arriving at solutions, finding creative ways of thinking, and learning by making mistakes without any fear of failure or pressure for success.

Through play, people dare to take risks, explore possibilities and test boundaries (Resnick 2007). If people are not enjoying learning, they will only learn the minimum required to accomplish standardised goals. Such goals and tests are necessary to guarantee certain levels of education. However, in a world of globalisation and international competition, it is important to have people who can think 'out-of-the box'. Innovation and creativity will be more and more important for a successful life in this world (Friedman 2005, Resnick 2007, Shaffer 2006).

The first parts of this chapter focus on current challenges in research about playful learning in digital environments in school settings. The second part deals with future possibilities in the area of playful digital learning environments from a learner-centred approach.

Are you playing or learning?

Computer games are mostly seen as entertainment rather than as educational. In this section, computer games for learning and playful learning environments are defined. Based on this definition, the ongoing debate about learning effects in games is analysed.

Playful learning environments

The basis of playful learning environments (as interpreted in this chapter) lies in social constructivist theory. A playful learning environment consists not only of a game, but also of activities outside the game-player context (Figure 9.1).

A playful digital learning environment is defined as a number of components, the game system, players and the social environment, that interact strongly with each other. Learning happens through several communication

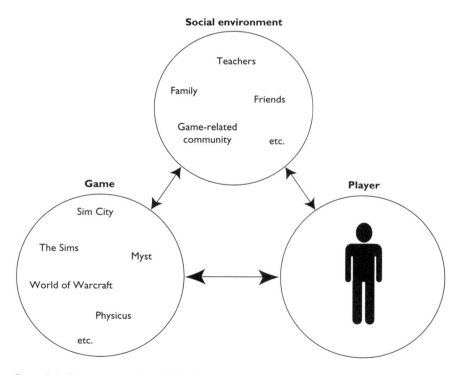

Figure 9.1 Components of a playful digital learning environment.

and interaction channels around a game (chat, community forums, etc.), not only directly between the game system and the player.

In this chapter, I will not distinguish between games and simulations. According to Shaffer (2006), children run simulations of worlds they want to learn about in order to understand the rules, roles, and consequences of those worlds. Every kind of play consists of a set of rules, even open-ended games that have no specific goals. Rules can be defined by game designers or be expanded and changed by players. By playing according to a set of rules, players take over certain roles. Thus, Shaffer reduces the definition of game to two single aspects: rules and roles. Commercial games like *Sim City*, an urban planning game where players take over the role of a mayor, consist of vast numbers of rules. *World of Warcraft*, a massive multi-player online game where thousands of people chat and resolve quests in a virtual world, is so complex that even after 50 hours of play time the player does not fully know all the rules and stories in the game. Learning in games is understood as an integral part of the game. This means that the better players understand the rules and can identify with their roles, the better they master the game and thus the intended learning content.

Games and their learning effect

Play is not always naturally related to learning in school environments. Reaching level 40 out of 70 levels in *World of Warcraft* takes a vast time of hard work (several days or weeks); nevertheless, players enjoy the game. Why should this not be possible with learning a school subject? Gee (2005) analysed existing commercial games and the learning principles found in them, and compared these to general learning theories for educational games. According to Gee, game-like learning provides deep conceptual knowledge obtained in a situated way. Feedback is seen as instructions given 'just in time' or 'on demand'. Knowledge is distributed among learners, objects or characters in the game.

Research is needed to investigate the relationship between learning, playing and the social context:

* How does the social context influence the learning progress in the game? Can this influence be quantified?
* Can the social environment somehow be manipulated or directed to support the player/learner?
* Can a model or a framework be developed that describes the relationships among the three systems: player, game and social environment?

Designing games for learning purposes

Despite the views of some sceptics, there are teachers who use games in their classrooms. A study by Sanford *et al.* (2006) found the application of commercial computer games in a classroom environment very challenging. A game like *Sim City* can take ten to twenty hours of playtime. For a deeper understanding, up to 100 hours may be required. Normally, one classroom lecture takes 45 minutes. The integration of such a game would thus fill a whole semester course. Commercial computer games are very motivating and encouraging, but the learning effect for traditional schools will be quite low if there is no thorough debriefing of the students by the teachers. Commercial games cannot be used for self-regulated learning unless they are modified for specific learning needs. Therefore, the quality and use of commercial games in classrooms largely depends on the teachers' teaching styles and their knowledge of games (Sanford *et al.* 2006).

On the other hand, there are special situations such as after-school programs that are not tied to the traditional classroom structure. Students can take their own time for playing a computer game, and it can result in very positive effects on learning outcomes (Squire 2008).

This area still needs more research. There should be more experiments, with different kinds of methods, on the use of games for school. Questions remaining to be answered include:

- How can a commercial computer game be structured and fitted for learning within a classroom environment?
- Should the classroom perhaps be structured around games? If so, how should this setting be designed in order to provide a playful learning environment?

More empirical studies are needed to investigate the impact of games on learning and the requirements of the surrounding classroom structure.

Some games are specifically developed for learning a certain subject such as physics or biology. *Physicus*, for instance, is part of a game series that also teaches biology or chemistry. The game style very much resembles *Myst* or *Riven*, well-known graphic adventure games. Designing a game that has an engaging effect similar to a commercial game, specifically for learning purposes, is very challenging. Certain motivational aspects, such as flow, curiosity, and fantasy (Malone and Lepper 1987), must be considered in the design of a game for learning. The term 'flow' describes a subjective, positive state at which people arrive when they are completely involved in something. They lose their sense of time, do not get tired or hungry and are absolutely concentrated on the task. Flow also leads to an increase of learning success (Csikszentmihalyi and Csikszentmihalyi 1988). A virtual world for learners must satisfy their curiosity and inspire them to explore it.

Designers of games for learning face additional challenges. Commercial games are designed for a specific target audience: gamers. Learning environments have to be designed for a much wider audience. The 'learner group' consists of various kinds of people such as hardcore and casual gamers, as well as non-gamers. If a learning environment resembles a famous commercial game too closely, gamers might reject it because of its likeness to the original. On the other hand, for non-gamers, it might be difficult to understand the concept of learning through a game; goals in the game must make sense.

There is also the matter of development costs. Games are very expensive to create. A commercial game like *World of Warcraft* would cost $40 million or more. A good educational game does not necessarily have to cost millions of dollars. Designers just have to be even more creative in taking into account simple but effective design issues in a game. Some examples are described in David Shaffer's book *How Computer Games Help Children Learn* (2006).

Even though the most important elements of designing a game are known (flow, fantasy, curiosity etc.), more research is needed on target group analysis and on how these aspects impact learning. Questions to be addressed include:

- What can we learn from good examples of successful games? What can we learn from bad examples? What are the elements in games that are engaging? What affects learners?
- What would motivate non-gamers in a playful learning environment? Do their motives differ from those of gamers, and in what way?
- How can IT support more cost-efficient methods of developing games for learning?

The more we know about the design of games for learning, the impact of motivational aspects, and learners' understandings, the better the games for learning that can be developed for school settings.

A learner-centred approach for more enjoyment

This second part of the chapter will look at some areas connected with playful learning: creative thinking and adaptation of the game system to users' behaviour.

Playful learning and creativity

Creative thinking is important in order to succeed in a world of rapid change and global competition (Resnick 2007). Creativity is a powerful aspect of playful learning. This approach is mostly applied in open-ended games or in so-called game 'modding', i.e. modifying a game. Many commercial games provide a development kit where players can create their own game level or their personal game character; these are called evolutionary games (Spring-Keller and Ito 2007). The creations are published on the Internet, which invite users to add ever more sophisticated modifications. Perhaps the most extreme example of an open-ended game is *Second Life*, which has hardly any rules or roles. Users can create and develop everything themselves, even their own games within this environment.

Research in this field is mostly concentrated on how learning occurs in such environments and how it could be transferred to other settings. What is hardly known is the impact the social environment (the game-related community, a teacher or friends, for instance) or the game system itself could have on the learners to foster their creative abilities. Certain aspects are known to destroy creativity and should thus be taken into account in the design of playful learning environments (Goleman *et al.* 1993):

- *Time:* Lack of time is the most important impediment to creativity. Every person has a different feeling for time. A classic classroom structure is thus unsuitable for supporting this state. On the other hand, we also should analyse creative thinking under time pressure. Many people in creative jobs (e.g. marketing, advertising) need to be innovative on demand or are most creative when under pressure.
- *Evaluation and assessment:* Learners should be trained to become capable of self-assessing and of asking themselves if they are satisfied with their personal performance. It has become increasingly common in learning environments to define a personal learning goal (Spring-Keller and Ito 2007). Measuring learning success is still a widely discussed topic with no clear outcomes.
- *Restriction of decision making:* Children lose curiosity and motivation to find alternative solutions if the choices of solutions for a problem are restricted. Designers of digital learning environments can define how someone should learn a specific subject, instead of letting learners find their own learning strategies. In order for learners to discover personal learning styles, the environment has to provide a setting where it is possible to experiment.

Nevertheless, some creative solutions are found under constraints and under time pressure. A balance must be found between a framework of constraints and an open environment.

This leads to the following research questions:

- Can new methods to engage creative thinking be developed from observing behaviour of users in a playful environment?
- What is the impact of the social environment on a learner's creativity?
- What kind of guidance is suitable that is not patronising? How do we know if someone needs guidance by just observing the user's behaviour?
- How can creative thinking be measured? Do we need new requirements for measuring learning success in regard to creativity?
- How can learning progress generally be measured in an open environment such as open-ended games? Do we need a more deliberate definition of learning success?

Learning and adaptation

Engaging creativity and guiding people in playful environments differs from one individual to another. Every person has a different approach to retrieving and processing information and to learning. Table 9.1 lists some of the attributes of learners.

Research in the field of learner attributes and their influence on learning is very controversial. Some studies argue that prior knowledge is the main influence on learning outcomes (Jonassen and Grabowski 1993), but games for learning could change the meaning of these attributes. Learning types such as 'visual' or 'verbal' become less relevant because both are supported in games. Introverted persons may suddenly appear open and talkative to other players.

Failure takes on a different meaning in a playful learning environment. In classic school settings, making mistakes was seen as weakness to be eradicated. Playful learning allows failure without punishment. This enables experimentation. There are people who mainly learn by their mistakes. How can behaviour be analysed and measured in complex game systems?

There are also different ways of dealing with frustration over failure. There are very few studies about the tolerance of frustration in learning settings. Adults seem to need more assistance in solving a problem than children, and for them frustration appears earlier (Milis 1990). We have to analyse learning strategies and understand what causes a person to become frustrated.

For research, this means that play styles and their relation to learning need further investigation. Some of the questions to be posed are:

• Are there any play styles that can be related to learning in games? If so, is there a learning benefit from adapting to these play styles?
• Instead of applying existing theories of learning and play styles, what kind of methods could be used in order to gather data for player/learner observation?

Table 9.1 Learner attributes (based on Jonassen and Grabowski 1993)

Attributes	Description	Examples
Personality	Characteristics of human behaviour	Extroversion, introversion, anxiety, achievement motivation, etc.
Cognitive style	Problem-solving, sensory and perceptual abilities	Impulsive, reflective, focused, distracted, etc.
Knowledge	Content knowledge	Deep conceptual, structural, factual, etc.
Experience	Experience in the subject and its corresponding environment or related areas	Had a bad maths teacher, was teased for asking questions, etc.
Attitude	Stance toward the subject	Emotions – frustration, fear, excitement

- Are there technologies or algorithms that manage to deal with dynamic adjustments to behavioural patterns?

It could also be valuable to analyse learner groups as a whole and adapt the game system to their behaviour. In multi-player games, the composition of a group can say much about successful team-work. Since the adaptation of game systems to groups is uncharted territory so far, there are many open questions.

- How can a playful environment be adapted to team characteristics in this specific environment (depending on the subject)?
- How can soft skills in effective team work be measured, analysed and enforced?
- If there exist interpersonal problems among group members, what kind of interventions are possible? Is there a benefit of a computer-generated intervention compared to a personal intervention?
- What influence does the social context have on virtual group work in a playful environment?

Conclusion

There are many challenges and open questions to be analysed in the research field of playful digital learning environments. The meaning of learning and play cannot be simply separated. Learning is an active process and needs to be a part of play. For games, this means learning is integrated into the game's system – the better the player masters the game, the better the learning outcome. Also it is important to see learning as a holistic process including the social context. Excitement is triggered through collaborative activities or sharing information and creations. However, the individual as player/learner should not be forgotten. We have to better understand learners and their fears and needs. What makes them curious? What frustrates them? Knowing the learners' strengths and weaknesses might not be enough. There is a need for a model describing crucial requirements for a playful digital learning environment. If we face the challenges described, we can transfer the enjoyment of learning from kindergarten to later childhood, youth, and even into adulthood.

References

Csikszentmihalyi, M. and Csikszentmihalyi, I. (1988) *Optimal Experience*, Cambridge: Cambridge University Press.

Friedman, T.L. (2005) *The World is Flat*, New York: Farrar, Straus and Giroux.

Gee, J.P. (2005) 'What would a state-of-the-art instructional video game look like?' *Innovate*, 1. Online. Available HTTP: <http://innovateonline.info/?view=article&id=80> (accessed 15 March 2009).

Goleman, D., Kaufman, P. and Ray, M. (1993) *The Creative Spirit*, New York: Penguin Books.

Jonassen, D.H. and Grabowski B.L. (1993) *Handbook of Individual Differences in Learning and Instruction*, Hillsdale, NJ: Lawrence Erlbaum.

Malone, T.W. and Lepper, M.R. (1987) 'Making learning fun: a taxonomy of intrinsic motivations for learning', in R.E. Snow and M.J. Farr (eds) *Aptitude, Learning, and Instruction, III: cognitive and affective process analysis*, Hillsdale, NJ: Lawrence Erlbaum.

Milis, M. (1990) 'Leaving the known for the unknown', *Parabola*, 15: 39–47.

Resnick, M. (2007) 'All I really need to know (about creative thinking) I learned (by studying how children learn) in kindergarten', paper presented at the 6th ACM SIGCHI Conference on Creativity & Cognition, Washington, DC., June.

Sanford, R., Ulicsak, M., Facer, K. and Rudd, T. (2006) *Teaching with Games: using commercial off-the-shelf computer games in formal education*, Bristol: Futurelab.

Shaffer, D.W. (2006) *How Computer Games Help Children Learn*, New York: Palgrave Macmillan.

Spring-Keller, F. and Ito, T. (2007) 'Combining personalisation and adaptation in game-based learning systems', paper presented at the IASTED European Conference on Internet and Multimedia Systems and Applications, Chamonix, France, March.

Squire, K. (2008) 'Open-ended Video Games: a model for developing learning for the interactive age', in K. Salen (ed.) *The John D. and Catherine T. MacArthur Foundation Series on Digital Media and Learning*, Cambridge, MA: MIT Press.

Part 2

Theoretical underpinnings to inform research design

Chapter 10

Models for exploring and characterising pedagogy with information technology

Mary Webb
King's College London, UK

Introduction

Models can help to clarify and communicate ideas, processes and relationships. They may act as conceptual lenses through which to view the world. They can help researchers to identify, classify and characterise objects and situations they are studying and to decide their importance and significance. Some models support statistical analysis, some are applied to qualitative data, while others support conceptual understanding.

Models are needed when researching pedagogy with IT to investigate, analyse, understand and evaluate the following interrelated phenomena:

- teachers' pedagogy and pedagogical practices when using IT
- the affordances that various types of IT may provide for learning and teaching
- the potential for developing pedagogy with IT
- current and future roles for teachers, students and the technology.

This chapter examines and compares models that have been developed for researching these areas and those that have been applied to explain data. In addition, selected models from other areas of research are considered where they facilitate understanding the research into pedagogy with IT in a broader context.

The term IT is used to describe a broad range of hardware and software resources for learning including desktop PCs, mobile devices, interactive whiteboards, simulations, web-based materials, modelling environments, etc. When using the models examined here it is almost always necessary to specify the nature of the IT used, as the pedagogical opportunities supported by various types of IT can be very different.

Pedagogy in perspective

In order to understand models for researching pedagogy with IT in an appropriately broad context this section will first review briefly some key

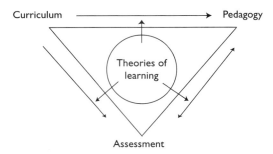

Figure 10.1 The Triangle of Learning: a formative approach (based on Wilson 2007).

ideas about the nature of pedagogy and pedagogical change. The term pedagogy usually refers to the science or theory of educating and that is the intention here.

Within a framework of educational practice Alexander (1992) identified teaching methods and pupil organisation as the two facets of pedagogy. Relationships between pedagogy and other aspects of educational practice are characterised further in Wilson's (2007) triangular causal model for understanding pedagogy (Figure 10.1), in which the curriculum provides a 'road map' for pedagogy, developments in formative assessment practices enable a productive relationship between pedagogy and assessment, and teachers' theories of learning mediate the effects of curriculum and assessment on their pedagogy.

Conceptions of pedagogy have become more complex as our growing knowledge has become both more differentiated and more integrated (Watkins and Mortimore 1999). In particular, recent developments in our understanding of cognition and meta-cognition have led researchers to develop a complex model differentiated by details of context, content, age and stage of learner, purposes etc. This model also incorporates learning communities in which knowledge is actively co-constructed. Therefore, in considering models that relate IT and pedagogy, it is important to remember that both pedagogy and IT in education are changing in response to other factors as well as to each other.

Models that characterise computer-student interaction

One of the earliest attempts to characterise pedagogy with IT that has remained influential was by Kemmis *et al.* (1977) who described four paradigms for computer assisted learning (see Figure 10.2).

Kemmis's framework focused on learning and how the technology could support it, whereas Taylor (1980) concentrated on modes of computer use (see Figure 10.3).

Instructional Paradigm
• based on Skinnerian/behaviourist theory
• programmed learning
• drill-and-practice
Revelatory Paradigm
• based on theorists such as Bruner (spiral curriculum)
• activities where things are revealed gradually to learners
• discovery or experiential learning: simulation, problem-solving
Conjectural Paradigm
• based on constructivist theories (Piaget, Papert)
• learner has control, tries to teach the computer, or
  creates models
• computers as tools: word-processing, data-handling, modelling
Emancipatory Paradigm
• reducing workload
• occurs in tandem with one of the other three
• removes the need for 'inauthentic learning' i.e. that which is
  not relevant to the learning intention of the activity
  e.g. classifying and sorting large amounts of data

Figure 10.2 Kemmis's Paradigms for computer assisted learning (based on Kemmis *et al.* 1977).

Computer as tutor
Computer presents the student with some subject-matter
content and a set of questions or directions; the student
responds and the computer evaluates the response, before
presenting further content.
Computer as tool
Using generic software applications e.g. word processor for
writing in English; spreadsheet to help with analysis of data
in a maths problem or data-handling tool to help analyse
geographical information.
Computer as tutee
User 'teaches' the computer through programming,
modelling, multimedia authoring etc.

Figure 10.3 Modes of computer use (based on Taylor 1980).

While beginning to characterise possible roles for the technology and thus helping researchers and educators in these early developments to understand the possible value of IT, these technocentric models failed to take account of other elements in learning environments that are explored in the next section.

Models incorporating wider interactions

Squires and McDougall (1994) argued that to evaluate software for its peda-gogical potential, it is essential to consider actual or potential classroom interactions. Therefore their Perspectives Interactions Paradigm (PIP) focused on the interactions between three key actors: student(s), teacher and designer (as embodied in software). In Laurillard's (1993) 'conversational framework' (Figure 10.4) the essential features are two actors (teacher and student) both operating at two levels (conceptual and experiential). The 'designer' element embodied in the PIP is at first glance missing, but is actu-ally spread throughout the conversational framework. Thus, when designing software or analysing learning activities, the framework encourages a focus on the interactions and their locations. Using this model Laurillard *et al.* (2000) identified two extreme instructional forms: 'narrative guidance' which is the more teacher-controlled form of learning; and 'narrative construction' which is the more student-controlled form. Ideally, teachers aim for bridging forms between these two extremes, where teacher and students share responsibility for progressing the learning. However, when they used the framework to analyse student interactions with multimedia software, Laurillard *et al.* iden-tified a clear need for guidance from the teacher and/or software to promote meaningful learning. This framework could be applied to any learning inter-action, between teacher and student(s) or between students, whether or not it involves use of computer media and communications (Laurillard 2002).

This conversational framework provides a useful starting point that focuses on interaction and has proved useful for designing learning resources in higher education (Laurillard 2002). However, the complexity of interactions and their importance in pedagogy has led to many different approaches to analysis (Alexander 2006, Mercer 2007, Mercer *et al.* 2004, van Lier 1996, Dillon 1988). In a multi-disciplinary study (Dillon 1988), transcripts of five

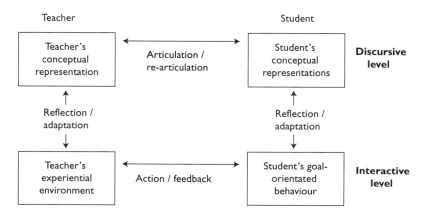

Figure 10.4 Overview of Laurillard's conversational framework.

classroom discussions were the subject of twelve different types of analysis and commentary: six of these appraised the pieces from different pedagogical perspectives, under such headings as 'models of discussion', 'questions and wait-time', and 'questioning vs student initiatives'. Van Lier (1996) mapped out classroom interactions and suggested that they can vary along a number of dimensions that determine their learning power. Dimensions potentially important for pedagogy with IT include transmission to transformation, monologic to conversational, non-contingent to contingent, and product-oriented to process-oriented.

Models enabling quantitative analysis of computer use

Twining's (2000) 'Computer Practice Framework (CPF)' provides for quantitative analysis of computer use and embodies categorisation of how the use of the computer is interacting with the content and/or processes of the curriculum. Twining proposes that the computer can be used to support the existing objectives, to enhance or extend the objectives, perhaps to alter their priorities or to enable new objectives to be set (such as the improvement of a piece of writing through re-drafting), and to transform the objectives (for example, 'a hypermedia authoring package could be used to transform the mode of communication and our definition of literacy') (Twining 2000: 9).

A number of other frameworks and models have been developed for measuring computer use. For example, the first Impact Study (Cox *et al.* 1993) developed a ten-point scale for recording and analysing the uptake and use of IT. However, this did not include any measure of the quality of the IT work of the teachers, but only the frequency and extent of IT use. Research over a period of years at the Research and Development Center for Teacher Education in Austin, Texas, on the development of a 'Concerns based adoption model' has produced an extensive 'levels of use' scale (Loucks *et al.* 1998) relating to various categories of quality of use, which has been used to record, rate and assess the extent of integration of innovation in teaching. The model has been used in several studies to characterise the uptake and use of IT in teaching, for example Griffin and Christensen (1999) have developed a self-evaluation tool for teachers. Castillo (2006) has developed a methodology for classifying teachers into levels of IT use according to the range of IT types used. This reflects the number of software types being used by teachers, but not the quality of the software itself or its curriculum effect.

These models are useful for characterising computer use within pedagogical practices, but for understanding teachers' pedagogy and pedagogical decision-making there is also a need to understand the processes involved and teachers' planning for how they expect the computer to support, enhance or transform learning and how this is achieved in practice. This means identifying teachers' perceptions of the features that will contribute to affordances, and evidence of affordances in practice and/or perceptions of the pupils.

Affordances

Affordance is a term coined by Gibson (1979) and derives from his ecological theory of perception. As the term has been adopted in both the human computer interaction (HCI) field (Norman 2002), and the education literature (Kennewell 2001, Laurillard *et al.* 2000, Downes 2002), and used to develop frameworks and models of pedagogy in IT-based learning environments, its meaning will be examined in some detail. Gibson (1979) explained how an affordance depends not only on the environment, but also on the possible actions of an organism: 'affordance implies the complementarity of the animal and the environment' (Gibson 1979: 127). In Gibson's definition the same environment can enable different affordances for different organisms.

Gibson (1979) discussed how features of a range of different aspects of the environment may compound together to provide an affordance. In addition, events may provide affordances or may contribute to an affordance. Just as in an ecological system in which affordances for a particular organism depend on the potential interaction between the organism and the physical environment and interactions with other organisms, so in an IT-supported learning environment affordances for learning are provided by interactions between the hardware, software, other resources, teachers and other students.

Norman (2002) introduced the term 'perceived affordance' to emphasise that in the design of a computer interface what the user perceives is crucial, whereas for Gibson the affordance exists whether or not it is perceived: 'The Observer may or may not perceive or attend to the affordance, according to his needs, but the affordance, being invariant, is always there to be perceived' (Gibson 1979: 138). Whether or not a person perceives an affordance may depend on the information available. McGrenere and Ho (2000), working in the context of software design, identified two factors that are important in the usability of an affordance as the degree of perceptual information and the degree of affordance (see Figure 10.5).

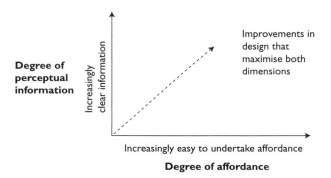

Figure 10.5 Affordance and information specifying the affordance (based on McGrenere and Ho 2000).

Greeno (1998) redefined affordances in the context of situation theory in terms of constraints where affordances of the physical environment, together with abilities of individuals, act as conditions for constraints. Thinking about knowing how to do things can then be described as attunement to constraints.

Given this range of definitions, when using models incorporating affordances it is important to be clear about how the term is being used. In this chapter, Gibson's original concept of affordance being a property of the environment and the possible actions of the learner is used. In educational environments affordances are provided not by IT alone but by the totality of the environment, including the teacher, the other students and other resources and their interactions through classroom processes (Webb 2005, Webb and Cox 2004). An overview of this framework is shown in Figure 10.6. A focus on affordances for learning in an IT-rich environment may be a useful way of thinking about the conditions needed for learning to occur. In order to understand how to create those conditions we need to examine in depth the processes that have led up to and contributed to these affordances, including the pedagogical reasoning involved in planning and teaching. Figure 10.6 is a dataflow diagram showing an outline of key processes. Each process

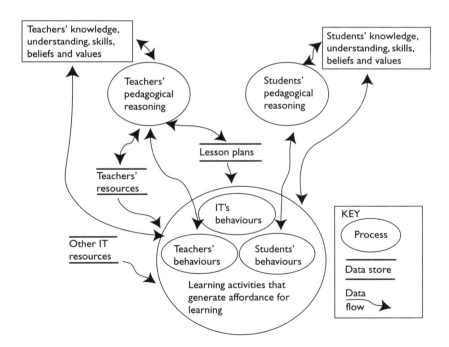

Figure 10.6 Framework for pedagogical practices relating to IT use (based on Webb and Cox 2004).

circle could be expanded to show details of sub-processes, such as the pedagogical reasoning process that is discussed in the next section. Processes involved in the learning activities are complex and include the interactions discussed earlier.

Pedagogical reasoning

The processes of planning, teaching, assessing and evaluating, and the knowledge needed for these processes, are described in Shulman's (1987) model of pedagogical reasoning which was further developed by Webb (2002) to incorporate IT use and teachers' ideas, beliefs and values (Alexander 1992). A crucial sub-process in this model is the process of transformation of knowledge (see Figure 10.7), which according to Shulman occurs not only prior to the instructional process, but also throughout classroom teaching and during evaluation of teaching. This process of transformation also equates to Perrenoud's (1998) model of interactive regulation of learning processes that describes how teachers regulate learning through two levels of management:

1.   the setting up of situations that favour the interactive regulation of learning processes
2.   interactive regulation of these situations.

During the cycle of processes in pedagogical reasoning, pedagogical content knowledge (PCK) is used and generated. PCK has subsequently been defined for particular subjects, for example Linn and Hsi:

> Pedagogical content knowledge refers to knowledge about a topic that enables improved teaching of that discipline. In science such knowledge involves an understanding of the ideas students bring to class, the context in which students apply their science knowledge, and the multiple models of the same topic used by students and experts in the various contexts of application.
>
> (Linn and Hsi 2000: 337)

Koehler and Mishra (2005) introduced a further term, Technological Pedagogical Content Knowledge (TPCK), which they represent as an intersection between Content knowledge (C), Pedagogic knowledge (P) and knowledge of Technology (T). With this model they aimed to capture the dynamic, transactional relationship between knowledge of content, pedagogy and technology. Koehler and Mishra argue that teachers can develop TPCK through design-based professional development activities. However, while such activities are desirable, the amount and range of this knowledge makes it unmanageable for individual teachers to achieve a sufficiently comprehensive knowledge set in this domain.

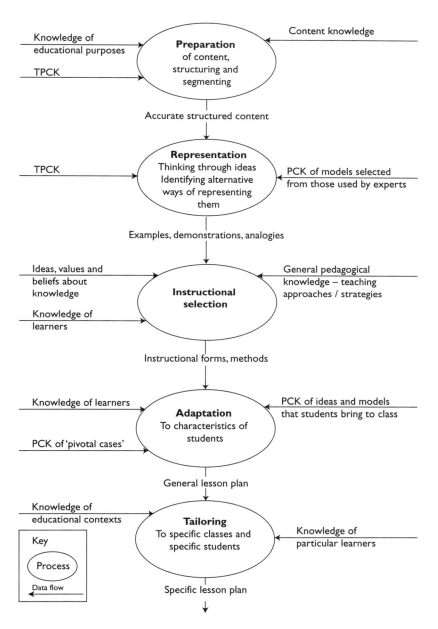

Figure 10.7 Transformation of knowledge within teachers' pedagogical reasoning (based on Webb 2002).

One approach to resolving this dilemma is to develop software tools to support resource selection during pedagogical reasoning, such as digital assistants and search engines. Another approach is to reduce reliance on the knowledge of an individual teacher by empowering students and sharing pedagogical reasoning with them (Webb 2005). For example, in the model illustrated in Figure 10.6 the importance of students' thinking about and planning their own learning is incorporated in 'student pedagogical reasoning'. According to Black *et al.* (2003) the development of formative assessment pedagogy has enabled students themselves to identify their needs, and hence play a larger role in planning for their learning. Students could become aware not only of what they do not understand, but also of how they learn and what kind of materials they prefer to use. Thus students are undertaking a pedagogical reasoning process in which they use knowledge of their own learning abilities and styles and their achievements to make decisions. This, combined with digital assistants and search engines to facilitate students' access to resources, might obviate the need for teachers to develop extensive knowledge of functionalities of content-specific software.

These models focused on analysing interactions at different levels of granularity in order to inform the design of learning environments and the opportunities for IT-supported learning. Other research has developed models to analyse changes associated with using technology to enhance learning.

Models that focus on analysing change

As developments in IT provided new learning opportunities, the need for a new 'integrated pedagogy' was identified (Cornu 1995). For example, McLoughlin and Oliver (1999) defined pedagogic roles for teachers in a technology supported classroom including setting joint tasks, rotating roles, promoting student self-management, supporting metacognition, fostering multiple perspectives and scaffolding learning. A dynamic model for such a transforming pedagogy for IT was developed by Somekh and Davies (1991), who identified various dimensions of pedagogic change, including from a sequential to an organic structuring of learning experiences.

Understanding people's behaviour in communities that are undergoing change may be enabled by psychological theories such as the theory of planned behaviour (Ajzen 1991). For example Koutromanos (2004) carried out a quantitative study using the theory of planned behaviour to identify important factors affecting teachers' decisions to use IT.

Changes associated with IT use can be analysed using Activity Theory, which provides 'a framework for understanding transformations in collective practices and organizations' (Engeström *et al.* 2002: 211). Engeström's third generation of activity theory (Engeström 2001) incorporates principles of

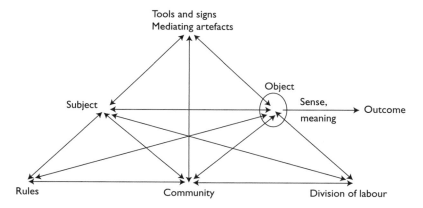

Figure 10.8 Structure of a human activity system (based on Engeström, 2001: 135).

interacting activity systems, multi-voicedness, historicity, a central role for contradictions as sources of change and development, and the possibility of expansive transformations.

According to Engeström *et al.* (2002), the key to understanding activity systems is their object-orientedness. An activity system is commonly represented graphically as a set of elements in a triangular arrangement as shown in Figure 10.8. In this representation 'the object is depicted with the help of an oval indicating that object-oriented actions are always, explicitly or implicitly, characterized by ambiguity, surprise, interpretation, sense making, and potential for change' (Engeström 2001: 134).

One advantage of activity theory for understanding pedagogy with IT derives from the first principle being that the prime unit of analysis is a collective, artefact-mediated object-oriented activity system. Therefore, it suits analysis of systems where people are engaged in purposeful activities mediated by artefacts such as IT resources. In the diagram shown in Figure 10.8, IT resources can be mediating artefacts but can also act as support for any of the other nodes in an activity system (Kuutti 1995), for example by enabling communication within the community.

Activity theory can be used as an analytical framework to enable the identification of important contradictions that produce tensions and conflicts in a changing system, but also may provide driving forces for change. For example, Figure 10.9 shows conflicts that were identified in the activity systems of teachers of English for Business Purposes (EBP) in Chinese Higher Education where IT had been introduced into the curriculum (Hu and Webb 2009). The analysis was based on open coding of data from interviews and lesson observations, and identifying key themes that were then classified as nodes and relationships within the activity system. Bold arrows indicate

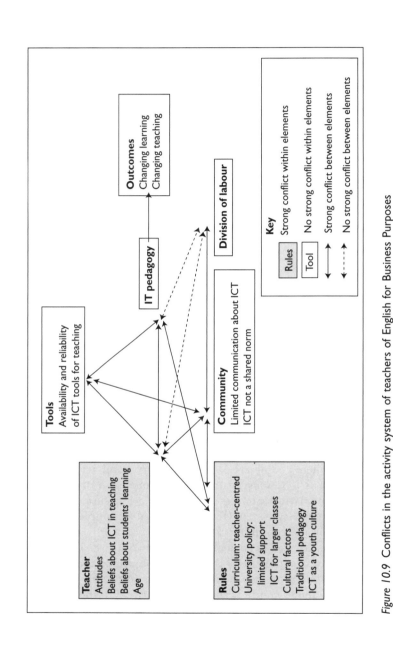

Figure 10.9 Conflicts in the activity system of teachers of English for Business Purposes (EBP) in Chinese Higher Education (adapted from Hu and Webb 2009).

major contradictions and consideration of these can support effective design of professional development programmes for enabling pedagogy with IT.

Using Activity Theory as explained by Leont'ev (1978), in which activities can be broken down into sequences of actions, more detailed frameworks have also been developed to investigate classroom based sequences of actions and the roles of mediating artefacts including IT tools (see for example Wells 2002, Stevenson 2008). Furthermore, in order to support intervention-based research that aims to bring about change, Engeström (2001) developed a 'Change Laboratory' that uses third generation Activity Theory to model proposed solutions as well as existing systems. Somekh (this volume) has developed a 'Generic Pedagogic Framework' incorporating aspects of Activity Theory and taking account of the location of pedagogical activity between the home and school with a primary purpose of communicating with the participants in a development project.

Choosing a model for researching pedagogy

All of the models reviewed here can be valuable tools when they are suited to the research aims. Understanding pedagogy with IT involves understanding pedagogy within a broader framework while investigating current and changing classroom interactions and learning, as well as the thinking and planning that supports them. Therefore researching pedagogy with IT generally requires various combinations of the models reviewed here together with adaptations of other general pedagogical models.

The choice of models for any particular piece of research obviously depends on the purpose and degree of granularity of the study. In order to facilitate comparison of the value and features of the models discussed in this chapter, they are listed with their features in Table 10.1. These models can contribute to researching pedagogy with IT through supporting specific tasks, as shown in Table 10.1, which can be summarised as follows:

- placing pedagogy in a broader context
- characterising computer use
- analysis of interactions between designers, teacher and students
- quantitative analysis of computer use for specific learning purposes
- identifying factors affecting teachers' and students' behaviours towards IT
- measuring and analysing the uptake and levels of use of IT
- analysing pedagogical practices and pedagogical reasoning relating to IT use
- understanding the nature of knowledge developed through and required for pedagogical reasoning about the use of IT
- analysing and characterising systems that are undergoing change relating to IT use
- involving teachers and students in researching and developing IT use.

Table 10.1 A comparison of models for examining pedagogy with IT

Name of model	Reference	Intended purpose	Features and measures	Value for researching pedagogy with IT in future?
Curriculum, Pedagogy and Assessment	Wilson 2007	Theoretical view of interrelationships between curriculum, pedagogy and assessment	Conceptual view	Characterising computer use
Paradigms for computer assisted learning (CAL)	Kemmis et al. 1977	To classify ways in which computers support learning	Conceptual view	Characterising computer use
Modes of computer use	Taylor 1980	To classify ways in which computers can be used for learning	Conceptual view	Characterising computer use
Perspectives Interactions Paradigm	Squires & McDougall 1994	For evaluating educational software	Conceptual view	Taking account of importance of interactions between designer, teacher and students
Conversational framework	Laurillard et al. 2000	To characterise teacher–student interactions in order to design software	Interactions with computer. Interactions between teacher and pupils	Framework for analysing teacher–student interactions
Computer Practice Framework	Twining 2000	To analyse computer use in a curriculum context	Conceptual view. Amount and types of IT use	Framework for quantitative analysis of computer use for specific learning purposes
Educational practice: a conceptual framework	Alexander 1992	To represent a theoretical overview of educational practice	Conceptual view	Placing pedagogy in broader context
Theory of planned behaviour	Ajzen 1991	To understand factors affecting people's behaviour	Conceptual view. Pedagogical decision making. Analysing change	Identifying key factors affecting teachers' and students' behaviours towards IT
ImpactI framework	Cox 1993	To record and analyse the uptake and use of IT	Amount of IT use	Recording and analysing the uptake and use of IT

Model	Reference	Description	Features	Purpose
Concerns based adoption model	Loucks et al. 1998	To measure people's levels of use of IT	Amount of IT use	Measuring teachers' and learners' levels of IT use
Concerns based adoption model	Griffin and Christensen 1999	Self-evaluation tool for teachers' levels of IT use	Amount of IT use	Self-evaluation tool for teachers' levels of IT use
Teachers' IT Use model	Castillo 2006	Classifying teachers into levels of IT use according to the range of IT types used	Amount and types of IT use	Classifying teachers into levels of IT use according to the range of IT types used
Framework for pedagogical practices relating to IT use	Webb 2005	Conceptual framework for pedagogical practices relating to IT use	Conceptual view. Interactions with computer. Interactions between teacher and pupils	Framework for analysing pedagogical practices relating to IT use
Model of pedagogical reasoning	Webb 2002	Conceptual model for analysing teachers' pedagogical reasoning processes	Conceptual view. Types of IT use between teacher and pupils. Pedagogical decision making	Analysing teachers' and students' pedagogical reasoning processes
Dynamic model for a transforming pedagogy	Somekh and Davies 1991	Conceptual model of pedagogic change with IT change	Conceptual view. Types of IT use. Interactions with computers. Interactions between teacher and pupils. Analysing change	Analysing the extent to which pedagogy with IT in different situations matches this model
The components of technological pedagogical content knowledge	Koehler and Mishra 2005	To capture the dynamic, transactional relationship between knowledge of content, pedagogy and technology	Conceptual view	Understanding the nature of knowledge developed through and required for pedagogical reasoning about the use of IT

(Continued)

Table 10.1 (Continued)

Name of model	Reference	Intended purpose	Features and measures	Value for researching pedagogy with IT in future?
Activity Theory framework	Engeström 2001	Analytical framework for identifying tensions and contradictions in systems	Conceptual view. Analysing change	For identifying tensions and contradictions in systems that are undergoing change relating to IT use
Change Laboratory	Engeström 2001	Analytical framework for identifying tensions and contradictions in systems	Conceptual view	Framework for involving teachers and students in developing IT use
Pedagogy model	Stevenson 2007	Analytical framework for characterising sequences of actions in activity systems where IT is used	Conceptual view. Types of IT use. Interactions with computers. Interactions between teacher and pupils	For characterising actions and sequences of actions in activity systems where IT is used
Generic Pedagogic Framework	Somekh and Davies 1991	Framework for communicating with the participants in an IT development project	Conceptual view. Types of IT use. Interactions with computers. Interactions between teacher and pupils	Framework for communicating with the participants in an IT development project

The number and variety of models is indicative of the complexity and the changing nature of the research community's understanding of pedagogy as well as of developing understanding of opportunities provided by technological developments. This climate of change means that models that enable understanding of change are particularly valuable for researching pedagogy with IT. Therefore Activity Theory, which provides a conceptual framework that can be combined with various qualitative techniques to enable analysis of changing systems and to model proposed systems, has gained in popularity in the IT research community. Furthermore, the multilayered nature of Activity Systems and their interactive nature support modelling of the complexity of IT-enabled learning activities.

Future developments

In the current educational climate in many countries, pedagogy is constrained by high stakes assessments, but the dynamics of this relationship could be altered by a stronger curriculum with clear 'road maps' for development and more focus on formative assessment (Wilson 2007). Developments in pedagogy with IT have focused on a range of different approaches including online learning, blended learning and efforts to characterise teaching interactions and assessment processes to support the design of applications that are intended to take over significant aspects of the teaching role. These latter applications include intelligent tutoring systems that have been used successfully to teach in fairly limited technical areas, such as algebra, but have not achieved the widespread application that was once envisaged. Nevertheless, developments in software agent technology are proceeding (Callaghan *et al.* 2004) and a significant future role is envisaged for them as digital assistants in education. Pedagogy for online learning is also developing, particularly where distance learning is the only viable option. A major focus for developments in pedagogy with IT in the near future is to understand pedagogy for 'blended learning', where a range of types of IT are used in various combinations of face-to-face teaching and online support for learning. These developments enable 'anytime, anywhere learning' and extend pedagogy beyond the classroom, giving more opportunities for changing roles of teachers and students. Contributions of various players and resources in these scenarios need to be analysed and characterised.

At the same time pedagogy as it is understood more generally in education, where IT use may be more limited, continues to adapt and evolve, not only in response to new understanding of theories of co-construction of knowledge and cognition, but also in association with developments in our understanding of formative assessment practices or 'assessment for learning' (see for example Black and Wiliam 2009). This approach to assessment differs from the more traditional assessment of learning, through feedback from the assessment process into teachers' planning and students' learning. These processes of teacher and peer assessment can enable students to understand their own learning in relation to the curriculum and to become more autonomous in their learning by focusing on what they need to learn and how to learn it.

As indicated earlier, pedagogical reasoning processes for teachers have become more complex as the developing capabilities of technology have provided new affordances for learning. At the same time the knowledge domain associated with understanding the pedagogical value of technology for learning different content areas (TPCK) is becoming unmanageable for an individual teacher. One way forward towards resolving this issue is to develop distributed models for both the knowledge domain and the pedagogical reasoning process. Assessment for learning may enable students to share pedagogical reasoning with their teachers as suggested in Figure 10.6. Thus the teacher-directed processes envisaged by Shulman (Figure 10.7) could be gradually transferred to student control as their knowledge of the curriculum as well as their knowledge of the nature of their own learning developed. Furthermore, TPCK may be distributed among teachers, learners and software agents.

The nature and dynamics of distribution of TPCK might vary with a number of factors, particularly the age and experience of students, the nature of the content and the sophistication of any digital assistants. Typically, experienced teachers might draw on a wealth of pedagogical knowledge including knowledge of a range of learners and extensive PCK, whereas learners would be enabled to develop pedagogical knowledge of their own learning. Many learners may have better technological knowledge than their teachers, so their technological pedagogical knowledge could become very important. The scope for such distributed models and their development is potentially a rich area for research and development.

Communication and interaction between teachers and students is obviously one aspect of development of TPCK. Understanding interactions in classrooms that can lead to effective assessment for learning is a focus of continuing research (Black and Wiliam 2006, Webb and Jones 2007). This research is building on Perrenoud's (1998) model of interactive regulation of learning processes and Mercer's models of exploratory talk and sequencing of dialogic interaction (Mercer 2000, Mercer 2007).

As our understanding of classroom talk (Mercer 2000) and dialogic learning (Alexander 2006) develops, questions emerge as to how these are best supported through new technologies. For example, when is whole class discussion valuable and how can this be supported by display technologies or electronic whiteboards? How can teachers and/or computer software support and enable small group discussion? What are the relationships between whole class and small group interaction in terms of, for example, modelling of effective interactions and bridging between the two?

In IT-enabled learning environments the situation may be more complex in that elements of the interactive regulation of learning processes may be built into the design of software. Teachers can build on these software resources in various ways, using their own pedagogical reasoning to provide blended learning scenarios. Students can become more proactive in pedagogical reasoning and planning as they become more autonomous in their learning, and as technologies provide more support for self-regulation of learning. These developments provide opportunities for changes in pedagogy and present challenges for researchers to investigate the potential for learning and the effects of these changes. Careful selection from the models presented in this chapter together with further development of models, particularly models of 'distributed pedagogy' where knowledge and pedagogical reasoning is co-developed and shared between teachers, learners and digital assistants will be necessary to support research into IT-enabled pedagogy in the future.

References

Ajzen, I. (1991) 'The theory of planned behavior', *Organizational Behavior and Human Decision Processes*, 50: 179–211.

Alexander, R. (1992) *Policy and Practice in Primary Education*, London: Routledge.

Alexander, R. (2006) *Towards Dialogic Teaching: rethinking classroom talk*, York: Dialogos.

Black, P., Harrison, C., Lee, C., Marshall, B. and Wiliam, D. (2003) *Assessment for Learning: putting it into practice*, Buckingham, UK: Open University.

Black, P. and Wiliam, D. (2006) 'Assessment for learning in the classroom', in J. Gardner (ed.) *Assessment and Learning*, London: Sage.

Black, P. and Wiliam, D. (2009) 'Developing the theory of formative assessment', *Educational Assessment, Evaluation and Accountability,* 21: 5–32.

Callaghan, V., Clarke, G.S., Colley, M.J., Hagras, H.A.K., Chin, J.S.Y. and Doctor, F. (2004) 'Inhabited intelligent environments', *BT Technology Journal*, 22: 233–247.

Castillo, N. (2006) 'The Implementation of Information and Communication Technology (ICT): an investigation into the level of use and integration of ICT by secondary school teachers in Chile', unpublished PhD thesis, King's College, London.

Cornu, B. (1995) 'New technologies: integration into education', in D. Watson and D. Tinsley, (eds) *Integrating Information Technology into Education*, London: Chapman and Hall.

Cox, M.J., Johnson, D.C. and Watson, D. (1993) *The Impact Report: an evaluation of the impact of information technology on children's achievements in primary and secondary schools*, London: King's College, The University of London.

Dillon, J.T. (1988) *Questioning and Discussion: a multi-disciplinary study*, New York: Ablex.

Downes, T. (2002) 'Blending play, practice and performance: children's use of the computer at home', *Journal of Educational Enquiry*, 3: 21–34.

Engeström, Y. (2001) 'Expansive learning at work: toward an activity theoretical reconceptualization', *Journal of Education and Work*, 14: 133–155.

Engeström, Y., Engeström, R. and Suntio, A. (2002) 'Can a school community learn to master its own future? An activity-theoretical study of expansive learning among middle school teachers', in G. Wells and G. Claxton (eds) *Learning for Life in the 21st Century: sociocultural perspectives on the future of education*, London: Blackwell.

Gibson, J.J. (1979) *The Ecological Approach to Visual Perception*, Boston: Houghton Mifflin.

Greeno, J.G. (1998) 'The situativity of knowing, learning, and research', *American Psychologist*, 53: 5–26.

Griffin, D. and Christensen, R. (1999) *Concerns-Based Adoption Model (CBAM) Levels of Use of an Innovation (CBAM-LOU)*, Denton, Texas: Institute for the Integration of Technology into Teaching and Learning.

Hu, L. and Webb, M. (2009) 'Integrating ICT to higher education in China: from the perspective of activity theory', *Education and Information Technologies* (forthcoming).

Kemmis, S., Atkin, R. and Wright, E. (1977) *How Do Students Learn? Working papers on computer assisted learning*, Norwich: Centre for Applied Research in Education.

Kennewell, S. (2001) 'Using affordances and constraints to evaluate the use of information and communications technology in teaching and learning,' *Journal of Information Technology for Teacher Education*, 10: 101–116.

Koehler, M.J. and Mishra, P. (2005) 'What happens when teachers design educational technology? The development of technological pedagogical content knowledge', *Journal of Educational Computing Research*, 32: 131–152.

Koutromanos, G. (2004). 'The effects of head teachers, head officers and school counsellors on the uptake of information technology in Greek schools', unpublished PhD thesis, King's College, London.

Kuutti, K. (1995) 'Activity theory as a potential framework for human computer interaction research', in B. Nardi (ed.) *Context and Consciousness: activity theory and human computer interaction*, Cambridge, MA: MIT Press.

Laurillard, D. (1993; 2nd edn 2002) *Rethinking University Teaching: a framework for the effective use of educational technology*, London: Routledge.

Laurillard, D., Stratfold, M., Luckin, R., Plowman, L. and Taylor, J. (2000) 'Affordances for learning in a non-linear narrative medium', *Journal of Interactive Media in Education*, 2.

Leont'ev, A.N. (1978) *Activity, Consciousness, and Personality*, Englewood Cliffs: Prentice-Hall.

Linn, M.C. and Hsi, S. (2000) *Computers, Teachers, Peers: science learning partners*, London: Erlbaum.

Loucks, S.F., Newlove, B.W. and Hall, G.E. (1998) *Measuring Levels of Use of the Innovation: a manual for trainers, interviewers and raters*, Austin, Texas: Southwest Educational Development Laboratory.

McGrenere, J. and Ho, W. 'Affordances: clarifying and evolving a concept', paper presented at Graphics Interface 2000, Montreal, May 2000. Online. Available HTTP: <http://www.graphicsinterface.org/proceedings/2000/177/> (accessed 4 March 2005).

McLoughlin, C. and Oliver, R. (1999) 'Pedagogic roles and dynamics in telematics environments', in M. Selinger, and J. Pearson (eds) *Telematics In Education: trends and issues*, Oxford: Elsevier Science.

Mercer, N. (2000) *Words and Minds: how we use language to think together*, London: Routledge.

Mercer, N. 'Time for learning: examining the temporal development of classroom talk', paper presented at the American Educational Research Association Annual Meeting, The World of Educational Quality, Chicago, Illinois, April 2007.

Mercer, N., Littleton, K. and Wegerif, R. (2004) 'Methods for studying the processes of interaction and collaborative activity in computer-based educational activities', *Technology, Pedagogy and Education*, 13: 195–212.

Norman, D.A. (2002) *Affordances and design*. Online. Available HTTP: <http://www.jnd.org/dn.mss/affordances_and.html> (accessed 4 March 2005).

Perrenoud, P. (1998) 'From formative assessment to a controlled regulation of learning processes. Towards a wider conceptual field', *Assessment in Education*, 5: 85–102.

Shulman, L. (1987) 'Knowledge and teaching: foundations of the new reform', *Harvard Educational Review*, 57: 1–22.

Somekh, B. and Davies, R. (1991) 'Towards a pedagogy for information technology', *The Curriculum Journal*, 2: 153–170.

Squires, D. and McDougall, A. (1994) *Choosing and Using Educational Software: a teachers' guide*, London: The Falmer Press.

Stevenson, I. (2008) 'Tool, tutor, environment or resource: exploring metaphors for digital technology and pedagogy using activity theory', *Computers & Education*, 51: 836–853.

Taylor, R.P. (1980) *The Computer in the School: tutor, tool, tutee*, New York: Teachers College Press.

Twining, P. (2000) 'The computer practice framework: a tool to help identify the impact on education practice of investments in information and communication technology', paper presented at ALT-C 2000, Manchester, October. Online. Available HTTP: <http://www.jcu.edu.au/asd/docs/conference/confAherran.htm#twining> (accessed 4 March 2005).

Van Lier, L. (1996) *Interaction in the Language Curriculum: awareness, autonomy and authenticity*, Harlow: Pearson Education.

Watkins, C. and Mortimore, P. (1999) 'Pedagogy: what do we know?', in P. Mortimore (ed.) *Understanding Pedagogy and its Impact on Learning*, London: Chapman.

Webb, M.E. (2002) 'Pedagogical reasoning: issues and solutions for the teaching and learning of ICT in secondary schools', *Education and Information Technologies*, 7: 237–255.

—— (2005) 'Affordances of ICT in Science learning; implications for an integrated pedagogy', *International Journal of Science Education*, 27: 705–735.

Webb, M.E. and Cox, M.J. (2004) 'A review of pedagogy related to information and communications technology', *Technology, Pedagogy and Education*, 13: 235–286.

Webb, M.E. and Jones, J. (2007) 'Developing assessment for learning: how teachers' and students' beliefs and experiences affect changing classroom practice', paper presented at the American Educational Research Association Annual Meeting, The World of Educational Quality, Chicago, Illinois, April.

Wells, G. (2002) 'Dialogue in activity theory', *Mind, Culture, and Activity*, 9: 43–66.

Wilson, M. (2007) 'Developing new approaches to classroom assessment: recognizing how teachers work with formative practices', paper presented at the American Educational Research Association Annual Meeting, The World of Educational Quality, Chicago, Illinois, April.

Chapter 11

Analysing the impact of information technology on activity and learning

Steve Kennewell
Swansea Metropolitan University, UK

Introduction

Since the early days of using computers to aid learning, much of the research has been focused on what the technology can do and what difference this can make to learning. However, IT is just one component of the educational arena, and any attempt to focus only on the role of IT in enhancing learning is likely to produce results that show little effect compared with the influence of all the other factors involved. On the other hand, large-scale studies that attempt to isolate the impact of IT from all the other variables statistically will not produce large effect sizes because of the sheer variety of the ways in which IT is used in different cases; some uses of IT may lead to learning gains, others will make little difference and some may well be inferior to traditional methods.

In order to explore the potential of new technologies for improving learning in educational activity systems, a suitable framework for analysis of relationships between teacher, learners and resources is needed. The ideas of cultural–historical activity theory provide a framework for analysing organisational work and characterising changes in terms of the activity taking place and the subjects, goals, tools, roles, rules and communities involved in the activities (Engeström 1987, Somekh 2001). This sort of analysis has been applied to classroom settings (Stevenson 2004) and online learning communities (Lim 2002), but it does not fully capture the level of detail needed concerning the nature of IT as mediational means, the mental processes which may be stimulated and supported using IT, and the key role of the teacher in managing the process. Quite different effects would be expected from a teacher showing a PowerPoint presentation, from a student using game or quiz software, and from a group of students collaboratively developing a concept map. In order to capture such effects, a more fine-grained approach to the study of learning has been developed (Kennewell *et al.* 2008) which weaves together a number of perspectives on learning and activity. In this chapter, the theoretical basis for this approach is set out.

Features of educational activity settings

Learning takes place in many different environments, and the focus here is on educational activity settings: the physical and cultural environments which form part of activity systems whose object is education. These include classrooms in schools and colleges, online learning environments, and workplace training provision, although in this chapter the main focus for discussion will be the classroom. The nature of activity in classrooms is influenced by the socio-cultural features of the setting, including the prevailing ethos and available tools, and the characteristics of the participants in the activity system.

The people participating in such settings will characteristically include the teacher, other learning support staff, and the learners themselves. The relevant features of the practitioners can be classified as knowledge, beliefs, values and behaviours (Cox and Webb 2004). Students also exhibit features such as these. The ethos is influenced by school policies and practices, subject culture, classroom rules, and the social background of students. These can exert a strong influence on IT functions as a means of mediation (Olson 2000). The media and instruments available may be those based on language, such as discussion, or physical tools such as coloured pens and paper. IT is a particularly versatile medium, and is not easy to classify in nature or function. It can be compared with other educational resources, such as books, posters on the wall, information sheets, worksheets, video and audio recordings which help stimulate, structure and support activity in the classroom. IT does not necessarily replace these more familiar resources; in some situations the traditional medium may be more appropriate, or it may be used most effectively in combination with IT.

Other variables include participants in the activity system, the object of the activity, the goals of the individuals and groups involved and the actions carried out in pursuit of the goals. These actions will, of course, be dependent on the culture, the mediational means and the roles of the other people (students, teachers, other adults) participating in the activity. The classroom is non-typical as an activity system, in that the primary intention is for learning to take place rather than a product to be created or a service to be provided.

Most often, however, task completion will dominate learners' actions (Lings and Desforges 1999, Somekh 2001, Rabardel and Samurçay 2001), and students will focus on producing a recognisable outcome. This task outcome may be a physical (or electronic) artefact, such as the solution of a mathematical exercise or a table comparing nutritional values of different meals. It may involve performance, such as responding to questions, reporting on behalf of a group discussion, or playing a role. The teacher's intention is that the students will learn from such a task, but if the learners' only goal is one of task completion, it is likely that learning will be limited. Learning, then, is not the same kind of action as writing, browsing the Internet, or performing a play; rather it is a by-product of such action and may not be intended by the student. Nevertheless, the learning that results from the action will manifest itself as a change in the student's abilities.

It is important, therefore, to focus on the learners (as individuals, as classes and in other more temporary groupings selected for learning purposes) and what abilities they bring to the action. The abilities required of the learner in order to achieve their goals will be some combination of knowledge (factual and conceptual), skills, values, beliefs and dispositions in the target subject matter (Cox and Webb 2004) together with generic skills (such as literacy, IT capability and working in teams). Students' metacognitive abilities and disposition towards learning will be particularly important.

Affordances for action

One way of analysing the effect of features of the setting is in terms of their *affordances* for people carrying out goal-related actions. This idea was developed by Gibson (1979) to help analyse visual perception and adapted by Norman (1998) to characterise features of machines. The common ground in the most explicit views published in the field of IT education (Laurillard *et al.* 2000, Webb 2005, John and Sutherland 2005) concerns the opportunities or *potential for action* inherent in features of the setting, usually in the form of tools that indicate how they might be used, or models and examples that may be copied. In the field of IT, for example, a hyperlink on a word or image in a web page is an affordance for finding more information about the idea represented by the word or image.

The use of the related idea of *constraint* (see for example Greeno 1998), in conjunction with affordance, provides a more comprehensive characterisation of the relationships between the environment and the people acting in and on that environment. The term constraint refers to a boundary, guide or *structure for action*. It may take the form of a prompt or question, rather than a physical property. Using the web page example again, a navigation bar is a constraint on action; it limits the user to exploring the ideas listed on the bar. The structure provided by constraints can take a positive form (guidance) or a negative form (barrier or obstacle to be overcome) depending on the person's perspective. The same feature will contribute both potential and structure, as in the case of the navigation bar that provides potential for finding information on the site, as long as the information required is amongst the options listed. The person acting may or may not perceive the affordances and constraints that are inherent in the features, and so the potential and structure for action depend on the abilities and goals of the person(s) acting. For instance, the hyperlink on the web page will only have potential for action for a person who is familiar with the sign conventions of a web browser and has the physical control to move and click a mouse.

In order to simplify the text in this chapter, the term 'affordance' will be used to represent the constraining as well affording aspects of the relationship between a person and the environment.

Orchestration

From socio-constructivist theories concerning 'scaffolding' (see for example Wood 1998: 99), it would be expected that the most effective learning should occur when the intended task outcome is comprehensible (and ideally motivating) to the students but not easily achievable without support. In order to complete the task, some cognitive effort on the part of the students will be required if learning is to occur. If students have difficulty with their task, the teacher acts to increase the potential and/or structure for action in a minimal way so that learners have opportunity to achieve as much as possible for themselves. For example, when students are using a search engine to investigate an issue, the teacher may constrain them to particular keywords. It is expected that the learner will be able to achieve the goal with less help in future as the assistance is 'faded' (see Wood 1998: 100). So next time the students are to use a search engine, the teacher may discuss the sort of words to use as keywords without making specific suggestions. Subsequently, students may be expected to devise search terms with no prompts at all. In this view, the role of the teacher is one of setting tasks which present some challenge to the learners and then 'orchestrating' (Wood 1998: 98, Kennewell *et al.* 2008) the affordances by continuously manipulating features of the classroom in response to students' operations, so as to ensure successful task completion. The teacher uses knowledge of the learners' abilities to set a level of cognitive effort that will stimulate the desired learning.

It is not only teachers who orchestrate affordances in the classroom, however; learners also may actively seek and evaluate resources to help them achieve their goals, decide on who to approach for advice, and impose structure on their action. This is commonly seen in young people's leisure activity with IT (Facer *et al.* 2003), but can be fostered in the classroom, too. The child who is moving images on the board at the front of the class can gain feedback on whether she is positioning them correctly by gauging the reaction of her classmates, and adjusting her operation accordingly. One of the challenges for the teacher is to orchestrate the affordances of the setting with a sufficiently light touch to allow students to take initiatives, make decisions and maintain a degree of autonomy over their learning.

Reflection

The role of reflection is also seen as crucial in learners' internalisation of socially mediated ideas, and the cycle of learning involves a reflection stage, when conceptual knowledge production occurs within individual students' minds (Rabardel and Samurçay 2001). The student's goal switches from production to learning.

Schön (1983) characterises two different forms of reflection associated with goal-related action:

- *reflection-in-action,* which corresponds to the process of orchestrating affordances to provide potential and structure for action;
- *reflection-on-action,* which corresponds to evaluation of the outcome, and analysis of the action itself.

Reflection-in-action is characteristic of autonomous work settings and may not occur naturally during classroom learning situations in which the students have little responsibility for monitoring the progress of their actions. However, reflection-in-action may be stimulated when teachers use a more dialogic approach, such as uptake questioning or focusing dialogue, that gives students more influence over the course of the lesson (Kennewell *et al.* 2008).

Reflection-on-action may lead to the construction of conceptual knowledge through analysis of invariant properties and relations in the subject matter of the task. This individual knowledge may well be idiosyncratic initially (John and Sutherland 2005), but the interactivity within the classroom setting generates collective knowledge, a process carefully manipulated by the teacher's orchestration of the whole-class setting to provide affordances for reflection on key issues. Students consider together what they have achieved, how they have achieved it and what they have learned from the action. For example, teachers may provide a writing frame for a report, focusing questions for a group discussion, a request to produce a concept map for a formative assessment portfolio, or challenges to informal ideas about changes in the state of matter shown by the arrangements of items on the interactive whiteboard. Students may learn to carry out the evaluation process independently and engage in self-regulated learning. IT can make important contributions to this process; as well as the collation of group presentations, the storage feature of IT facilitates the revisiting of material generated previously by the class (Kennewell and Beauchamp 2007).

Construction of knowledge completes the loop, whereby what is learned from an action influences the learner's ability to engage in future actions. Figure 11.1 indicates the role of orchestration in activity on both the active and reflective plane.

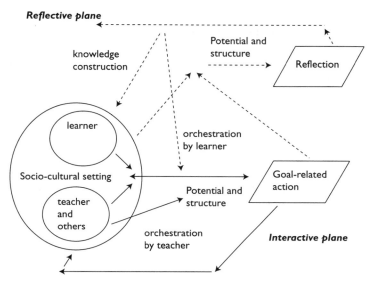

Reflective plane

Solid arrows represent influences related directly to action, broken arrows represent influences related to reflection

Figure 11.1 Reflection and knowledge construction during goal-related action.

Application of the framework

This approach to researching teaching and learning complements the use of the cultural–historical activity theory framework. The focus on orchestration and reflection provides a structure for interpreting and comparing educational activity settings and the impact of pedagogical practices at a detailed level. This level of analysis shows that IT has a number of features that are new or enhanced in comparison with non-digital educational media, including multimodality, capacity, automation, provisionality and feedback (Kennewell and Beauchamp 2007). It should not be taken for granted that the affordances of these features can just be assimilated into teachers' existing pedagogical knowledge and orchestrated in the same way as for traditional resources, however. The teacher needs to make appropriate decisions about when and how to use IT, when to use other media, and when to delegate decisions to students. For example, the feature of automation enables teachers' planned orchestration to be represented in the form of a slide presentation with video and animation, instead of the teacher having to repeatedly write and draw on a board, organise tapes, etc. This could have the effect of freeing the teacher to respond to learners' interests and difficulties, but it could alternatively have the effect of restricting the teacher to following a predetermined path. For students to make effective use of the autonomy that they may have in an IT-rich environment, they will need an intention to learn rather than merely complete tasks, together with IT capability and generic learning skills.

This analysis points future empirical research towards investigating the effects of developing jointly teachers' ability to teach interactively, students' ability to learn intentionally, and the IT capability of both so that they can exploit the features of IT when it is appropriate to do so. The framework is general in scope, and can be applied to planning, evaluation and research in distance learning and work-based training settings as well as classrooms. Because of its focus on goals and the orchestration of affordances for action, it is sensitive to the small differences, both in the student task and in the support provided, that can make a major difference to learning (see for example Kennewell *et al.* 2008). It is in this detailed analysis that the impact of IT will really be brought into focus.

References

Cox, M. and Webb, M. (2004) *A Review of the Research Evidence Relating to ICT Pedagogy*, London: Becta / DfES.

Engeström, Y. (1987) *Learning by Expanding: an activity-theoretical approach to developmental research*, Helsinki: Orienta-Konsultit.

Facer, K., Furlong, J., Furlong, R. and Sutherland, R. (2003) *ScreenPlay: children and computing in the home*, London: Routledge Falmer.

Gibson, J.J. (1979) *The Ecological Approach to Visual Perception*, Boston, MA: Houghton Mifflin.

Greeno, J.G. (1998) 'The situativity of knowing, learning and research', *American Psychologist*, 53: 5–26.

John, P. and Sutherland, R. (2005) 'Affordance, opportunity and the pedagogical implications of ICT', *Educational Review*, 57: 405–413.

Kennewell, S. and Beauchamp, G. (2007) 'The features of interactive whiteboards and their impact on learning', *Learning, Media and Technology*, 32: 227–241.

Kennewell, S., Tanner, H., Jones, S. and Beauchamp, G. (2008) 'Analysing the use of interactive technology to implement interactive teaching', *Journal of Computer Assisted Learning*, 24: 61–73.

Laurillard, D., Stratford, M., Luckin, R., Plowman, L. and Taylor, J. (2000) 'Affordances for learning in a non-linear narrative medium', *Journal of Interactive Media in Education*, 2: 1–19.

Lim, C. P. (2002) 'A theoretical framework for the study of ICT in schools: a proposal', *British Journal of Educational Technology*, 33: 411–421.

Lings, P. and Desforges, C. (1999) 'On subject differences in applying knowledge to learn', *Research Papers in Education*, 14: 199–221.

Norman, D. (1998) *The Design of Everyday Things*, New York: MIT Press.

Olson, J. (2000) 'Trojan horse or teacher's pet? Computers and the culture of the school', *Journal of Curriculum Studies*, 32: 1–8.

Rabardel, P. and Samurçay, R. (2001) 'From artefact to instrument-mediated learning', paper presented at New Challenges to Research on Learning, International Symposium, University of Helsinki, March.

Schön, D. (1983) *The Reflective Practitioner*, New York: Basic Books.

Somekh, B. (2001) 'Methodological issues in identifying and describing the way knowledge is constructed with and without information and communications technology', *Journal of Information Technology for Teacher Education*, 10: 157–178.

Stevenson, I. (2004) *Measures for Assessing the Impact of ICT Use on Attainment*, Coventry: Becta.

Webb, M. (2005) 'Affordances of ICT in science learning: implications for an integrated pedagogy', *International Journal of Science Education*, 27: 705–735.

Wood, D. (1998) *How Children Think and Learn*, Oxford: Blackwell.

Chapter 12

Transformative application of research and learning praxis in education

Trends in information technology integration

Paul T. Nleya
University of Botswana, Botswana

Introduction

This chapter traces theoretical constructs that attest to the paradigm shift, albeit gradual, from techno-centric to more socio-technical approaches, through social constructivism to social cognitive theories as applied in education. The author argues that transformative applications of IT that could lead developing nations to go beyond traditional uses of these technologies in education practice would need fundamental changes in the way education is conceived and delivered, and the way developmental research is conducted. If appropriately used, IT tools have the potential to optimise learner-centred pedagogical methods that ascribe to higher order metaphors of learning; Cultural–Historical Activity Theory (CHAT), Developmental Work Research (DWR) and Change Laboratory (CL) conceptual frameworks have rendered valuable outcomes. The World Information Technology Forum (WITFOR) pilot project in Botswana is cited to exemplify the praxis of these frameworks. The chapter focuses on a socio-cognitive approach that emphasises the socio-cultural nature of human cognition.

Cultural–Historical Activity Theory (CHAT)

Activity Theory (AT) emphasises that internal mental activities cannot be understood if they are analysed separately, in isolation from external activities, because there are mutual transformations between these two kinds of activities: internalisation and externalisation. The principle of tool mediation plays a central role within the approach. First, tools shape the way human beings interact with reality. Second, tools usually reflect the experiences of other people who have tried to solve similar problems at an earlier time and invented or modified tools to make them more efficient. Tools are means for the accumulation and transmission of social knowledge, and they influence the nature of both external behaviour and the mental functioning of individuals (Bertelsen and Bodker 2003a). In human activity theory, the basic unit of analysis is human (work) activity. Human activities are driven by certain needs where people wish to achieve a certain purpose. The activity is usually mediated by one or more instruments or tools. Individuals holding some praxis (e.g. carpentry or nursing) continue the praxis, and change it as well, by inventing new ways of doing things. In other words, we can talk about the appropriateness of a certain tool for a certain praxis (Bertelsen and Bodker 2003b). According to Vygotsky (1978), the Zone of Proximal Development occurs during adoption of socio-cultural practices within a community. The notion of 'trialogue' has its basis in activity theory's notion of a mediation and object oriented activity system. Trialogue means that by using various mediating artefacts (signs, concepts and tools) and mediating processes (such as practices or the interaction between tacit and explicit knowledge) people develop common objects of activity.

The knowledge society no longer adheres only to individual cognitive competencies, but also to joint or shared competence. Another contention pertains to bridging the existence of two persistent gaps in educational research: between educational theory and teaching praxis, and between the praxis of research and the praxis of teaching. Teaching, learning, and researching are regarded as constitutive parts of daily classroom praxis rather than separate entities; and IT is inherently a powerful tool to assist nations to adapt to the knowledge society (Roth 1998, 2000).

From taxonomies of learning to metaphors of learning

According to Hakkarainen *et al.* (2004), providing an educational system with a list of skills that should be facilitated could end up with a situation where educators develop instructional strategies teaching certain selected skills, and methods for assessing students' mastery of these skills. What is likely to be learned in this context is the ability to show indications of the skills in question in familiar situations involving practices at school, probably without the ability to deal with meaningful and complex real-world situations.

Learning taxonomies and competence

The discourse on skills and competencies is not a new phenomenon in educational contexts. Taxonomies and lists of desirable skills have been created and defined as educational objectives. Bloom's domains of learning (cognitive, affective and psycho-motor) include six levels within the cognitive domain (knowledge, comprehension, application, analysis, synthesis and evaluation). These range from the simple recall of facts as the lowest level, through increasingly more complex and abstract mental levels, to the highest order classified as evaluation (Bloom 1956, cited in OfficePort undated).

However, as outlined above, taxonomies usually elicit low quality education. This cognitive approach upholds the viewpoint of an individual's cognition and this tendency may be named the 'cognitivist bias'.

Contemporary socio–cognitive research on human expertise and competence has emphasised the socio-cultural nature of human cognition, unlike traditional cognitive models that are both individualistic and mentalistic. The development of networked expertise is a necessary requirement for the knowledge society. This type of competence cannot only be understood by referring to individual cognitive competencies, but must also include joint or shared competence. When expertise is examined only at the individual level, explanation of the development of expertise becomes not only difficult but also mysterious (Engeström 1992).

Networked environments entail complex and reciprocal relations between individuals and collective competencies. In order to understand the challenges to human competence emerging from the knowledge society, it is essential to re-examine the basic assumptions about how learning occurs and how human competence develops.

Constructivist learning theory

Constructivism holds that, by reflecting on our experiences, we construct our own understanding of the world. Learners generate their own 'rules' and 'mental models', which they use to make sense of their experiences. Learning, therefore, is simply the process of adjusting mental models to accommodate new experiences. Constructivist teachers encourage students constantly to assess how activities help them gain understanding. Through questioning themselves and their strategies, students in the constructivist classroom ideally become 'expert learners'. With a well-planned classroom environment, the students learn how to learn.

While constructivism has similarities with the more recent approaches, constructivism has tended to carry many versions and interpretations, so that the term by itself has become rather uninformative without further qualification (Steffe and Gale 1995). Given that knowledge will be, or already is, the most important critical resource for social and economic development, a competitive edge emerges from adding value to and creating new knowledge rather than by simply exploiting existing knowledge resources (Bereiter 2002, March 1999). Many investigators have argued that a challenge to every employee is to engage in activities that add value to knowledge, rather than just producing physical goods. Educational institutions and knowledge organisations are obliged to find new models and practices for facilitating the creation and sharing of knowledge as well as the dynamic development of expertise, and to develop new technologies to cope with these challenges. The qualifications individual employees would need to acquire in order to be productive in the knowledge society need careful scrutiny.

However, Paavola *et al*. (2004) have argued that the problem with a constructivist stance in psychology and education is that it often does not involve specific analysis of constructive process, particularly with respect to innovation, and that as a consequence, the understanding of these processes has not become more specific during the past two decades. They propose that metaphors of learning (knowledge acquisition, participation, and knowledge creation) have recently provided a road map serving as heuristic knowledge useful in understanding the development of expertise both within work places and education (Paavola and Hakkarainen 2005). These metaphors of learning and models of innovative knowledge communities would further the constructivist agenda and support innovative practices in education such as IT integration.

An emergent epistemological approach to learning

An emergent epistemological approach to learning has recently been proposed. Paavola and Hakkarainen (2005) have argued that beyond metaphors, according to which learning is a process of knowledge acquisition by individual learners (a 'monological' approach) or a participatory approach to social interaction (a 'dialogical' approach), one should distinguish a 'trialogical' approach: learning as a process of knowledge creation where common objects of activity are developed collaboratively. The third metaphor helps to elicit and understand processes of knowledge advancement that are important in a knowledge society. They argue that cognition and knowing are distributed over both individuals and their environments, and learning is 'situated' in these relations and networks of distributed activities of participation. The argument is that knowledge and knowing cannot be separated from situations where they are used or where they take place.

Paavola *et al*. (2004) have proposed a knowledge-creation metaphor that addresses processes of deliberate transformation of knowledge and corresponding collective social practices. The metaphor views learning as analogous to

Table 12.1 Summary of three metaphors of learning

No.	Metaphors	Characteristics of the metaphors
1	Knowledge Acquisition metaphor ('monological' approach)	Individual learners construct knowledge from past experience
2	Participation Metaphor ('dialogical' approach)	Individual derives knowledge through participation in social interaction
3	Knowledge creation metaphor ('trialogical' metaphor)	Learning as process of knowledge creation where common objects of activity are created – concentrates on mediated processes

innovative processes of inquiry where new ideas, tools, and practices are created and the initial knowledge is either substantially enriched or significantly transformed during the process. The metaphor addresses processes, practices and social structures that are likely to encourage the formation of new knowledge and innovations. This metaphor is quite appropriate for the diffusion of IT and the information society.

Developmental work research praxis in education

The Center for Activity Theory and Developmental Work Research, within the University of Helsinki in Finland, has developed and registered the Change Laboratory (CL) method to deal with problems created by a separation of theory and research from teaching. Activity Theory and associated approaches hold that it is inherently futile to attempt to understand human activity independent of contexts, and that human practices can best be understood from the perspective of praxis. Human beings and their environment, including researchers, are theorised as being part of a fundamental unity. When we consider learning environments in terms of activity, we simultaneously theorise research and its object (e.g. praxis of teaching and learning), thereby removing the gap between theory and praxis that research seeks to explain. Teaching, learning, and researching are regarded as constitutive parts of daily classroom praxis (Holzkamp 1991, Roth 1998, 2000). CHAT is therefore explicitly based on the premise that humans are co-creators of their learning environment.

Educators have recently levelled a methodological critique against traditional forms of classroom research because they both objectify teachers and students and lead to results that do not enhance praxis. A different way of doing classroom research grounded in Developmental Work Research (DWR), which has its basic value in the primacy of human agency, has been adopted. This includes the capacity of individuals to participate in creating their lived-in world, rather than merely being determined by it. The DWR methodology relies on interventions aimed at helping practitioners analyse and redesign their activity system. An important theoretical framework in CHAT is that of expansive learning. The major objective is to ascribe an approach to research on learning environments that, among others, contributes to overcoming two persistent gaps in education: between educational theory and teaching praxis, and between the praxis of research and the praxis of teaching (Roth *et al.* 2001). This perspective provides researchers with a radically different view of classroom events and classroom environments (Engeström 1987).

In classroom research, students are the subject of the activity and their primary object is an aspect of the world. Teaching is motivated by the intent to assist students to change their relation to the world, thereby providing them with increased potential to act in the world. This increased potential to act is the outcome of the activity. Activity theory is thus portrayed as non-reductionist in that subject, object and tools participate in other mediated relations. The society (community) also mediates the relationship between student (subject) and pedagogy (tool); that is, because tools have cultural-historical origins (see Webb, Figure 10.7).

Such praxis enables researchers to co-generate theory together with teachers and students with whom they already share the classroom experiences for the purpose of improving the practices of teaching and learning. The CL method therefore assists researchers with DWR. It is a reflective team-building approach where video data is collected for longer term reflection, analysis and intervention. The videos are viewed, questions asked and modification of existing norms, procedures, policies and objectives of the institution made to achieve the desired outcomes. The desired changes only come when the whole cycle of the learning metaphors are covered. Within the CL method, teaching and research are different aspects of one overarching activity system intended to assist students to learn.

Transformative applications of IT in schools

Many developing countries' policies promote the necessary transition from agro-based societies to ones that recognise people and the investment in their education and training as a necessary condition for national development. Technologically, Finland is amongst the most advanced countries in the world. According to an OECD (2001) evaluation, Finland produces the best results in the world in many areas. The rapid growth and modernisation of Botswana's economy has created demands for certain kinds of educated and skilled labour which are not being met at present. The Botswana Commission on Education (Republic of Botswana 1994) decided that the nation's resource is its people, and that investment in their education and training is a necessary condition for national development. The commission recognised the application of technology as increasingly important and that the workforce needed to be adaptable and receptive to change. The Botswana ICT policy in pursuance of the nation's vision 2016 has noted that Botswana would be a globally competitive, knowledgeable and informed society where lasting improvements in social, economic and cultural development would be achieved through effective use of ICT, (Republic of Botswana 2004).

This policy provides Botswana with a clear and compelling roadmap to drive the transformation process through the effective use of IT. Botswana, through the Botswana Technology Center (BTC) also launched a national policy on Science and Technology (Republic of Botswana 1998). This policy recognises IT as being vital in Botswana's technological developments.

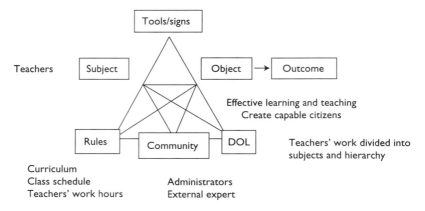

Curriculum
Class schedule
Teachers' work hours

Administrators
External expert

Figure 12.1 Molefi school initial ICT plan on activity system.

Developmental work research in the WITFOR pilot project

DWR and CL approaches are integral aspects of the World Information Technology Forum (WITFOR) Education Commission project launched in Botswana in 2005. WITFOR has proposed research that promotes the primacy of human agency and that is both innovative and sustainable. Figure 12.1 depicts an activity system developed by Molefi Senior School (MSS) at a post-WITFOR 2005 workshop held in Botswana. The pilot school team identified their outcome, the rules, division of labour and members of the community to be involved in their computer integration process.

Results of DWR outcomes on the activity system

Wilson (2007) reported that MSS teachers, students and administrators co-generated some basic theory which they used to improve the initial activity system of the school (Figure 12.2). The improved activity system was a product of participants' past experience (monological), through participating in the case study (dialogical), and the knowledge created was a result of social interaction and involvement in the DWR process (trialogical). Aspects of the DWR approach are exemplified in this case study where outcomes were collaboratively developed through the research praxis, rather than by the researcher alone.

The findings show that some significant improvement was made on the activity system shown in Webb Figure 10.8. However, the findings also suggested the establishment of a CL at MSS, to enable further DWR so as to achieve the desired transformation and outcomes concomitant with the

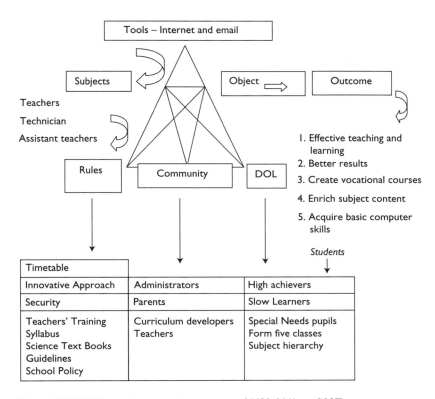

Figure 12.2 DWR results on activity system of MSS (Wilson 2007).

participation and knowledge-creation learning metaphors. A CL is currently in progress at MSS to continue developmental work research.

Conclusion

An eclectic and comprehensive theory of human competence, that derives new skill and competence requirements from the socio-cognitive theories of expertise, is now achievable in part (Hakkarainen *et al*. 2004). Transformative application of IT in education and research, using pedagogically meaningful ways of learning and research, would respond to the challenges of the knowledge society. Learning would then become an integral and inseparable aspect of the praxis of teaching, learning, and even research. Historically, there has been a tradition of people undertaking research in a relatively non-participatory manner. However, CHAT and associated frameworks portray some praxis in which teaching and research are different aspects of one overarching activity system.

References

Bereiter, C. (2002) *Education and Mind in the Knowledge Age*, Hillsdale, NJ: Erlbaum.

Bertelsen, O.W. and Bodker S. (2003a) 'Activity theory', in J.M. Carroll (ed.) *HCI Models, Theories and Frameworks: toward a multidisciplinary science*, San Francisco: Morgan Kaufmann.

Bertelsen, O.W. and Bodker, S. (2003b) 'Beyond the interface: encountering artifacts in use', in J.M. Carroll (ed.) *HCI Models, Theories and Frameworks: toward a multidisciplinary science*, San Francisco: Morgan Kaufmann.

Bloom (1956) 'Bloom's Taxonomy', in OfficePort (undated). Online. Available HTTP: <http://www.officeport.com/edu/blooms.htm> (retrieved on 12 March 2009).

Engeström, Y. (1987) *Learning by Expanding*, Helsinki: Orienta-Konsultit.

—— (1992) *Interactive Expertise: studies in distributed working intelligence*, Research Bulletin 83, Helsinki: University of Helsinki.

Hakkarainen, K., Palonen, T., Paavola S. and Lehtinen, E. (2004) *Communities of Networked Experience: professional and educational perspectives*, London: Elsevier.

Holzkamp, K. (1991) 'Societal and individual life processes', in C.W. Tolman and W. Maiers (eds) *Critical Psychology: contributions to an historical science of the subject*, Cambridge, UK: Cambridge University Press.

March, J.G. (1999) *The Pursuit of Organizational Intelligence*, Oxford: Blackwell.

OECD (2001) *Knowledge and Skills for Life – first results from programme for international student assessment 2000*, Paris: OECD.

Paavola, S. and Hakkarainen, K. (2005) 'The knowledge creation metaphor: an emergent epistemological approach to learning', *Science & Education* 14: 535–557.

Paavola, S., Lipponen, L. and Hakkarainen K. (2004) 'Models of innovative knowledge communities and three metaphors of learning', *Review of Educational Research*, 74: 557–576.

Republic of Botswana (1994) *Report of the National Commission on Education*, Gaborone: Government Printer.

Republic of Botswana (1998) *National Policy on Science and Technology*, Gaborone: Government Printer.

Republic of Botswana (2004) *Maitlamo ICT Policy*, Gaborone: Ministry of Communication Science and Technology.

Roth, W. M. (1998) 'Teaching and learning as everyday activity', in B.J. Fraser and K.G. Tobin (eds) *International Handbook of Science Education*, Dordrecht: Kluwer.

Roth, W.M. (2000) 'Learning environment research, lifeworld analysis, and solidarity in practice', *Learning Environment Research*, 2: 225–247.

Roth W.M., Robin, K. and Zimmermann, A. (2001) 'Coteaching/cogenerative dialoguing: learning environments research as classroom praxis', *Learning Environments Research*, 5: 1–28.

Steffe, L.P. and Gale, J. (eds) (1995) *Constructivism in Education*, Hillsdale, NJ: Erlbaum.

Vygotsky, L. S. (1978) *Mind and Society: the development of higher psychological processes*, Cambridge, MA: Harvard University Press.

Wilson S. (2007) 'An assessment of computer integration into the teaching and learning of science: a case study of Molefi senior secondary school', Unpublished thesis, University of Botswana.

Chapter 13

The practical power of theoretically informed research into innovation

Bridget Somekh
Manchester Metropolitan University, UK

Introduction

> Nothing is as practical as a good theory.
>
> (Kurt Lewin 1951)

This chapter seeks to clarify the importance of theory in informing the purposes and design of research. It argues also for the importance of distinguishing research into IT in education from other kinds of research, and the need, in particular, to ground research into IT in theoretical knowledge about the process of innovation. Many researchers assume that the same methods can be applied to any situation, and they tend to see knowledge as a set of established propositions which are equally 'true' in all contexts. Paradoxically, those who apply these methods to research into IT in education are often little concerned with 'theory' which they tend to dismiss as unimportant and unnecessary when what is needed, as they see it, is systematic application of methods – often surveys involving the administration of questionnaires – to establish facts about the uptake and use of IT, the amount of in-service training delivered to teachers, and the test score results of the students who have been taught in IT-rich classrooms compared with those who have not received this 'treatment'. This chapter contests this view and argues, with Lewin (1951), that for knowledge to be practical – that is, powerful in changing the social practices of human beings – it needs to be grounded in a coherent body of theory. Moreover, this body of theory should inform the research methodology and methods which generate the knowledge, as well as the analysis of the situations under study.

Research into IT in education is always research into innovation

Research into IT in education, at least in the recent past and foreseeable future, is research into the process and impact of innovation. To generate useful knowledge that will inform policy and practice in IT in education, we need a methodology that integrates research with development, because we need knowledge about how the process of change itself shapes practice. Research that attempts to measure the impact of an IT innovatory initiative without researching the factors which enabled or constrained its implementation can never be valid, because it cannot provide evidence of exactly *what* was being measured; such research at best provides knowledge of the impact of a partially implemented initiative, and at worst of an initiative that when implemented bears little relation to its original aims and vision.

This chapter suggests a methodology for researching IT in education grounded in a theoretical framework for understanding and analysing innovations in human behaviour and social practices. I am defining methodology in Sandra Harding's terms as 'a theory and analysis of how research should proceed' which involves exploration of 'issues about an adequate theory of knowledge or justificatory strategy' and is distinct from methods that are 'techniques for gathering evidence' (Harding 1987: 2). Methodology and methods are closely inter-related because methods are shaped by an underpinning methodology in both their design and implementation.

There are some special features of innovative initiatives in education involving IT that need first to be noted. They involve two quite separate strands of innovation: a technical strand involving procurement, installation and configuring of new equipment and systems; and a personal/social strand involving implementation of the new equipment by users who must acquire skills in its use and learn how to integrate its use with their practice. Both strands involve participants in action and decision-making over time, but they are not necessarily the same participants, indeed often not. Theories of innovation that focus on organisational change ought to take both of these strands into account, but often fail to distinguish between them.

The technical strand usually has several components: it begins with major procurement decisions – involving the spending of large sums of money relative to other initiatives – which are often fraught with uncertainty because of lack of any available evidence of how the equipment has been successfully used in other educational settings. Procurement is followed by installation of the new equipment which may involve construction work to adapt existing buildings; at this stage a number of decisions have to be made about apparently inconsequential matters (e.g. the location of power sockets) that later prove to be crucial to ease of use of the new equipment. Installation is best carried out by people with a high level of technical expertise, but the extent to which they take advice from the teachers and educational leaders who will use the equipment varies; in practice, even when they consult users fully they are unlikely to configure the new digital systems in ways that best support their future use, because users can have only a limited understanding of what might be possible. In other words, there is necessarily 'an imagination gap' at the configuration stage which leads to unforeseen constraints in later use. Organisational leaders often focus more attention on the technical strand because of the high cost of procurement, but they are often unable to manage the technical decision-making well because of lack of technical knowledge.

The technical strand is necessarily the main focus of endeavour in the initial stages and usually takes considerably longer than planned. It is crucial to enabling the personal/social strand of innovation in which teachers, educational leaders and students embark on the dual process of learning skills in using the IT equipment and systems and exploring the possibilities they offer for working in new ways. Unfortunately, the effort and delays involved in the technical strand often lead to the importance of the personal/social strand of the innovation being underestimated. In reality, it is when people start using the new systems that the most demanding phase of the innovatory initiative begins. This is where considerable energy and resources need to be focused. Training in how to use the new equipment is only the first step; much more important is the management at organisational and department level of the whole change process, whereby all those involved are able to: explore its possibilities; develop initial routines for its use; locate or develop resources that extend its possibilities; share their experiences with one another; try out expanded or different routines for its use; and over time develop new social practices in which IT is no longer an add-on to the way things were done before, but has become for its users what McLuhan (1964) called an extension of the self.

There is often a clash in values between those who are involved in the technical and personal/social strands of IT innovation. Those who are involved in the technical strand value efficiency and simplicity of system design, which they see as the best ways of ensuring ease of use (for teachers, students and administrators), security of infrastructure, and efficient system maintenance. The personal/social strand of IT innovation is most successful when its leaders value exploration, diversity of approach, cooperation between users (teachers, students and administrators) and flexibility of technical provision and support. The clash between these two sets of values, when not understood and managed at the organisational and system levels, may result in misunderstandings and frustrations for all concerned.

A theoretical framework for understanding and researching innovation

Theories of innovation in the existing literature focus on the need for reform to be 'bottom up', providing teachers with professional development 'on the job' supported by strong leadership (see Fullan and Stiegelbauer1991). There has also been an emphasis on categorising personality types according to teachers' preparedness to undertake innovation, and tracking the process of innovation through stages in organisational development (see Rogers 2003). These theories of innovation have tended to divert attention away from the processes through which social practices develop and become embedded in cultural–historical activity systems; as a result little attention has been paid to how heavily teachers' work and school organisation are dependent upon the larger structures of the education system.

This has been particularly problematic in the field of IT in education where factors that affect the implementation of innovations are magnified by the extent of both structural change (at national/state and organisational levels) and change in teachers' practice (at the school level) that they necessitate (Voogt and Pelgrum 2005). Even when attention is paid to factors such as the need to invest in teacher development and strong organisational leadership, the innovation of IT in education has not led to transformations in pedagogy and learning. The forces of cultural reproduction work to maintain the *status quo*, and this is particularly the case in schools which are very resilient structures (Bidwell 2001). There is an assumption that reforms should 'start where teachers are at' and as a result too many initiatives have been too strongly predicated on a theory of incremental change which, as Cuban *et al.* (2001) show, does not remove the constraints to effective use of IT.

This chapter presents a theoretical framework for understanding and researching innovation drawn from a range of socio-cultural and systemic theories that have been largely ignored by the innovation literature (Somekh 2007). It enables a more fine-grained understanding of the relationships between ITs, the social practices of schools and classrooms, and the inter-relationships between innovations in schools and the visions of policy-makers. These theories shed light on the social practices of individuals and groups, and extend our understanding of innovation. They are normally presented and understood as independent bodies of knowledge, but in the framework presented here the overlap between them is clear and provides confirmation of their explanatory power.

The theoretical framework consists of seven guiding principles

Principle one

Social practices are culturally constructed through patterns of behaviour and are interdependent with the social practices of others. Social interaction is largely a performance of routinised practices by individuals and social groups who give each other a sense of identity and belonging through this interaction.

Innovation can be understood as dependent on social interaction if we adopt a theory of the self as inter-dependent with others, as in Mead's (1934) three-part model of mind or consciousness: the 'I' (active), the 'me' (the object of self-scrutiny) and the 'generalised other' (comprising the social group within which the self acts). According to this theory, self is not an independent agent because the generalised other of the community 'exercises control over the conduct of its individual members' (Mead 1934: 155). Following Mead, the work of Goffman (1959) and Garfinkel (1984) shows how strongly our actions depend on the responses of others, so that much group behaviour can be interpreted as a choreographed performance of inter-actions. Groups conform to culturally-historically constructed rules and roles which pre-determine norms of behaviour, tasks and responsibilities ('divisions of labour') (Engeström *et al.* 1999). It follows that we are only partly in control of our own actions which, as a result, are likely to have many unintended consequences. Intentional changes in behaviour are not easy. Integral with this process of control that locks individuals and groups into particular forms of social practice are the values and beliefs that shape the group's thinking.

Principle two

All human activity is oriented towards achieving an object; and this relates to the fact that humans always seek to make meaning of whatever they experience.

Cultural-historical activity theory (CHAT) has at its core a theory of human activity as oriented towards an object, which may incorporate specific stated aims, but operates also at a more fundamental level of orientation (Engeström *et al.* 1999). In groups there is often fundamental lack of clarity about the object of activities. For example, in schools the object may be assumed to be students' learning, but may also be a number of other things such as the development and display of personal identity, or the establish-ment and enactment of social control and power. Students and teachers may in fact have different objects and be making different meanings from their experience. Wittgenstein, whose ideas are usefully explicated by Burbules and Smith (2005), provides a similar analysis when he describes all social practice as 'rule-governed' and the acquisition of social and technical skills as a process of 'learning how to go on'. Innovation cannot be attempted, there-fore, until current practices are understood in relation to the rules that govern them 'from the inside'. The overlapping and conflicting objects in apparently organised activity systems such as education systems, schools and classrooms add hugely to the complexity of innovation, which needs always to take account of how to negotiate changes in the object. Without effective strate-gies for negotiating the object of activity, innovation will struggle to hold together disparate individuals and groups.

Principle three

Tools such as ITs are cultural tools that have been produced by technologists and design-ers to enable new ways of doing things. They mediate human activity, yet their affordances remain latent until individuals and groups find how to embed them in new social practices as 'extensions of themselves'.

Vygotsky's theory of human development as a process of social interaction extends to a concept of human activity as integrally dependent on cultural tools such as language, physical artefacts and mental concepts. These tools can be said to have affordances which are best understood as latent possibilities which humans can appropriate to develop new ways of doing things, rather than features which in themselves have any power to determine changes in human behaviour. Nevertheless, major changes in social and economic patterns throughout history can be seen to be linked to changes in technology such as the telegraph (McLuhan 1964) and the Internet (Lankshear 2003), and this has direct relevance to understanding the potential that IT offers for transforming education. Wertsch (1998) suggests that tools and agents cannot be separated as components of human activity but need to be conceptualised as 'a single unit of analysis'; he draws the analogy of a pole vault, in which neither the agent nor the pole can be said to carry out the jump without the other. Cole and Engeström (1993) locate cultural tools as central components of the human activity system, showing how agent, object and cultural tool are historically-socially enmeshed in community structures, rules and divisions of labour which can either constrain or enable human activity. To become skilled in using new tools we need to have access to them so we can explore how to use them in a variety of ways in different contexts and for different purposes.

Principle four

Innovation in social practices to make use of the affordances of a new tool depends on the development of a vision of what might be possible.

When the World Wide Web was first developed in the early 1990s it was impossible to envisage the uses to which it has been put today. What we now call 'googling' is much more sophisticated than anyone could have imagined from using one of the early search engines. The rapid and widespread take-up of sites like *Facebook* and *YouTube* has fundamentally changed the way we understand communication and publication. These radical shifts in the way our community, worldwide, uses the Internet have depended on a continuing process of envisioning new possibilities, developed through ten years of exploratory designs, coupled with transformations of the power of the Internet to transmit images and handle enormous data sets. Radical new social practices with an IT tool always depend on the development of a vision through individuals and groups exploring its possibilities over a period of time in an unstructured, even playful, manner, and building up skills in its use alongside mental models of how to use it. Wartofsky (1979) presents a theory of perception as an active process in which we draw on cultural and personal experience to use tools (primary artefacts) skilfully guided by our mental models of their use (secondary artefacts), and are further able to go 'offline' to imagine and creatively reorganise these representations of the tools (tertiary artefacts) and envision completely new ways of using them (Wartofsky 1979). Recent research into the introduction of interactive whiteboards into primary schools in England suggests that the development of a new social practice passes through overlapping stages: first, *initial appropriation* in which humans try to fit the tool's use to their existing practice; second, *exploratory implementation* in which they become skilful through frequent use; third, *pedagogical innovation* in which they adapt their practice to make novel uses of the tool's affordances (Lewin *et al.* 2008). Vision, made possible in Wartofsky's model by the development of 'tertiary artefacts', begins to develop somewhere around the third stage and is fully developed at a fourth stage.

Principle five

Human activity is inter-related across all phenomenal levels of social structures and systems, as well as at the level of the social interactions of individuals and groups. Hence, change at any one phenomenal level depends upon it being enabled by changes at other phenomenal levels.

The inter-dependence of human interactions and the nature of their routinised, mutually affirming performances, extends between all levels of social structures. Indeed, complexity theory suggests that everything in our world, including physical and chemical elements, is inter-related and oriented towards maintaining equilibrium (Davis and Sumara 2005). This means that changes introduced by individuals or small groups are always subject to unforeseen pressures that attempt to spontaneously reorganise the system to regain its stability. Teachers cannot change the curriculum in their classrooms to incorporate innovative uses of IT without changes at the school level to re-allocate resources of time, rooms and equipment; neither they, nor their larger grouping of colleagues and the school as a whole, can change the curriculum if there is no change in the assessment system and other accountability mechanisms in the education system; the expectations of students, their parents, and the media (e.g. newspapers and television) constitute further mechanisms to enforce conformity to expected norms. Failures to embed the use of IT in teaching are therefore much more likely to result from lack of change at the systemic level than from teachers' resistance to change.

Principle six

Change is naturally occurring and to a large extent unpredictable as systems spontaneously self-organise to maintain equilibrium. As a result, planned innovations, for example in schools and education systems, are likely to have unintended consequences and need to be monitored and continuously adjusted.

Chaos theory takes this notion of the interconnectedness of all things a step further, suggesting that even minor changes such as Lorenz's famous example of the flapping of a butterfly's wing will have unpredictable consequences on other parts of the system. Kompf (2005) uses chaos theory as a framework for interpreting the impact of IT in education. He concludes that there is a danger that the education system may be overwhelmed by the larger social, economic and global changes that IT is bringing to our world. We may be naïve in assuming that we have any control over the education system. In line with these ideas, Davis and Sumara (2005) suggest that the role of educators is to nurture spontaneously occurring change that we judge beneficial by creating contexts that support learning and personal flourishing through group interactions.

Principal seven

Social science knowledge is contingent on context, culture and researcher subjectivity. Knowledge that is co-constructed by participants, and validated by its use to inform action and change, provides the best possible basis for innovation.

Cultural-historical activity theory (CHAT) assumes that current cultural practices have developed historically through human beings' ability to develop lifestyles that make use of available artefacts and lead to the production of an ever increasing number of cultural tools. Knowledge and ideas are not separate from this process but are, by means of thinking and language, culturally constructed tools that increase human capacity for (mental and physical) activity and creativity. Kurt Lewin famously said, 'If you truly want to understand something, try to change it' (See SourceWatch 2008).

Langemeyer and Nissen describe CHAT methodology as taking the form of setting up a prototype and researching it 'to objectify and inscribe the processes into data' and use these to analyse the practices, seeking out 'contradictions' and working with participants to seek ways to 'mediate and resolve contradictions'. The process should be, 'produced and treated as the property of all participants, mediating a critical dialogue that transforms relevant cultural elements in participants' lives' (Langemeyer and Nissen, 2005: 191). The resulting knowledge is both robust and actionable because it is sensitive to context and can be generalised to similar settings where it is validated and appropriated by those who recognise its immediate usefulness (Somekh, 2007).

Using the framework to design research into innovation

The framework was developed through a process of praxis: action informed by knowledge and reflection. The practicality of the framework as a means of researching innovation was tested and refined in a series of projects through which the following methodological principles for research design were developed.

Methodological principles

Research into IT innovation needs to:

- take the form of a participatory (intervention) study in which partici-pants are supported in exploring ways of changing taken-for-granted rules of behaviour, roles and divisions of labour;
- involve participants in developing knowledge about their social practices, and brokering their new understandings with others through collabora-tion and discussion;
- involve participants at all the phenomenal levels so that they understand how practice at their own level (e.g. policy/administration) needs to change to enable change at other levels (e.g. schools and classrooms);
- involve participants with different status and roles (e.g. teachers and stu-dents) in negotiating the object of their activity with one another;
- involve participants in discussion of the theoretical framework to enable them to develop the vision necessary to develop new practices;
- ensure that access to ITs are ubiquitous and continuous, so that partici-pants have a genuine choice over when and how to use them and for what purposes.

Table 13.1 presents these principles for research design and the theoretical principles from the Framework as a matrix that can be used for project planning.

Between 2003 and 2006, researchers at Manchester Metropolitan University collaborated with teachers and students in the Developing Pedagogies with E-Learning Resources project (PELRS) (Pearson and Somekh 2006; Somekh 2007). Participating schools were equipped with relatively high levels of IT, including for example digital video cameras, interactive whiteboards, 'banks' of laptops, and wireless networks. PELRS research both refined the framework and methodological principles and tested them out in practice. It established prototype innovatory practices through its focus on the research question: 'Could we organise teaching and learning in radically different ways now that we have digital technologies?' Work started with brainstorm-ing ideas. Strategies were adopted to change the traditional roles of teachers and students by giving them new roles. The object of classroom activities was negotiated with the students at the beginning of each learning event. PELRS working methods and transformative learning aims were diagram-matically represented in a Generic Pedagogic Framework (GPF) (Figure 13.1) which served as a planning tool for teachers planning learning events, as well as being the interface for the website (www.pelrs.org.uk). The GPF and the four Pedagogic Strategy themes provided working documents as the basis for discussing PELRS research and its underpinning theories with teachers, the Advisory Boards and participants at conference presentations.

Table 13.1 Matrix for designing research into innovations such as IT in education

Features of Research Design	1: A participatory (intervention) study	2: Participants develop knowledge and broker understanding	3: Involvement of participants at all levels of the education system	4: Negotiation of the objective of activity between all participants	5: Participants develop understanding of the seven theoretical principles – and how to test them out	6: ICT is ubiquitous and participants have continuous access
Principles of the Theoretical Framework						
1: Behaviour is patterned in inter-related performances						
2: Activity is object-oriented						
3: Activity is mediated by tools						
4: Vision and skilled use are essential before tools can mediate new actions						
5: Activity is inter-related at all phenomenal levels						
6: Change is unpredictable and self-organising						
7: Knowledge is co-constructed and validated in action						

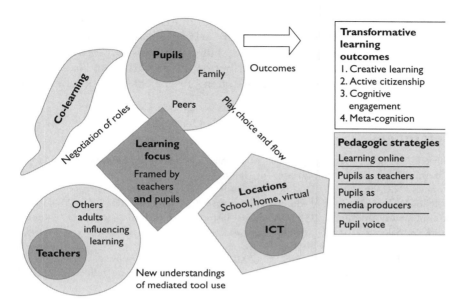

Figure 13.1 The Generic Pedagogic Framework.

As co-researchers with the university team, the teachers and students were knowledge producers. PELRS was sponsored by the General Teaching Council for England (GTC) which established an Advisory Board with representatives from all the key agencies responsible for developing education policy and supporting practice. In this way, PELRS was brought to the attention of policy-makers and its research was used to inform the GTC's responses to government consultation documents on policy and practice for IT in education.

Conclusions

This chapter has presented a theoretical framework for understanding and researching innovations in human behaviour and social practices, and a set of methodological principles to inform the design of research. The final section of the chapter provides a brief example of how the framework and methodological principles were used in the Developing Pedagogies with E-Learning Resources (PELRS) project.

As a result of the rapid changes in the uptake of digital technologies, research into IT in education is always, in our time, research into innovation. To provide a sound base for decision making in educational policy and practice, there is a need for a research methodology grounded in theories of innovation in social practices: specifically, how collaborative practices such as pedagogy can be transformed when new digital tools are introduced and cultural-historical features of the activity systems enable or constrain such development. All change is not good, but a robust theory of innovation enables researchers to make a contribution to nurturing and sustaining changes whose novelty may otherwise often prevent potential benefits from being recognised.

References

Bidwell, C.E. (2001) 'Analyzing schools as organizations: long-term permanence and short-term change', *Sociology of Education*, 74: 100–114.

Burbules, N.C. and Smith, R. (2005) 'What it makes sense to say: Wittgenstein, rule-following and the nature of education', *Educational Philosophy and Theory*, 37: 425–430.

Cole, M. and Engeström, Y. (1993) 'A cultural-historical approach to distributed cognition', in G. Salomon (ed.) *Distributed Cognition: psychological and educational considerations*, Cambridge: Cambridge University Press.

Cuban, L., Kirkpatrick, H. and Peck, C. (2001) 'High access and low use of technologies in high school classrooms: explaining an apparent paradox', *American Eductional Research Journal*, 38: 813–834.

Davis, B. and Sumara, D. (2005) 'Complexity science and educational action research: towards a pragmatics of transformation', *Educational Action Research*, 13: 453–466.

Engeström, Y., Miettinen, R. and Punamaki, R-L. (eds) (1999) *Perspectives on Activity Theory. Learning in Doing: social, cognitive, and computational perspectives*, Cambridge UK: Cambridge University Press.

Fullan, M. and Stiegelbauer, S. (1991) *The New Meaning of Educational Change*, New York: OISE/Teachers College Press.

Garfinkel, H. (1984) *Studies in Ethnomethodology*, Cambridge: Polity Press.

Goffman, E. (1959) *The Presentation of Self in Everyday Life*, London: Penguin.

Harding, S. (1987) *Feminism and Methodology*, Bloomington: Indiana University Press.

Kompf, M. (2005) 'Information and communications technology (ICT) and the seduction of knowledge, teaching, and learning: what lies ahead for education', *Curriculum Inquiry*, 35: 213–233.

Langemeyer, I. and Nissen, M. (2005) 'Activity theory', in B. Somekh and C. Lewin (eds) *Research Methods in the Social Sciences*, London: Sage.

Lankshear, C. (2003) 'The challenge of digital epistemologies', *Education, Communication and Information*, 3: 167–186.

Lewin, K. (1951) *Field Theory in Social Science: selected theoretical papers*, New York: Harper Row.

Lewin, C., Somekh, B. and Steadman, S. (2008) 'Embedding interactive whiteboards in teaching and learning: the process of change in pedagogic practice,' *Education and Information Technologies*, 13: 291–303.

McLuhan, M. (1964) *Understanding Media*, New York: Routledge and Kegan Paul.

Mead, G.H. (1934) *Mind, Self and Society*, Chicago: University of Chicago Press.

Pearson, M. and Somekh, B. (2006) 'Learning transformation with technology: a question of social-cultural contexts? *International Journal of Qualitative Studies in Education*, 19: 519–539.

Rogers, E.M. (2003) *Diffusion of Innovations*, 5th edn, New York: Free Press.

Somekh, B. (2007) *Pedagogy and Learning with ICT: researching the art of innovation*, London: Routledge.

SourceWatch (2008) 'Kurt Lewin'. Online. Available HTTP http://www.sourcewatch.org/index.php?title=Kurt_Lewin (accessed 10 March 2009).

Voogt, J. and Pelgrum, W.J. (2005) 'ICT and curriculum change', *Human Technology*, 1: 157–175.

Wartofsky, M. (1979) *Models: representation and scientific understanding*, Dordrecht: Reidel.

Wertsch, J.V. (1998) *Mind as Action*, Oxford: Oxford University Press.

Chapter 14

Global interdisciplinary research into the diffusion of information technology innovations in education

Niki Davis
University of Canterbury, New Zealand

Introduction

Taken as a whole, the wide range of research on innovation and change with IT in education is confusing. Reviews of the change literature by Ferster (2006) and Surry and Farquhar (1997) noted that the interdisciplinary literature on diffusion of innovations tends to be deterministic, focusing on innovation primarily from the perspective of those who want the innovation adopted, whereas the educational perspective tends to be more instrumentalist by taking the perspective of the educator considering adoption. For example, Cuban (2001) was the educator who coined the phrase that IT was 'oversold and underused'. While both perspectives are valid, the evidence reviewed in this chapter suggests that neither goes far enough to inform educational renewal with IT. Comprehensive studies of the impact of IT in schools, such as ImpaCT2 in the UK (Harrison *et al.* 2003), provide a picture of complex processes with many factors interacting. Therefore, it is timely to seek a more useful theoretical perspective for research and theoretical models to inform the diffusion of IT innovations in education.

Ecology was developed to analyse the living world. It provides a means to interpret IT in education that may encompass the complex processes engaged in, by both individuals and organisations. This chapter reviews the diffusion of IT innovations in education through an ecological perspective, to examine the fit.

Ecological perspective

Figure 14.1 provides a simple Venn diagram of the ecologies that will be discussed. The teacher's classroom is at the centre (an ecosystem), nested within the school (another ecosystem), nested within the region or nation (an ecozone), and the global biosphere (the world). Additional ecosystems that span multiple school systems are also illustrated: a college of teacher education and a multinational IT company. The latter also spans countries and their educational systems, as does UNESCO. Before research evidence

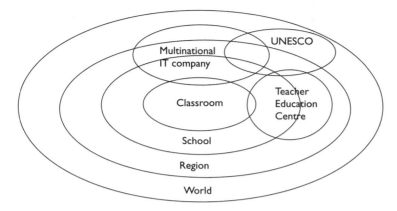

Figure 14.1 Venn diagram of a teacher's classroom nested within a school ecosystem and regional ecozone in the Global Biosphere: Ecosystems for a multinational IT company, a teacher education college and UNESCO illustrate overlapping ecosystems (not to scale).

is presented, the diffusion of an IT innovation in education is briefly illustrated from an ecological perspective. A teacher who decides to adopt digital storytelling in her curriculum must change her classroom ecology by adding at least one digital camera and routines for its safe use. Access to a computer with software for editing and presentation is also part of the cluster of innovations, along with curriculum development and assessment. The teacher's adoption of digital storytelling will be facilitated by similar practice in her department, school and related ecosystems, including assessment systems external to her school.

Leadership support and professional development will also facilitate adoption. In ecological terms, such conditions would result in ecological forces that 'optimise' this teacher's 'inclusive fitness' in her school environment. Conversely, without some or all of these conditions, the adoption of digital storytelling would not be the most adaptive strategy for this teacher. Similar processes occur in higher education, although the ecosystems are less constrained.

Educational researcher Zhao and ecologist Frank (Zhao and Frank 2003) provided evidence of IT in education to support an ecological perspective. Their framework conceptualised a teacher who used IT as an 'invasive exotic species' interacting with and displacing a traditional teacher as the 'keystone species' in the classroom of a school ecosystem. My criticism of Zhao and Frank's framework is their misleading use of the term 'extinct'. A teacher who adapts his or her practice to adopt IT, does not become extinct – after all the teacher remains. What has occurred is that the teacher, plus their leaders and supporters, have adapted both pedagogical and organisational practices with the diffusion of IT innovations into education. The term adaptation is more accurate.

Zhao and Frank (2003) used ecologists' modelling analysis on teachers' uses of IT over time in a 'contained educational system' of nineteen schools in four districts in the US. They found evidence of co-evolution of both IT and teachers' pedagogies. Change was more likely when there was an 'empty niche', for example telecommunications was exploited to communicate with parents where there had been little communication before. However, IT was rarely exploited for curriculum purposes where it competed with existing curriculum activities. Zhao and Frank identified four basic mechanisms that support adoption of IT in the school system: recruitment/selection of new teachers with IT among selection criteria; training/socialisation supportive of IT; the provision of opportunities to explore and learn with IT; and leveraging change within the social context, including engaging opinion leaders with IT innovations.

The school ecosystem

Zhao and Frank's evidence is in accord with Rogers' (2003) seminal axioms for the diffusion of innovations. Organisations move through stages in the adoption (and/or rejection) of innovations. Rogers' terminology for his five stages of organisational change is: agenda-setting; matching; redefining/restructuring; clarifying; and routinising (Rogers 2003: 420).

However, IT is not a benign innovation and, as a result, organisations that adopt one or more IT-related innovations tend to experience further changes stimulated by the adoption of IT. That is, Rogers' clarifying and routinising processes are disrupted by further innovations with IT. Golden *et al.* (2006) use the term 'eMaturity' to denote the development and embedding of the e-learning infrastructure and processes that they observed in UK further education. This sequence starts with localised exploitation by one or more teachers' adoption of one or more IT innovations and then, as the number of adopters increases and activity proliferates, the increasing demand for resources stimulates administration to appoint an IT coordinator to manage demand and coordinate internal resources. The range of innovations continues to expand and they become further embedded into the organisation through the work of the IT coordinator and other adopters, who network together to redesign their curriculum and educational practice.

The next stage involves IT in a redesign of the school's external networks, which often leads to further embedding of IT with external organisations such as partner schools and educational authorities that require information and provide support. The first three stages moving from localised exploitation to internal process redesign are common. In contrast, organisations with embedded IT, such as virtual universities and schools, start at an eMature stage of embedded IT or innovative design with an educational scope that reaches further, often to include underserved populations (Davis 2008).

Early diffusion studies in education found that a predictor of school innovativeness was educational expenditure on students (Rogers 2003). Rogers also recognised that organisations as well as individuals may reject innovation after earlier adoption. Contextual factors vary with normal rhythms of personal and organisational lives, such as the school year, as well as being subject to external shocks such as imposed reforms and weather-related disasters. Today in the US and the UK high stakes assessment has reduced opportunities for IT innovation. Hargreaves (2003) provided an illustration of a knowledge-society school in Canada, Blue Mountain, which was set up as an exemplary 'learning organisation' with state-of-the-art technology used effectively in learning, teaching, and administration, with support from an IT coordinator. This organisational structure appeared to be at the educational process redesign stage, but that was not sustained following external shocks of budget cuts and changes in leadership. The school reverted to a more traditional approach with localised exploitation and internal integration of IT.

Additional factors are involved when collective decisions are made about clusters of innovations. The first to innovate (both individuals and organisations) are unlikely to be perceived as similar by others. This is supported by an international study of innovative schools, which found that these innovative schools were unlikely to provide a model for schools that adopted IT later (Yuen et al. 2003).

The teacher's classroom ecosystem

The teacher is the key individual in education, and in ecological terms 'the keystone species' (Zhao and Frank 2003). The process of innovation takes time and the stages in adoption and/or rejection can be characterised for the individual and/or the community or communities in which they work. Teachers' concerns often start with the technology (hardware and software), but come to relate more strongly to content and pedagogic knowledge. This blend of different types of knowledge has recently become known as 'technological pedagogical content knowledge' or TCPK (AACTE 2008).

Building on earlier research, Sherry et al. (2000) identified five stages of teachers' pedagogical innovation with IT: teacher as learner, teacher as adopter, teacher as co-adopter, teacher as re-affirmer or rejecter, and teacher as leader. The later stages promote other teachers' adoption. The final stage of 'teacher as leader' describes a teacher who advocates for IT and provides support to others and this is likely to increase the permeation of IT in other classrooms.

The lack of equitable access to IT, and related socio-technical change forces, impact on teachers and their schools differentially because of differences in their ecologies. Software design and pedagogy are not culturally neutral and tend to fit better with the practices of the majority. In addition, minority teachers typically have less access to IT in school and at home (Resta and Laferriere 2008, Clark and Gorski 2001). One strategy to reduce the tendency to decrease equity is to begin the introduction of IT with a disadvantaged group and adapt the innovation to their ecology before introducing it to the majority.

Attributes of innovations and essential conditions for adoption

As noted earlier, species adapt as their ecologies develop. Teachers' adoption of IT in education is impacted by both the characteristics of IT innovations and their conditions of work. Rogers (2003) identified five attributes that influence the speed of the adoption and/or rejection of an innovation: relative advantage, compatibility, complexity, trialability, and observability. The same five attributes also apply to the process of innovation with IT in education (Ferster 2006).

Another way of describing this is through Ely's (1990) conditions that facilitate IT innovation: dissatisfaction with the status quo, knowledge that skills exist, commitment by those involved, resources are available, time is available, participation is expected and encouraged, and leadership is evident. Further evidence for both Rogers's (2003) attributes and Ely's (1990) conditions, comes from research on leadership strategies, because leaders manipulate these attributes and conditions to promote or retard adoption of IT (Yee 2001, Jenson et al. 2002).

Ecosystems that impact multiple ecologies

Commercial marketing and politically-motivated promotion of IT innovations also play a role in IT diffusion in education. Figure 14.1 is a simplified diagram of the educational biosphere that includes examples of two organisations that promote diffusion of IT innovations across multiple ecosystems. Davis (2008) provides a more detailed perspective with four axes spanning the biosphere: commercial, political, bureaucratic and professional. An example of a commercial organisation is a multinational IT company and an example of a professional organisation is a teacher education college. The literature includes evidence relating to both types of organisation. Selwyn's (2002) discursive deconstruction of educational computing provides evidence of the socioeconomic forces that have pushed IT diffusion in the UK. Selwyn provides evidence that IT vendors saw multiple benefits from the educational sector: profit, educational branding for sales to the much larger home market, employable people for their IT sector, and building of a future consumer base.

Institutions of teacher education also impact multiple ecosystems. Goodlad (1994) recognised the need for 'simultaneous renewal' of both teacher education and K–12 schools. Teacher education institutions also appear to progress through similar maturation stages with IT, but the process is more complex because changes in learning and teaching must also involve partnering K–12 schools where students practise teaching. The first national project that diffused IT into preservice teacher education provides insights into the change process in five institutions. The micro-politics of institutional change moved all five institutions one stage forward in organisational maturation with IT from the localised stage to coordinated integration of IT (Somekh and Davis 1997). Drawing on that and other research, Somekh (2007) summarised five key factors linked to research of successful innovation with IT in higher education: messiness; the power of individuals to make a positive contribution to bring about change; partnership; making teacher professional development central to the process of planning and implementing change; and the integration of theory and practice.

The re-analysis of the national initiative to train all teachers in England to become competent with IT undertaken by Davis *et al.* (2009) confirms these factors. The most highly rated model was organic, in that it 'grew' out of existing partnerships led by teacher educators and IT leaders in schools. The Internet was used to facilitate the training of teacher trainers, who were able to work with colleagues in their own schools. In contrast, computer-based training supported by remote online trainers was ineffective and disruptive.

Consideration of these intersecting ecosystems emphasises the complexity of the diffusion of IT innovations in education, because ecosystems are not isolated from each other. The global biosphere of education has ecozones that follow political borders because most countries provide bureaucratic directions to their schools. In addition, IT innovations are also communicated across these educational ecozones by organisations such as UNESCO, through its guidance documents and meetings; the UNESCO (2002) planning guide for IT and teacher education has been translated into at least six languages. Thus, all four axes (commercial, political, bureaucratic and professional) that Davis (2008) identified as spanning the biosphere can be seen to influence IT diffusion in education.

Conclusion and recommendations

This chapter's analysis of the literature on the diffusion of IT innovations finds that an ecological perspective does fit the available evidence. This gives rise to a number of recommendations that are summarised below. The key point is that the diffusion of IT in education is naturally complex, because IT impacts multiple ecologies and it is also impacted by these ecologies. Knowledge of the processes of diffusion may also be used to speed (or retard) adoption.

One important lesson: it is time for researchers in IT in education to rise to this theoretical challenge and adopt appropriate methodologies with research questions that recognise that change in one ecosystem is likely to impact related ecologies. Conversely, lack of change in the organisational ecologies will impede change in the classrooms and curricula linked to that ecosystem. The implications for future research are twofold:

- Published research should be re-evaluated and critiqued from an ecological perspective. Many generalisations that have been accepted are less than half the story and may be misleading. Randomised trials that assume there is one system are not appropriate.
- Researchers need to rise to the interdisciplinary challenge of ecology: to ask more sophisticated questions and to use stronger methodology that systematically gathers evidence in the multiple ecologies that may be impacted by IT innovations. Such research will recognise that change is complex and that ecosystems take time to evolve and continue to evolve in unexpected ways.

References

AACTE (2008) *Handbook of Technological Pedagogical Content Knowledge (TPCK) for Educators*, New York: Routledge and AACTE.

Clark, C. and Gorski, P. (2001) 'Multicultural education and the digital divide: focus on race, language, socioeconomic class, sex and disability', *Multicultural Perspectives*, 3: 39–44.

Cuban, L. (2001) *Oversold and Underused: computers in the classroom*, Cambridge, MA: Harvard University Press.

Davis, N.E. (2008) 'How may teacher learning be promoted for educational renewal with IT?' in J. Voogt and G. Knezek (eds) *International Handbook of Information Technology in Primary and Secondary Education*, Amsterdam: Springer.

Davis, N.E., Preston, C. and Sahin, I. (2009) 'ICT teacher training impacts multiple ecologies: evidence from a national initiative', *British Journal of Educational Technology*, 40: 135–148.

Ely, D. (1990) 'The diffusion and implementation of educational technology in developing nations: cross-cultural comparisons of Indonesia, Chile and Peru', *Instructional Developments*, 1: 9–12.

Ferster, W. (2006) 'Towards a Predictive Model of the Diffusion of Technology into the K–12 Classroom', Charlottesville, VA: unpublished thesis, University of Virginia.

Golden, S., McCrone, T., Walker, M. and Rudd, P. (2006) *Impact of e-Learning in Further Education: survey of scale and breadth*, London: NFER. Online. Available HTTP: <http://www.dfes.gov.uk/research/data/uploadfiles/RR745.pdf> (accessed 17 April 2009).

Goodlad, J. (1994) *Educational Renewal: better teachers, better schools*, San Francisco, CA: Jossey-Bass.

Hargreaves, A. (2003) *Teaching in the Knowledge Society: education in the age of insecurity*, New York: Teachers College Press.

Harrison, C., Comber, C., Fisher, A., Haw, K., Lewin, C., Lunzer, E., McFarlane, A., Mavers, D., Scrimshaw, P., Somekh, B. and Watling, R. (2003). *ImpaCT2: the impact of information and communication technologies on pupil learning and attainment*, Coventry: Becta.

Jenson, J., Lewis, B. and Smith, R. (2002) 'No one way: working models for teachers' professional development', *Journal of Technology and Teacher Education*, 10: 481–496.

Resta, P. and Laferriere, T. (2008) 'Digital equity', in J. Voogt and G. Knezek (eds) *International Handbook of Information Technology in Primary and Secondary Education*, Amsterdam: Springer.

Rogers, E. (2003) *The Diffusion of Innovations*, 5th edn, New York: The Free Press.

Selwyn, N. (2002) *Telling Tales on Technology. Qualitative Studies of Technology and Education*, Burlington, VT: Ashgate.

Sherry, L., Billig, S., Tavlin, F. and Gibson, D. (2000) New insights on technology adoption in schools. *Technology Horizons in Education (T.H.E. Journal)*, 27: 43–46.

Somekh, B. and Davis N.E. (eds) (1997) *Using IT Effectively in Teaching and Learning: studies in pre-service and in-service teacher education*, London and New York: Routledge.

Somekh, B. (2007) *Pedagogy and Learning with ICT: researching the art of innovation*, London: Routledge.

Surry, D.W. and Farquhar J.D. (1997) 'Diffusion theory and instructional technology', *Journal of Instructional Science and Technology*, 2. Online. Available HTTP: <http://www.usq.edu.au/electpub/e-jist/docs/old/vol2no1/article2.htm> (accessed 17 April 2009).

UNESCO (2002) *ICT in Teacher Education. A Planning Guide*, Paris, France: UNESCO. Online. Available HTTP: <http://unesdoc.unesco.org/images/0012/001295/129533e.pdf> (accessed 17 April 2009).

Yee, D. (2001) 'The many faces of ICT leadership', in B. Barrell (ed.), *Technology, Teaching and Learning: issues in the integration of technology*, Calgary, Canada: Detselig.

Yuen, A.H.K., Law, N. and Wong, K.C. (2003) 'ICT implementation and school leadership: case studies of ICT integration in teaching and learning', *Journal of Educational Administration*, 41: 158–170.

Zhao, Y. and Frank, K.A. (2003) 'Factors affecting technology uses in schools: an ecological perspective', *American Educational Research Journal*, 40: 807–840.

Part 3

Methodological approaches and applications

Chapter 15

Educational information technology research methodology

Looking back and moving forward

Peter Twining
The Open University, UK

Introduction

This chapter examines some of the key methodological trends in the educational IT literature in order to help us gain a better understanding of existing research and to inform future research design. The issue of research methodology is crucial to any study, as it underpins the types of questions that can be addressed and the nature of the evidence that is generated (Clark, *et al*. 1984, Shulman 1986). The approach employed also has implications for the uses that can legitimately be made of research outcomes. For example, within an empiricist approach it would be assumed that one could make generalisations based on research findings, while this may not even be a goal for many interpretivist researchers (Schofield 1993). Thus, the purposes underpinning one's research need to inform the methodology employed (Underwood and Underwood 1997).

Robson (1993) described three different purposes underpinning research in the social sciences: exploratory research, which aims to seek new insights, ask questions and find out what is happening; descriptive research, which aims to provide an accurate profile of the situation or phenomenon being studied; and explanatory research, which aims to explain the phenomenon being studied, often in the form of causal relationships. All three purposes are evident in the educational IT literature.

Robson went on to suggest that the purpose of the research helps to determine the most appropriate research strategy. He loosely linked case studies with exploratory work, surveys with descriptive studies, and experiments with explanatory research. The use of experimental approaches in educational research, which by definition rely upon the control of variables, have been widely criticised from both pragmatic and philosophical perspectives. While even advocates of experimental approaches to research in education recognise the limitations of the use of artificial contexts, experimental approaches based within authentic educational settings have been criticised because of practical and ethical problems associated with attempts to control the variables in such contexts (e.g. Hammond 1994; Venezky 2001). Philosophically, experimental approaches have been criticised on the basis that they ignore the differences between people and the objects of study of the natural sciences (Fenstercacher 1986), and thus the assumptions underlying experimental approaches are argued to be invalid, at least when applied to the study of social phenomena. Conversely, qualitative approaches have been said to lack validity or reliability due to the subjective nature of the data collection and analysis. These are paradigmatic arguments, which are often expressed as a debate about the extent to which quantitative and qualitative approaches can be combined (Bryman 1988). Understanding and coming to a view about this argument is an important step in deciding upon the most appropriate research methodologies for studying educational IT.

The quantitative vs qualitative debate

Robson (1993) noted that quantitative research is typically seen as involving approaches to data collection such as experiments and surveys. He also identified that qualitative research is typified as involving case studies, observation and interview.

Bryman (1988), in summarising the debate about the extent to which one can legitimately combine quantitative and qualitative research, identified two different ways of viewing them. The first sees the distinction between qualitative and quantitative research as relating to different ways of collecting data, and claims that one needs to choose the best method on the basis of the technical constraints of each. The alternative stance is that quantitative and qualitative research represent incompatible views on how the social world should be studied: 'they are essentially divergent clusters of epistemological assumptions, that is, of what should pass as warrantable knowledge about the social world' (Bryman 1988: 5).

Thus, at one extreme there are researchers who argue that one can mix and match between quantitative and qualitative research (e.g. Tesch 1990; Underwood and Underwood 1990). At the other extreme are those who argue that quantitative and qualitative research, because of their different underpinning assumptions about ontology and epistemology, represent distinct and incompatible paradigms (e.g. Scott and Usher 1999). In the middle are researchers, such as Hammersley (1992), who dispute the significance of the differences between the philosophical underpinnings of quantitative and qualitative research and thus argue that they are not mutually exclusive, and others, such as Willis *et al.* (1999), who while appearing to acknowledge paradigmatic incompatibilities, still argue that we should attend to research from all paradigms.

Examination of this debate suggests that one could consider research at a number of different levels. For example, Strauss and Corbin (1998) distinguish between methodology and methods, while Scott and Usher (1999) differentiate between ontology, epistemology, strategy and methods (see Table 15.1).

Table 15.1 Different 'levels' at which one can consider research

Strauss and Corbin (1998)	Scott and Usher (1999)
Methodology: a way of thinking about and studying social reality	**Ontology:** the nature of the world: how it is
	Epistemology: how we know the world: views of knowledge
Methods: a set of procedures and techniques for gathering and analysing data	**Strategy:** research design using certain types of reasoning
	Method: techniques for collecting and analysing data

Both these classifications distinguish between philosophical and technical levels at which one can consider research.

Figure 15.1, which is adapted from Scott and Usher's (1999) classification, shows another formulation of the different levels at which researchers operate and the ways in which these levels relate to each other. It illustrates the way in which different approaches to research are underpinned by different views of ontology and epistemology, and highlights that they make use of a variety

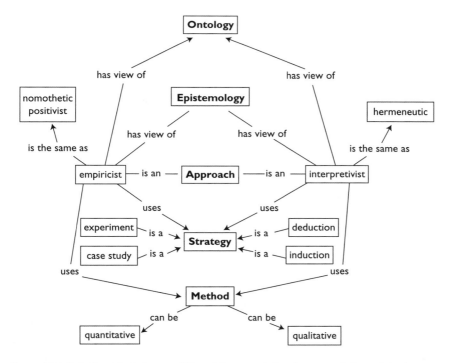

Figure 15.1 Relationship between different terms relating to research in social sciences.

of research strategies and methods. Figure 15.1 does not attempt to include all the different approaches, strategies or methods that are available, but provides illustrative examples.

Part of the explanation for the apparent disagreement about the extent to which quantitative and qualitative research could be combined appears to be due to ambiguity about the level of research that was being discussed and which paradigmatic labels should be applied. For example, Tesch (1990), unlike most authors, was only considering the Method level when she defined quantitative research as being that which uses numerical data, while qualitative research is any research that uses data that cannot be expressed in numbers. Willis *et al.* (1999), whilst applying the labels quantitative and qualitative at the Method level, argued that paradigms are not about data sources (quantitative vs qualitative) but about what you do with those sources. Scott and Usher (1999) made the paradigmatic distinction between qualitative and quantitative research at the Approach level, which they tied in closely with the ontological and epistemological levels.

Even more problematically, many researchers do not clearly distinguish between these levels. For example, Robson (1993) appears to merge the Approach, Strategic and Method levels, when he characterises quantitative research as being based on a 'scientific' approach in which theories are built through the formulation and testing of hypotheses through empirical means, as opposed to qualitative research, within which he states that the theories emerge from the enquiry, and boundaries between data collection and analysis are often blurred.

Further confusion comes from the different ways in which terminology is used within the literature. For example, Miller and Olson (1999) use the terms Methodology and Methods without making it clear what they mean by them. Ambiguity also arises where terminology is used differently by different authors, as illustrated in Table 15.2.

Despite the apparent differences between authors, there appears to be considerable agreement once confusion about terminology and the level being discussed are removed. For example, Erickson's (1986) argument is that two researchers could both use observation – writing descriptions of what they see happening – but end up with very different descriptions because their orientation (Approach) is different. Willis *et al.* (1999) agree with this, in that they

Table 15.2 Comparison of terminology used in the literature on research

Author	Terminology			
Strauss and Corbin (1998)	Methodology		Methods	
Scott and Usher (1999)	Ontology	Epistemology	Strategy	Method
Erickson (1986)	Method		Technique	

are essentially arguing that different techniques at the Method level (i.e. those that use numerical data and those that do not) are compatible but that there are incompatibilities as you move up to the Approach level and above.

Thus, there appears to be fairly wide agreement for the stance taken by Scott and Usher (1999) who argue that different approaches (as in Figure 15.1) represent different and incompatible paradigms. For example, empiricist and interpretivist approaches are based on different ontological and epistemological positions, as summarised in Table 15.3. However, research strategies and methods are not paradigmatic in themselves. For example, an interpretivist can use both quantitative and qualitative data. Scott and Usher (1999) make the case that it is not the method that is used that determines the approach, but the way in which that method is employed.

Taking this stance overcomes much of the apparent disagreement within the literature in relation to quantitative and qualitative research and allows one to take full advantage of the widest range of research methods, while remaining within the paradigmatic confines of one's particular research approach.

However, it does not mean that any strategy can fit within any approach. The ontological and epistemological stance underpinning each approach has implications for the research strategies that are deemed appropriate. For example, an experimental research strategy, involving control groups or laboratory conditions, would be linked with an empiricist approach and would not fit within an interpretivist one.

This exploration of the quantitative–qualitative debate helps to clarify the research methodologies that are appropriate to use within this field. In the next section, we take a more detailed look at the methodologies used in previous research.

Table 15.3 Comparison of ontological and epistemological stances of empiricists and interpretivists (based on Scott and Usher 1999: 2)

Empiricists	Interpretivists
One reality that can be known (determinancy).	Multiple realities.
No contradictory explanations (rationality).	Multiple accounts.
The more objective and the less subjective the better (impersonality).	All data collection involves subjectivity – in the sense that what one perceives is dependent upon one's beliefs, knowledge and interests.
Research is the making of knowledge claims in the form of generalisations from which predictions can be made, and events and phenomena controlled (prediction).	Research is about providing rich descriptions. All understandings are situated and thus not generalisable. At best one can establish consensus in certain contexts.

Historical overview of research methodologies in the field of educational IT

There has been a considerable amount of research into the use of computers in education (Moseley *et al*. 1999) and the literature within the field is extensive (McFarlane *et al*. 2000; Condie and Munro 2007). The research methodologies evident within the literature on computer use follow the methodological trends evident within educational research literature in general. This includes confusion about key differences between different research approaches, as illustrated for example by Willis *et al.'s* (1999) taxonomy of research approaches (Table 15.4), which appears to confuse key distinctions between them. For example, they seem to assume that the definitions of empiricism and interpretivism are based on methodological considerations compared with Critical Theory, which is defined in terms of ideology.

This confusion within the literature also involves ambiguity about the level of description of the research process, as discussed in the previous section. For example, Hadley and Sheingold (1993) identify two main types of research that are relevant to the question of the impact of IT in schools: case studies and surveys. Their description of case studies and surveys (see Table 15.5) suggests

Table 15.4 A taxonomy of research into IT in education (summarised from Willis *et al.* 1999)

Critical Theory	
Ideological stance, often focused on power relationships and equity issues	
Empiricism	**Interpretivism**
Methodological stance, based on a positivist notion of epistemology and belief in scientific methods. Generally making use of sampling techniques, survey methods and/or controlled variables.	Methodological stance, based on post-modernist notions of epistemology: 'realities are local, transitory, and contextually based' (Willis *et al.* 1999: 34). Often based on 'constructivist' views of learning. Tends towards qualitative methodologies.

Table 15.5 Summary of Hadley and Sheingold's (1993) categorisation of research on the impact of IT in schools

	Surveys	*Case studies*
Scale	Large	Small
'Sample' and hence generalisability	Representative and hence generalisable	Atypical and hence not generalisable
Timescale	Snapshot	Longer timeframe
Outcomes	Broad trends with little detail	Interesting insights
Implicit research approach	Empiricist	Interpretivist

that they equate case studies with an interpretivist approach and surveys with an empiricist one. These examples are typical of the lack of clarity about research methods within the field.

Within the educational research literature as a whole, there has been a shift from predominantly empiricist approaches to a greater reliance on interpretivist ones. Within the USA this shift was reversed as a result of the *No Child Left Behind Act* (US Congress 2002). This legislation placed a major emphasis on 'scientifically based research', which involved large quantitative studies and the use of control groups.

Clark *et al.* (1984), in their review of the school effectiveness literature, identified the initial shift from empiricist approaches which predominated pre-1970 to interpretivist approaches which were in the ascendancy post-1970. Walker (1992: 98) argued that 'the old order based on an empirical-scientific-positivist doctrine has lost its grip on the field,' but that 'no new doctrine has yet achieved dominance'.

In the area of computer use in schools these general trends apply, although it is still the case that survey based studies dominate the literature even in the period between 1970 and 2002 (Chalkey and Nicholas 1997, Miller and Olson 1999, Moseley *et al.* 1999, Willis *et al.* 1999, Cuban 2001, Pelgrum and Anderson, 2001). There have also been a small number of studies that combine survey and case studies (e.g. Watson 1993, Harrison *et al.* 2003, Somekh *et al.* 2005).

In the late 1990s a number of research papers began to appear that fit a Critical Theorist approach (e.g. Selwyn 2000). Willis *et al.* (1999) argued that critical theory was ideological rather than methodological (see Table 15.4) and this is true to the extent that its focus is on critiquing society in order to bring about change. However, Horkheimer (1937) in his seminal essay on critical theory makes it clear that critical theory rejects logical positivism and thus places it within an interpretivist approach.

Another development has been a greater emphasis on practitioner-based research, as evidenced in the UK by the provision of funding at a national level to support teacher-researchers (Foray and Hargreaves 2003). Practitioner-based research is often mistakenly labelled as action research. Action research is 'the study of a social situation with a view to improving the quality of action within it' (Elliott 1991: 69) and involves cycles of planning, acting, observing and reflecting. Whilst the aims of practitioner based research often correspond closely with those of action research, the strategies used often differ.

Somekh (2000) suggests that despite the changes in research strategies and methods over the previous twenty years, research findings within the field have not changed substantially. This view also seems to be supported by Twining *et al.* (2006) who go on to identify the need for more systematically implemented and longitudinal research using a mix of methods within an interpretivist approach.

hodological issues and future research

It is clear from the computer use in schools literature that there are a number of issues relating to the ways in which research has been carried out and the uses to which the outcomes of research can be put. For example, a number of researchers have identified trends within the field that need to be borne in mind when trying to make sense of this research. Moseley *et al.* noted that:

> When researchers initiate ICT activities for pupils they tend to use computer assisted instruction or computer assisted learning software where learning content is presented to pupils. By contrast, when teachers carry out action research, the preferred choice is more open ended or generic software.
>
> Moseley *et al.* (1999: vii)

Hadley and Sheingold (1993) noted two distinct features of research that used case studies: the introduction of technology for a particular purpose, which was often constructivist in orientation; and working in contexts where high levels of resourcing (equipment and staff) were available (e.g. the *Apple Classrooms of Tomorrow* project (ACOT)) and which looked over a long time frame. This analysis was echoed by Miller and Olson's (1999) classification of research in this area, which they argued fitted into three main categories:

- *Visions* – often tended to ignore or criticise teachers (e.g. Perelman 1992); investigators were often advocates rather than 'neutral researchers' (e.g. Becta).
- *Lighthouse projects* (e.g. ACOT) – atypical in terms of the level of resourcing and the enthusiasm and commitment to the technology of the people involved; often unclear which variables lead to changes.
- *Large scale studies* – often relied upon survey methods, though some (e.g. Watson 1993; Harrison *et al.* 2003; Somekh *et al.* 2005) used both qualitative and quantitative techniques.

This latter group they sub-divided into those that were investigating factors involved in innovation and those that were trying to bring about systemic change, often with a particular view of how technology should be used.

A number of issues emerge from these analyses that are relevant to the design of research into educational IT. These include practical concerns relating to experimental strategies, such as the control of variables, and questions about causality in educational contexts. Other issues include: the validity and reliability of data, particularly in the context of self-evaluation or self-reporting; the level of detail provided; and the stance of the researcher.

An experimental strategy is based on the notion of being able to control variables using one of two techniques. The first involves the use of artificial contexts, such as laboratory experiments, whilst the second involves the use of control groups in 'real world' contexts. Due to substantial problems with the external validity of using the results from artificial contexts to inform practice in schools, the use of laboratory experiments has become much less prevalent when it comes to research into computer use in schools, and would seem to be inappropriate for developing educational IT use.

The use of control groups in pure experimental designs involves the allocation of samples from the target population to different conditions. In 'real world' educational settings this is normally impossible for practical and ethical reasons. To overcome this problem researchers often adopt what Campbell and Stanley (1966) call quasi-experimental strategies in which existing groupings are used (e.g. whole classes of children). Efforts are then made to account for, and thus eliminate, the effects of differences between the groups that might otherwise render the findings invalid. However, the notion that one can control all of the variables within an educational context is highly problematic (e.g. Hammond 1994, Pisapia *et al.* 1999, McFarlane *et al.* 2000).

The related problem of the difficulties of establishing causal links pertaining to computer use in schools is commonly noted within the literature (e.g. Clark *et al.* 1984, Schrag 1999, Lewin *et al.* 2000, McFarlane *et al.* 2000, Venezky 2001). Underwood and Underwood (1997), while accepting the complexity of educational contexts and the problems associated with the control of variables, claim that experimental strategies are still appropriate in education, as they are in medical research. Their argument is that well-designed experimental studies can help to illuminate causal relationships. They argue that if computers lead to changes that in turn bring about educational benefits 'the understanding of the specific causes of change is a secondary issue, even if the causes are at all separable' (Underwood and Underwood 1997: 34). In other words, they are claiming that it does not matter that one cannot control all of the variables, so long as you can show that there is a learning gain associated with computer use.

Experimental and quasi-experimental strategies generally involve statistical analysis of the data. Underwood and Underwood (1997), for example, argue in favour of the use of certain statistical techniques, such as multivariant analysis, within the context of well-designed experimental studies, to reveal that an intervention has had an effect. The inappropriate use of statistical techniques has been criticised in the literature: for example, Mitchell (1997) identifies this as one of the key mistakes that is common in the field. One example of this is the use of correlations to draw conclusions about causal relationships. This is clearly illustrated by a number of related studies looking at the relationships between IT in schools and students' attainment (e.g. see Becta 2007). In some of Becta's own research (e.g. 2000, 2001, 2002) the key approach was to show a correlation between the level of IT resourcing in schools (as judged by OFSTED inspections) and the attainment of pupils on national tests (SATS or GCSEs). In each case, they reported finding correlations such as those illustrated in Figures 15.2 and 15.3.

The implication that because there was a correlation between the quality of IT resourcing and pupils' attainment there was a causal connection

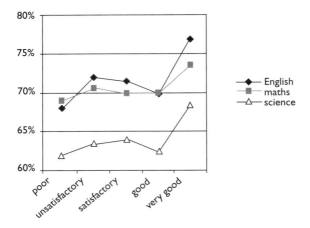

Figure 15.2 Percent children achieving L5 or above at KS3 (redrawn from Becta 2001: 11).

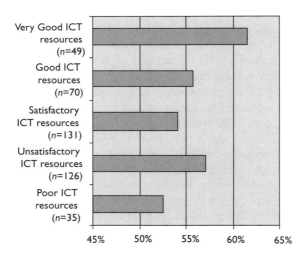

Figure 15.3 Percent children achieving 5 or more GCSEs at grade C or above against quality of IT resources (redrawn from Becta 2001: 11).

between them is flawed, because 'Even if a correlation can be established between two variables, it is still not possible to assert, in an unproblematic way, that the one caused the other to happen' (Scott and Usher 1999: 80). Indeed, following the publication of the first of these reports by Becta, the UK Publishers Association (Watson 2001) demonstrated even larger correlations between the levels of spending on books in primary schools and pupils' achievements on SATs, using the same statistical techniques that Becta had used.

Underwood and Underwood (1997) argue that quantitative methods can tell us if something has changed, but that in order to understand how or why the change took place one needs to use qualitative methods. Scott and Usher agree that understanding social phenomena requires the use of qualitative techniques:

> Quantitative researchers are not able to deal with the intentions, beliefs and propositional attitudes of social actors. If they try to, they are engaged in processes of reification, packaging and ultimately distortion. This suggests that data-collection processes which do not involve quantification will have to be employed to fully understand the nature of the social world.
>
> Scott and Usher (1999: 92)

As has already been identified, surveys are commonly used by researchers interested in computer use in schools. Whilst all surveys, by their very design, rely upon respondents to provide information, a particularly common form of response is self-assessment (Harris 1999; Cuban 2001). For example, using surveys to explore the impact of increased levels of computer resourcing on the quantity and quality of computer use would require teachers to self-assess the quantity and quality of computer use before and after the addition of extra equipment. There are a number of potential problems with self-assessment, including overly subjective responses and misrepresentation.

Where rating scales are not clearly explained, there is a danger that responses may be overly subjective (Harris 1999). For example, if asked to rate the impact of IT on pupils' learning on a scale that included the options 'None', 'Little' and 'Substantial' it would not be surprising if there was variation in the way in which respondents interpreted those terms. Not only is the boundary between 'Little' and 'Substantial' unclear, but the options are also skewed with little scope for discrimination. In particular, it is unclear how one would rate the impact of IT on pupils' learning on this scale if it fell somewhere between 'Little' and 'Substantial', as it easily might.

Cuban criticises surveys on the basis that they 'are essentially self-reports and so are prone to inflation and selective memory' Cuban (2001: 120). In essence, he is arguing that misrepresentation may take place either deliberately or unwittingly. For example, if a head teacher is asked to 'indicate on average how many minutes per week each child in your school spends using a computer', she is unlikely to know the answer or have enough information to be able to calculate the answer; it is much more probable that the best she can do is make a 'reasonable' estimate. In making that estimate, the head teacher may overestimate the amount of computer use, either by unconsciously giving too much weight to the times she has noticed children using computers or deliberately, perhaps because she is concerned about the under use of such an expensive resource. Indeed, Chalkey and Nicholas (1997: 98) found that 'there is a tendency for respondents to overestimate their use of computers'.

Inevitably, there are power-relationship issues in any research, and these may exacerbate misrepresentation issues. For example, the UK government carries out regular surveys of computer use in schools, which are based on self-reporting by head teachers (or their representatives). Given the UK government's position as the key funder of these schools, it seems possible that head teachers will be keen to respond in ways that will cast their school in a good light. Indeed, comparing the UK government data (DfES 2001) with that collected by an 'independent source' (BESA 2001) suggests that the government data on expenditure exaggerated the levels of investment (see Table 15.6).

In comparing these figures it is important to remember that the DfES data related just to England, whilst the BESA data covered the whole of the UK. One would thus have expected the BESA figures for total expenditure to be higher than the DfES ones, which was not the case. This suggests that caution needs to be exercised about the use of surveys that involve self-reporting, particularly in contexts where the respondents might be keen to be seen in a good light.

Another potential disadvantage of surveys is that they tend to provide a broad but shallow picture (Hadley and Sheingold 1993), which may lack the level of detail needed in order to differentiate between key factors that play an important part in computer use in schools. Lewin *et al.* (2000) identify this as

Table 15.6 Comparison of the levels of expenditure on IT in primary and secondary schools in 2001, based on data from different sources

	Primary schools		Secondary schools	
	UK (BESA 2001)	England (DfES 2001)	UK (BESA 2001)	England (DfES 2001)
Average total IT expenditure per school	£7,620	£10,300	£34,640	£60,300
Estimated total IT expenditure	£175.6 million	£186 million	£156.5 million	£210 million

being a particular problem in the context of identifying the impact of IT on learning because of the important role that the way in which software is used has on the learning outcomes and 'because the micro features that differentiate between classrooms or activities where effects are occurring and those where they are not are too specific to be picked up by the research design' (Lewin *et al*. 2000: 23).

The need for greater detail in the data on computer use in schools has lead to there being substantial support in the literature for the use of observational techniques (e.g. Chalkey and Nicholas 1997, Kent and McNergney 1999, Miller and Olson 1999, Moseley *et al*. 1999, Willis *et al*. 1999, Cuban 2001). This fits with the use of case studies, which enable aspects of educational IT use to be explored in depth, using a range of quantitative and qualitative techniques. Cohen and Manion (1989) highlight a particular strength of case studies as being that they allow the complexity and subtleties surrounding computer use in educational contexts to be described.

Action research, along with other forms of practitioner research, also tend to provide rich pictures of practice. Such accounts help to illuminate the ways in which technology is being used, which seems to be critical in determining the effects of technology in education (Wegerif 2003). In addition, Somekh (1995) argued that action research is particularly well suited to the study of innovations and in particular the use of IT in education because it is more likely than 'conventional' research to form the basis of recommendations that can be implemented easily in practice.

In their discussion of action research Selwood and Twining (2005) highlight a key distinction between evaluation and research as being that research is informed by and builds upon the wider body of knowledge in the field. One criticism that could be levelled at much so-called practitioner research is that if fails to meet this requirement. McDougall and Jones (2006: 355) extend this criticism to include much of the research in educational IT, which they identify as being determined to neglect or deliberately ignore its own history. They go on to quote from Underwood (2004: 140) when they say '[I]n the excitement of the new we appear not to want to look back and learn from the lessons of the past'.

Conclusions

From the brief overview provided in this chapter, it is clear that there has been a great deal of confusion within the educational literature in general, and the educational IT literature in particular about the nature of research and the methods that are most appropriate to use. This is partly due to confusion and lack of clarity in the terminology used, but also to the fact that the whole area of educational research is contested. Ultimately, this is due to paradigmatic differences in views of 'how the world is' (ontology) and views of knowledge (epistemology).

In order to make sense of the educational IT literature you need to bear in mind the contexts in which particular studies took place: the approach and underlying stance of the researchers should inform your interpretation of their work.

In deciding on how to conduct your own research, you need to be clear about your underpinning ontological and epistemological positions, as these will determine the overall approach that you will adopt. Your approach will, in turn, have a direct bearing upon the strategies that you can legitimately use, the ways in which you view different research methods, and the sorts of claims that you can make based upon your data. As will become clear in subsequent chapters of this book, there is no one agreed 'correct way' to research educational IT.

References

Becta (2000) *A Preliminary Report for the Dfee on the Relationship Between ICT and Primary School Standards*, Coventry: Becta.

—— (2001) *The Secondary School of the Future*, Coventry: Becta.

—— (2002) *Primary Schools – ICT and Standards: a report to the DfES on Becta's analysis of national data from OFSTED and QCA*, Coventry: Becta.

—— (2007) *Making a Difference with Technology for Learning: evidence for local authorities*, Coventry: Becta.

BESA (2001) *Information and Communication Technology in UK State Schools*, London: British Educational Suppliers Association.

Bryman, A. (1988) *Quantity and Quality in Social Research*, London: Routledge.

Campbell, D.T. and Stanley, J.C. (1966) *Experimental and Quasi-Experimental Designs for Research on Teaching*, Chicago: Rand McNally.

Chalkey, T.W. and Nicholas, D. (1997) 'Teachers' use of information technology: observations of primary school practice', *Aslib Proceedings*, 49: 97–107.

Clark, D.L., Lotto, L.S. and Astuto, T.A. (1984) 'Effective schools and school improvement: a comparative analysis of two lines of inquiry', *Educational Administration Quarterly*, 20: 41–68.

Cohen, L. and Manion, L. (1989) *Research Methods in Education*, London: Routledge.

Condie, R., Munro, B. with Seagraves, L. and Kenesson, S. (2007) *The Impact of ICT in Schools: a landscape review*, Coventry: Becta.

Cuban, L. (2001) *Oversold and Underused: computers in the classroom*, London: Harvard University Press.

DfES (2001) *Survey of Information and Communications Technology in Schools 2001*, London: DfES.

Elliott, J. (1991) *Action Research for Educational Change*, Milton Keynes: Open University Press.

Erickson, F. (1986) 'Qualitative methods in research on teaching', in M.C. Whittrock (ed.) *Handbook of Research on Teaching*, London: Collier Macmillan.

Fenstercacher, G.D. (1986) 'Philosophy of research on teaching: three aspects', in M.C. Whittrock (ed.) *Handbook of Research on Teaching*, London: Collier Macmillan.

Foray, D. and Hargreaves, D. (2003) 'The production of knowledge in different sectors: a model and some hypotheses', *London Review of Education*, 1: 7–19.

Hadley, M. and Sheingold, K. (1993) 'Commonalites and distinctive patterns in teachers' integration of computers', *American Journal of Education*, 101: 261–315.

Hammersley, M. (1992) *What's Wrong with Ethnography?* London: Routledge.

Hammond, M. (1994) 'Measuring the impact of IT on learning', *Journal of Computer Assisted Learning*, 10: 251–260.

Harris, S. (1999) *INSET for IT: a review of the literature relating to preparation for and use of IT in schools*, Slough: National Foundation for Educational Research.

Harrison, C., Comber, C., Fisher, T., Haw, K., Lewin, C., Lunzer, E., McFarlane, A., Mavers, D., Scrimshaw, P., Somekh, B. and Watling, R. (2003) *ImpaCT2: the impact of information and communication technologies on pupil learning and attainment*, Coventry: Becta.

Horkheimer, M. (1937) 'Traditional and Critical Theory', in M. Horkheimer (ed.) (1972) *Critical Theory: Selected Essays*, New York: Herder and Herder.

Kent, T.W. and McNergney, R.F. (1999) *Will Technology Really Change Education? From blackboard to Web*, Thousand Oaks, California: Corwin Press.

Lewin, C., Scrimshaw, P., Harrison, C., Somekh, B. and McFarlane, A. (2000) *ImpaCT2 Preliminary Study 2: promoting achievement: pupils, teachers and contexts*, Coventry: Becta.

McDougall, A. and Jones, A. (2006) 'Theory and history, questions and methodology: current and future issues in research into ICT in education', *Technology, Pedagogy and Education*, 15: 353–360.

McFarlane, A., Harrison, C., Somekh, B., Scrimshaw, P., Harrison, A. and Lewin, C. (2000) *ImpaCT2 Preliminary Study 1: establishing the relationship between networked technology and attainment*, Coventry: Becta.

Miller, L. and Olson, J. (1999) 'Research agendas and computer technology visions: the need for closely watched classrooms', *Education and Information Technologies*, 4: 81–98.

Mitchell, P.D. (1997) 'The impact of educational technology: a radical reappraisal of research methods', *ALT-J* 5: 48–54.

Moseley, D., Higgins, S., Bramald, R., Hardman, F., Miller, J., Mroz, M., Tse, H., Newton, D., Thompson, I., Williamson, J., Halligan, J., Bramald, S., Newton, L., Tymms, P., Henderson, B. and Stout, J. (1999) *Ways Forward with ICT: effective pedagogy using information and communications technology for literacy and numeracy in primary schools*, Newcastle, UK: University of Newcastle.

Pelgrum, W.J. and Anderson, R.E. (eds) (2001) *ICT and the Emerging Paradigm for Lifelong Learning: a worldwide educational assessment of infrastructure, goals, and practices*, Amsterdam: The International Association for the Evaluation of Educational Achievement.

Perelman, L.J. (1992) *School's Out: hyperlearning, the new technology, and the end of education*, New York: William Morrow.

Pisapia, J.R., Knutson, K. and Coukos, E.D. 'The impact of computers on student performance and teacher behavior', paper presented at the 44th Annual Meeting of The Florida Educational Research Association, Deerfield Beach, Florida, 1999, ERIC ED438323.

Robson, C. (1993) *Real World Research*, Oxford: Blackwell.

Schofield, J.W. (1993) 'Increasing the generalizability of qualitative research', in M. Hammersley (ed.) *Educational Research: current issues*, London: Paul Chapman.

Schrag, J.A. (1999) *Inputs and Processes in Education: a background paper*. Alexandria, Virginia: National Association of State Directors of Special Education.

Scott, D. and Usher, R. (1999) *Researching Education: data, methods and theory in educational enquiry*, London: Cassell.

Selwood, I. and Twining, P. (2005) *Action Research*, Coventry: Becta.

Selwyn, N. (2000) 'Researching computers and education – glimpses of the wider picture', *Computers & Education*, 34: 93–101.

Shulman, L.S. (1986) 'Paradigms and research programs in the study of teaching: a contemporary perspective', in M.C. Whittrock (ed.) *Handbook of Research on Teaching*, London: Collier Macmillan.

Somekh, B. (2000) 'New technology and learning: policy and practice in the UK, 1980-2010', *Education and Information Technologies*, 5: 19–37.

—— (1995) 'The contribution of action research to development of social endeavours: a position paper on action research methodology', *British Educational Research Journal*, 21: 339–355.

Somekh, B., Underwood, J., Convery, A., Dillon, G., Lewin, C., Mavers, D., Saxon, D. and Twining, P. (2005) *ICT Test Bed Evaluation*, Coventry: Becta.

Strauss, A. and Corbin, J. (1998) *Basics of Qualitative Research: techniques and procedures for developing grounded theory*, London: Sage.

Tesch, R. (1990) *Qualitative Research: analysis types and software tools*, London: Falmer Press.

Twining, P., Broadie, R., Cook, D., Ford, K., Morris, D., Twiner, A. and Underwood, J. (2006) *Educational Change and ICT: an exploration of priorities 2 and 3 of the DfES e-strategy in schools and colleges*, Coventry: Becta.

Underwood, G. and Underwood, J. (1997) 'Evaluating the educational impact of information technology on teaching and learning: the case against techno-romanticism', in J. Underwood and J. Brown (eds) *Integrated Learning Systems: potential into practice*, Oxford: Heinemann.

Underwood, J.D.M. and Underwood, G. (1990) *Computers and Learning: helping children acquire thinking skills*, Oxford: Blackwell.

Underwood, J. (2004) 'Research into information and communications technologies: where now?' *Technology, Pedagogy and Education*, 13: 135–145.

US Congress (2002) *Public Law 107–110–Jan. 8, 2002*, Washington DC: US Congress.

Venezky, R.L. (2001) 'Procedures for evaluating the impact of complex educational interventions', *Journal of Science Education and Technology*, 10: 17–30.

Walker, D.F. (1992) 'Methodological issues in curriculum research', in P.W. Jackson (ed.) *Handbook of Research on Curriculum*, New York: Macmillan.

Watson, D.M. (ed.) (1993) *The ImpacT Report: an evaluation of the impact of information technology on children's achievements in primary and secondary schools,* London: DFE and King's College London.

Watson, R. (2001) *Relationship Between School Book Spending and School Results*, London: Publishers Association.

Wegerif, R. (2003) *Literature Review in Thinking Skills, Technology and Learning*, NESTA Futurelab Series Report 2, Bristol: NESTA Futurelab.

Willis, J., Thompson, A. and Sadera, W. (1999) 'Research on technology and teacher education: current status and future directions', *Educational Technology Research and Development*, 47: 29–45.

Chapter 16

Looking in classrooms

Researching school use of information technology for teaching and learning

Anthony Jones
The University of Melbourne, Australia

Introduction

The basis for the methodological approaches described in this chapter are formed by the arguments put forward for educational researchers to make use of methodologies that appear most likely to be appropriate for answering the research questions of their projects. Whenever this author-researcher was confronted with the task of investigating uses of IT within the constantly shifting complexities of classroom interactions between a teacher and 25 or more learners, it was obvious that there was a multitude of variables that would impact on the research. In classrooms there are far too many variables to be treated using traditional approaches that involve attempting to keep some of them constant, and focus only on a few. The ecology metaphor proposed by Cobb *et al.* (2003) pragmatically accepts that because they are ongoing and constantly evolving, the interactions and interplay among classroom variables means that the variables cannot be isolated or ignored by researchers.

Why look in classrooms?

Recent criticisms of educational research into classroom uses of IT, for example by Underwood (2004) from the UK and by Roblyer and Knezek (2003) from the USA, are addressed by McDougall and Jones (2006) when they argue that the primary focus of such research should be to contribute to our understanding of teaching and learning. It is only when researchers, practitioners, and learners better understand the interplay between pedagogy, subject content, and IT that effective pedagogical strategies will be formulated and that purpose-specific educational software can be developed.

'[M]uch of teaching is still an art and . . . if teachers are to be successful, they must develop a way to see, comprehend, and respond to the complex, rapid flow of classroom behaviour' (Good and Brophy 1978: xii). Writing thirty years ago, Good and Brophy realised how difficult it was for teachers and observers to understand the complex interactions that constitute a classroom lesson. Because they were aware of the differences between intended actions, such as those shown in a lesson plan, and the actual actions and occurrences, one aim of their book was to offer teachers a range of techniques for observing, and tools for recording, classroom occurrences.

Making permanent records of classroom episodes and incidents has become easier since the time of Good and Brophy. However, there are still some significant factors, present to differing degrees in different classrooms, that impinge on educational research, including learning through incidental (or accidental) experiences as well as deliberately planned and implemented experiences, the perceptions students have of teacher practice, and the actual application of IT. How much technology is available? Where is it positioned? For what purpose is it to be used? Each of these can have consequences for classroom teaching and learning.

How can we look at classroom lessons involving IT?

Research in education must do much more than offer empirical evidence for what is 'good' or 'better' in current practice. To be meaningful, educational research must also assist in the development of theories linked to practice. Winn (2003) reminded the research community that no one methodological approach could provide all the answers researchers and practitioners were seeking. He 'reaffirms the importance of experimental research for answering some research questions [and] argues that non-experimental methods, such as design experiments . . . are useful for answering other kinds of research questions about learning in complex settings' (Winn 2003: 367).

The pioneering work of Ann Brown (1992) in defining and popularising design experiments is clearly acknowledged by both Winn (2003) and Cobb et al. (2003). The 'metaphor of an ecology to emphasize that designed contexts are conceptualised as interacting systems rather than as either a collection of activities or a list of separate factors that influence learning' is used by Cobb et al. (2003: 9). It is also proposed that design experiments cater for diverse settings as well as variations in size and scope. Among the settings described are 'one-on-one' design experiments that involve a small number of students and a teacher-researcher, and 'classroom experiments in which a research team collaborates with a teacher' (Cobb et al. 2003: 9). The approaches to data collection and analysis that are detailed in the following sections represent a pragmatic use of the concepts of design experiments.

Collecting data

Over many years of studying classroom occurrences, data has been collected through surveys, questionnaires or researcher notes. It is common at the start of a study for participating teachers and students to be asked to complete a questionnaire that will provide base-line data about what is to be studied. In many ways this practice is still essential, but it requires supplementary data to provide detail and to fill in areas not capable of being covered in a survey or questionnaire.

Video-recording of lessons is a method used to provide detailed information about classroom occurrences. The methodology proposed here evolved from large-scale studies such the Third International Mathematics and Science Study (Stigler and Hiebert 2000) and the International Centre for Classroom Research (ICCR) Learners' Perspective Study (Clarke *et al.* 2006). Clarke and his colleagues at the ICCR have pioneered the extensive use of multiple-camera video data collection and analysis, enabling case study-like approaches to be used in research into interactions within classrooms. For the Learners' Perspective Study, classroom video data was collected about the teacher, the class as a whole, and a pre-selected group of students. This involved having three cameras, one that followed the teacher, one that provided a panoramic view of the classroom, and a third that was focused on one table and a small group of students who worked at that table.

Two cameras have been used in some recent research projects, especially when lessons were recorded in computer rooms. Figure 16.1 shows a composite video image produced by superimposing a panoramic view of the room on an image of the teacher. This lesson was recorded in a primary school computer room, and because the focus of this research was on the actions and pedagogies employed by the teacher, no attempt was made to include children in the larger image. In this example, one camera recorded the actions and voice of the teacher as she moved around the room. The teacher carried a wireless microphone that enabled all oral communications to be recorded. A second camera was set up in a corner to provide a panoramic view of the classroom, to give an indication of what students were doing, no matter where the teacher was, but not to focus on individual students.

———— Superimposed image of the whole room.

———— Main image used for data collection. Note that the teacher and the projection screen are the centres of attention.

Figure 16.1 Composite video image.

In another series of studies, a single camera has been used for projects that recorded and analysed teacher and student activities around an interactive whiteboard in a classroom. Because the focal point of these projects was on who was using the interactive whiteboard and what they were doing on it, only one camera was needed to capture the required data. Overall, the number of cameras to be used depends on the research question being investigated, the nature of the planned lesson, and on the physical attributes of the classroom or computer room.

Analysing data

Many studies in which video data of classroom activities is collected use edited video highlights as a stimulus for interviews with participants. For example, researchers using the ICCR approach conduct video-stimulated interviews with teachers or students immediately following a lesson. Figure 16.2a represents this approach.

However, in the IT studies reported here, the videos were first analysed by researchers, and video-stimulated interviews were conducted several days after the lesson had been recorded. Figure 16.2a shows the action research cycle that many teachers follow when classroom practice is being researched along the lines suggested here. A number of additional stages appear, as in Figure 16.2b. The researcher observes and video-records lessons, and then away from the classroom conducts an initial analysis of the video data. This analysis raises some key questions that form the basis for a semi-structured interview with the teacher. The researcher uses edited highlights of the video data to structure the interview, rather than contemplating using all of the video-record. In some instances the researchers believed it was necessary to request a second interview in order to discuss parts of the video not used in the initial interview, or for clarification. The interviews with teachers, and where appropriate with students in small focus groups, is the final aspect of data collection. In the extracts that follow, the aim of the interviews was to probe the teacher's perceptions about student engagement and motivation and learning when IT was used.

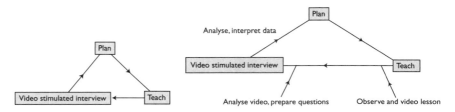

Figure 16.2a Teacher research cycle.

Figure 16.2b Researcher and teacher cycles.

Looking at classroom lessons involving IT

Since 2005 researchers from the University of Melbourne have undertaken several projects that involved video-recording lessons involving teacher use of IT. Initially, the focus was on lessons in computer rooms, and later data was collected on modes of use of interactive whiteboards. Most recently, the focus of research has shifted to the levels and nature of interactivity between teachers and learners when using an interactive whiteboard. All of these research projects involved the video-recording of lessons and subsequent video stimulated interviews. The comments that follow are from several projects, and consider the different types of lesson events that occur in classroom lessons that involve some teacher use of IT.

Sample results: categorising lesson events in classrooms

The examples that follow come from projects that investigated the pedagogical strategies employed by both primary and secondary level teachers when they used interactive whiteboards, laptop computers, or some other form of IT. By reviewing the video data several times, researchers identified events that were common to many of these lessons. These lesson events were named and categorised. Some lesson events were similar to those reported by mathematics education researchers, but the processes and structure were usually different in an IT context. For example, Mok and Kaur (2006: 147) described a 'learning task' lesson event as comprising discourse between teacher and students as they interact with a given task, often occurring at the start of a mathematics lesson when the teacher demonstrates a new concept or skill prior to students practising that concept or skill. Typically, in an IT lesson there is also a learning task lesson event. However, they differ considerably from the purpose and nature of the mathematics examples described by Mok. In the video data from IT lessons the teacher always attempted to provide a flavour of what was possible with the software the students would use, rather than providing a model for students to follow.

For example, a primary teacher working with a year 6 class commenced with a whole class demonstration with no preliminary warm-up or starter activity. During the interview a week after the lesson was taught, the teacher commented that students come into a computer class and expect to be working at set tasks involving computers. The teacher made use of a computer connected to a video-projector for her demonstration. In this lesson event, the teacher demonstrated for more than ten minutes at the start of the lesson. Her opening and concluding comments to the class are recorded below.

03:14	Teacher	*We are going to do three activities today. I will show the third activity first.*
15:14	Teacher	*Come and see me if you've got a question. Go!*

In contrast to this approach the researchers recorded several lessons involving interactive whiteboards, taught by different teachers but mostly with year 8 students, in which the lesson began with a puzzle or some other starter activity. There were instances where the starter activity was a form of revision of a previous lesson, others where student thinking was quickly channelled into a direction that linked to the lesson, and still others where the starter activity was almost a social occasion that got the class settled and ready for work, but did not obviously connect with lesson content.

In computer rooms teachers typically carried out management activities before a demonstration, including making sure students were logged-on correctly and pairing students to work at a computer. Then, in almost every lesson recorded, there was a teacher-led demonstration that covered a number of points, most often involving a revision of skills practised in a previous lesson and then information about the activity for the current lesson. This is exemplified by the primary teacher mentioned above who first presented what she called 'activity three', a quite sophisticated task that in her interview the teacher said she anticipated only the most competent students would reach in this lesson. The second activity she presented in her demonstration to the class was planned as the major activity for the lesson, and was based on skills and knowledge acquired in task one which had been started in a previous lesson. The third part of the demonstration was of a basic task that all students had to open and check they had completed before commencing activity two.

These comments suggest another strategy that was common in the lessons recorded – encouraging students to reflect on what they had learned in a lesson, and how this new knowledge or skills might be used in future computer sessions. The year 6 teacher, for example, a few minutes before the end, stopped the class in order to share a feature of the software found by one student, "Stop! Minimise for a sec[ond], please. Dillon is going to show us something he has discovered." (Teacher M: lesson 1:16:56) Dillon, one of the year 6 students, moved to the teacher's computer and via the video projector demonstrated a feature of the software that no one else in the class had found. The teacher asked questions of Dillon (for clarification) and of the class (for understanding and extension) during this demonstration. When the demonstration concluded, students were instructed to save their work and log off the computer. It was evident from the images from the second camera that not every student kept their hands away from the keyboard. Many students appeared to stop briefly, and then continue working with the keyboard.

Concluding comments

Video-recording lessons that focus on issues of management and pedagogy when IT is used, enables teachers to observe their own practice in a way that is not otherwise available. It also provides a rich vein of raw data for researchers. It is now three decades since Good and Brophy argued that teachers should be given video-recordings of their lessons to help them 'develop a conceptual system for labeling their own behavior' (Good and Brophy 1978: 30).

The data collected in these studies relied on extensive use of one or more cameras overtly visible in a classroom, and teachers using radio microphones. However, neither teachers nor students ever commented that they considered the technology to be intrusive. By placing a camera in a classroom for several lessons before actually collecting data, students (and teachers) become accustomed to its presence. This enabled the researchers to collect data that closely reflected normal classroom practice at the schools.

Categorising and analysing lesson events is only one possible avenue of research enhanced by our ability to easily video-record lessons in real classrooms. As a lesson event, the commencement of lessons involving IT tends to be influenced by the expectation that students will get to use the computers as soon as possible. Similarly, when teachers try and engage students in a plenary or reflective session to conclude an IT lesson, students do not want to leave their computers. The example briefly described here showed that strategies used by teachers to commence and conclude lessons with IT were different from those used in many other subjects, and constituted a rich and varied area for investigation and analysis.

The strength and significance of the approach presented in this chapter lie in the opportunity it provides to record some of the complexity of normal classroom practice, and for the researchers to re-analyse the video data at different times using different methodologies. We also believe it is well worth the time and effort involved in discussing with students part of a videoed lesson they participated in, and these video-stimulated interviews provide valuable insights for researchers.

References

Brown, A. (1992) 'Design experiments: theoretical and methodological challenges in creating complex interventions in classroom settings', *The Journal of the Learning Sciences*, 2: 141–178.

Cobb, P., Confrey, J., diSessa, A., Lehrer, R. and Schauble, L. (2003) 'Design experiments in educational research', *Educational Researcher*, 32: 9–13.

Clarke, D.J., Emanuelsson, J., Jablonka, E. and Mok, I.A.C. (eds) (2006) *Making Connections: comparing mathematics classrooms around the world*, Rotterdam: Sense Publishers.

Good, T. and Brophy, J. (1978) *Looking in Classrooms*, 2nd edn, New York: Harper and Row.

McDougall, A. and Jones, A. (2006) 'Theory and history, questions and methodology: current and future issues in research into ICT in education', *Technology, Pedagogy and Education*, 15: 353–360.

Mok, I.A.C. and Kaur, B (2006) 'Learning task lesson events' in D.J. Clarke, J. Emanuelsson, E. Jablonka and I.A.C. Mok, (eds) *Making Connections: comparing mathematics classrooms around the world*, Rotterdam: Sense Publishers.

Roblyer, M.D. and Knezek, G.A. (2003) 'New millennium research for educational technology: a call for a national research agenda,' *Journal of Research on Technology in Education*, 36: 60–76.

Stigler, J.W. and Hiebert, J. (2000) *The Teaching Gap: best ideas from the world's teachers for improving education in the classroom*, New York: Free Press.

Underwood, J. (2004) 'Research into information and communications technologies: where now?' *Technology, Pedagogy and Education*, 13: 135–145.

Winn, W. (2003) 'Research methods and types of evidence for research in educational technology', *Educational Psychology Review*, 15: 367–373.

Chapter 17

A cross-experiment methodology for networking research teams

Rosa Maria Bottino and Michele Cerulli
Istituto Tecnologie Didattiche – Consiglio
Nazionale delle Ricerche, Italy

Introduction

In the mathematics education research field, and, in particular, in that of mathematics teaching and learning with technologies, there is an increasing awareness of the difficulties that result from the diversity of theoretical frameworks (Artigue 2007). Since there are many constructs and theories, there are difficulties in collaboration and exchanges between teams adopting different frameworks as well as in understanding the research problems adopted and the results obtained. The diversity and fragmentation of existing theoretical frameworks makes it hard to understand what different research groups have in common and exactly what differentiates them. This also has repercussions on how educational practice is understood and designed.

These difficulties are often perceived at international conferences and workshops where the discussion at the end of a presentation may appear quite problematic: speakers and reacting listeners sometimes seem not to understand each other and remain tied to their specific frameworks. The problem of the language adopted is also crucial, since researchers do not usually share the same terminology or the same meanings for particular terms. This problem becomes crucial when teams belonging to different research cultures have to develop a joint project for which they are to collaborate from the beginning. This is the case, for example, with European Community (EC) funded projects like Networks of Excellence (NoE).

This paper refers in particular to the NoE Kaleidoscope (www.noe-kaleidoscope.org), an initiative funded (IST–507838) under the VI Framework Programme that brings together key European teams, promoting integration among them, with the aim of developing new concepts and methods to explore the future of learning with IT (Bottino 2007). Within Kaleidoscope, a number of different research activities, covering a wide range of topics, were carried out. Among these, the TELMA European Research Team specifically focused on Technology Enhanced Learning in Mathematics. Kaleidoscope involved six European teams and had as its main aim that of building a shared view of key research topics in the area of digital technologies and mathematics education, proposing related research activities, and developing common research methodologies. Each team brought to the project particular focuses and theoretical frameworks, adopted and developed over a period of time. Most of them had also implemented and tested computer-based systems for use in mathematics learning. In order to develop a shared and integrated view among teams, a methodology involving exchanges of IT-based tools was specifically developed by the TELMA group. This methodology is based on the following main phases sketched in Figure 17.1: [a] exchange of information among teams and development of a common perspective; [b] design, implementation and analysis of cross-experiments; [c] reflective interviews of the researchers involved in the previous phases.

TELMA teams started with the informative phase [a], where they exchanged research papers and reports, and then they moved towards a more concrete phase [b], where they jointly designed field experiments exchanging IT-based tools. Finally interviews [c] were conducted to reflect on the results of the cross-experiments.

In the following section the main phases of the methodology adopted within TELMA are presented.

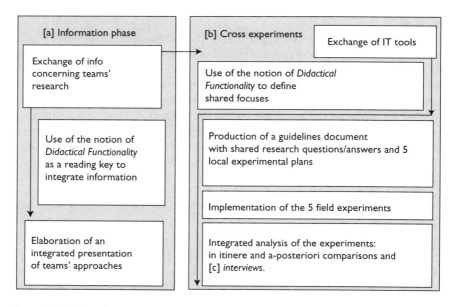

Figure 17.1 Main phases of the methodology adopted to support collaboration among different research teams.

A shared research methodology

Exchange of information to develop a common perspective

From the beginning of their collaborative work in the Kaleidoscope network of excellence, the teams involved in TELMA had to face the differences in their research approaches and theoretical frameworks. A first level of integration was pursued through the definition of the notion of 'didactical functionality of an IT-tool' to interpret and compare the different research projects (Cerulli *et al.* 2007a). This notion was used as a way to develop a common perspective among teams linking theoretical reflections to the real tasks that one has to face when designing or analysing the use of a digital technology in a given context. The notion of didactical functionalities is structured into three inter-related components:

- a set of features/characteristics of the IT-tool under consideration
- an educational aim
- modalities of use of the IT-tool in a teaching/learning process aimed at reaching this educational aim.

The different didactical functionalities designed and studied by each team were compared in an attempt to delineate how different theoretical back-grounds can influence the design of an IT-tool, the definition of the educational goals to be pursued, and the modalities of use of the tool to achieve such goals. At the beginning, this analysis was conducted on the basis of a selection of papers published by each team. This approach, although use-ful, was not considered sufficient to examine the less explicit aspects of the research work of each team. For this reason, TELMA researchers decided to move toward a strategy that would allow them to gain more intimate insights into their respective research and design practices. This strategy consisted of a 'cross-experiment' project where each TELMA team investigated an IT-based tool that was developed by one of the other teams.

Design, implementation and analysis of cross-experiments

The cross-experiment methodology is a new approach to collaboration that seeks to facilitate common understanding across teams with diverse practices and cultures and to elaborate integrated views that transcend individual team cultures. There are two principal characteristics of the cross-experiment pro-ject implemented within TELMA that distinguish it from other forms of collaborative research:

- the design and implementation by each research team of a field experi-ment making use of an IT-tool developed by another team

- the joint construction of a common set of questions to be answered by each team in order to frame the process of cross-team communication.

The aim of such cross-experiments was to acquire a better understanding of what happens when a field experiment is planned using a technological tool that has been designed and implemented under theoretical frameworks and in a context that is different from that of the experimenting team. The key idea was to take a further step in the following areas that are crucial in research into IT and education:

- understanding what it means to 'tune' the use of a tool to the specific pedagogical aims and research objectives of a team that has not developed it
- understanding similarities and differences in the educational contexts set up by each team to experiment with a particular tool
- understanding/discovering implicit aspects embedded in tools
- uncovering implicit theoretical assumptions that characterise the design and development of an experiment involving a tool.

Each team was asked to select an IT-tool among those developed by the other teams. This decision was expected to induce deeper exchanges between the teams, and to make the influence of theoretical frameworks more visible through comparison of the didactical functionalities developed by the designers of an IT-tool and those implemented by the team developing a field experiment using that tool. In order to facilitate the comparison between the different experimental settings, it was also agreed to address common mathematical knowledge domains, to carry out the field experiments with students between the 5th and 8th grade, and to perform them for about the same amount of time (one month).

The actual experimental phase was preceded by a reflective phase, mostly based on online exchanges, in which the teams reached an agreement on shared research questions to address during the experiments. On this basis, a 'Guidelines' document (Cerulli *et al.* 2007b) was built collaboratively. It contained all the research questions to be addressed (both questions to be addressed before the experiments and questions to be addressed after the experiments), and the experimental plans developed by each team. These plans included information on the experimental settings, on the modalities of employment of the tool, and on the methods to be used to collect and analyse data. During the experimental activity, the document was constantly updated and shared among the researchers involved. The researchers were periodically required to compare the different activities and the reflections brought forward by all the teams.

Reflective interviews

One of the more interesting results of the cross-experiment project was the fact that it helped to enlighten in concrete terms the relationship between theoretical assumptions and cases of practice. The theoretical frameworks underlying the work of each team affected the implementation of the experiments in different ways. They impacted on the analysis of the IT-tool and the definition of the didactical functionalities to be implemented; they also determined (more or less explicitly) the level of detail at which the experiments were planned in advance; moreover, they influenced the roles and responsibilities assumed during the classroom work by the teachers, the researchers and the students.

The analysis of the cross-experiments showed that sometimes there is a gap between theoretical assumptions and the decisions taken during the implementation of the field experiments. Thus, it appeared necessary to investigate such gaps in more depth in the a posteriori analysis. This was done by means of interviews; a senior researcher in each team, who was not directly involved with the experimental work, interviewed the researchers who carried out the field experiments. Interviews followed a specific technique called 'interview for explicitation' (Vermesch and Maurel 1997). Researchers were asked to say what they had done and how, but they were not questioned directly about the rationale for their actions. The main goal of the interview was to contribute to the understanding of the role played by theoretical frameworks in the planning and implementation of the classroom experiment and in the interpretation of its results. The interviews were designed using the guidelines document (Cerulli *et al.* 2007b).

Concluding remarks

The methodology adopted in the TELMA project allowed us to highlight interesting similarities and differences among the participating research teams. Even though it is not possible here to analyse specific results (see, for example, Cerulli *et al.* 2008, for a more in-depth analysis), it is nevertheless possible to make some general reflections. For example, it was found that all the teams were interested in investigating some common notions such as the notion of learning environment, the role played by social interaction and the mediating role of IT-based tools.

All teams shared the idea that when considering a learning environment all its components should be taken into account. Consequently, all teams attributed importance not only to the technological tool, but also to the pedagogical activities in which the use of the tool is integrated and to the way in which these activities are carried out. Moreover, they attributed importance to the different roles assumed during the experiments by the teachers, the students and the researchers themselves. Last but not least, all teams had an interest in the way in which the IT-tools used mediated students' evaluation of the work performed and the relationships established among the different actors during the activity.

A key aspect that was highlighted during the project is the gap between theoretical assumptions and the activities actually carried out. Such a gap may hide important aspects of a research study, making it difficult to interpret its results and making it difficult as well to communicate between different teams. The TELMA project showed that a valuable approach to such problems is to involve research teams in a self-reflection process aimed at sharing the assumptions made and the choices undertaken in as comparable a way as possible. In the cross-experiments each local experiment was thought of as part of a bigger project and had to be expressed in a way that could allow an easy comparison with others. Such an idea of focusing on comparison and supporting it by means of specifically developed instruments (e.g. guidelines, questionnaires) has also been adopted in another EC funded project (REMATH–IST–4–26751–STP) which followed the first TELMA work. The aim of the REMATH project is to extend the networking methodology adopted in TELMA in order to apply it also to the design of digital tools for mathematics learning.

References

Artigue, M. (2007) 'Digital technologies: a window on theoretical issues in mathematics education', in D. Pitta-Pantazi and G. Philippou (eds) *Proceedings of CERME 5: fifth conference of the European society for research in mathematics education*, Larnaca: Department of Education, University of Larnaca, Cyprus.

Bottino, R.M. (2007) 'On-line learning networks: framework and scenarios', *Education and Information Technologies*, 12: 93–105.

Cerulli, M., Pedemonte, B., Robotti, E. (2007a) 'An integrated perspective to approach technology in mathematics education', in M. Bosh (ed.) *Proceedings of CERME 4*, Sant Feliu de Guixols: IQS Fundemi Business Institute.

Cerulli, M., Pedemonte, B., Robotti, E. (eds) (2007b) 'TELMA cross experiment guidelines', *Internal Report R.I. 01/07*, Genova: Istituto Tecnologie Didattiche – Consiglio Nazionale delle Ricerche.

Cerulli, M., Georget, J.P., Maracci, M., Psycharis, G., Trgalova, J. (2008) 'Comparing theoretical frameworks enacted in experimental research: TELMA experience', *ZDM – The International Journal on Mathematics Education*, 40: 201–214.

Vermesch, P., Maurel, M. (eds) (1997) *Pratiques de l'entretien d'explicitation*, Paris: ESF.

Chapter 18

Methods for investigating young children's learning and development with information technology

Kleopatra Nikolopoulou
University of Athens, Greece

Introduction

Use of computers in early childhood settings was an issue of tremendous concern in the 1980s and early 1990s and views then were not as positive as those found in the current literature. Critics asserted computers would isolate children and negatively affect their social skills, as they are too abstract and difficult for young children to use appropriately (Goodwin *et al*. 1986). Later, Cordes and Miller (2000) argued that computers can interfere with healthy physical and mental development, except for special cases of children with disabilities. The debate is less polarized now. 'Evidence to support the claims that ICTs facilitate development may be unclear but a consensus is emerging that ICTs do have a contribution to make' (Stephen and Plowman 2003a: 232). Computers have become an increasingly recognised tool in the education of young children (Haugland and Wright 1997). Reviews of research (e.g. Clements and Sarama 2003; Siraj-Blatchford and Siraj-Blatchford 2006) have indicated the computer can be used as a tool to support learning and development, and assist communication, collaboration and language development in young children.

However, the body of existing research evidence has not been so conclusive and there is a need for more research to be undertaken. This chapter discusses methods commonly used in early childhood education research on IT, and addresses ethical and other issues that need to be taken into account when developing or adopting practical methods for investigating young children's learning with IT. The focus is on children aged three to six years old who attend early childhood education settings. Computer use is not recommended for children younger than three, and after the age of six children in many countries enter primary education. However, as the age range definitions of kindergarteners vary, this is identified as a methodological issue.

Ethics and early childhood education research

Ethical issues arise when investigating dependent, vulnerable members of society such as young children. Gaining informed consent from research participants is widely regarded as central to ethical research practice and in institutional settings such as schools, access tends to be mediated by gate-keepers (Heath *et al*. 2007). Within early childhood education settings, adult gatekeepers (teachers, managers etc.) frequently make decisions on behalf of the children in their care, including whether or not to provide access to researchers. It is common for gatekeepers to provide access, but then to dele-gate to children's parents the ultimate decision whether or not a child can participate. Flewitt (2005), conducting ethnographic video case studies with three-year-old children, discussed ethical considerations such as negotiating initial and ongoing consent, issues of anonymity when representing visual data, and keeping participants informed about research outcomes. Cameron (2005) reported that when interviewing young children, it is essential to examine the complex nature of confidentiality and consent. Participants need to feel free and safe to opt out whenever they wish to, in particular in the con-duct of longitudinal research.

There has been a shift within childhood studies from viewing children as objects of research towards a view that stresses their competence, often as co-participants in the research process (Heath *et al*. 2007). Researchers propose child-friendly research designs, such as using visual methods, drawings and stories as research tools, or choosing group interviews. Participants' names can be changed in written accounts and erased from audio recordings, while digital technology enables on-screen faces to be obscured to protect identity. Flewitt (2005) reported that three-year-old children were asked to watch the videos during data collection and their views on their activities were often very clear. Researchers must be aware of ethical issues involved, and negotiate ethical frameworks for their research with young children.

Commonly used methods in early childhood education research on IT

In early childhood education research on IT, qualitative approaches are used more frequently than quantitative approaches. Due to young children's lim-ited reading skills, relatively few research studies include instruments commonly used with older pupils, such as paper and pencil tests or question-naires. Qualitative approaches usually involve conducting in-depth case studies, using observations (observation schedules, video-cameras) and inter-views (with children, teachers and sometimes with parents). Case studies allow for diverse collections of facts, while researchers may closely observe interactions between children, IT and the teacher. Through observation, doc-umentation and interpretation of children's goals, strategies and theories, teachers and researchers gain insight into children's thinking. Interviews can reveal the 'how' and 'why' of the teaching and learning processes. These can be reliable methods of collecting data, but they require time and are difficult to accomplish with large samples of learners.

Table 18.1 shows aspects of methodology of specific early childhood research studies using IT. The table is structured by the methods used (quantitative or qualitative approaches), and within each section the order of research studies' appearance is based on children's ages. The range of IT use within a single study is usually narrow, while the programs used across all studies vary from wordprocessing to interactive multimedia. The duration of the intervention varies enormously, from two weeks to two academic years, and the IT sessions range from a few minutes to 40 minutes.

The aims of the research studies vary considerably, ranging from investigating the impact of a specific program on learning and the acquisition or development of specific skills (e.g. Moxley *et al.* 1997, Clements 2000), to designing-constructing and evaluating a child friendly program (e.g. Segers and Verhoeven 2002, Sung *et al.* 2008), up to investigating adult interventions in the IT environment (e.g. Nir-Gal and Klein 2004, Stephen and Plowman 2003b). The methods are linked to the study's aims. Qualitative approaches provide opportunities for in-depth study of the complex settings and the particular circumstances or context of each study. Although the small samples do not allow for generalisation of the results, such studies can tell us with greater accuracy the relationships between learning outcomes and IT activities. Close observations of children's interactions with the software/teacher may reveal specific software features beneficial for young learners (e.g. Labbo *et al.* 2000), as well as types of pedagogic strategies or lack of them (e.g. Stephen and Plowman 2003b).

Limitations of early childhood education studies that set up experimental and control groups include the lack of random assignment of subjects to groups, lack of any sort of intervention activities for the control group and the homogeneity of the sample (Carlson and White 1998). Din and Calao (2001) highlight the difficulty of designing age-appropriate tests and tasks.

Limitations of qualitative types of approaches include the nature and the quality of young children's discourse (children usually amplify their personal experiences) and the context-related learning experiences behind the observable data (Andrews *et al.* 2003).

Methods are linked to a variety of factors such as the aims of the study, the context and the ages of the children involved. Thus, it is restrictive to suggest a single practical method. The research studies illustrate some issues useful in designing or adopting practical research methods.

Issues to be considered when developing or adopting practical methods

The choice of research questions on which research is based is important in determining its value, and researchers should match the methods to learning objectives and learning outcomes they try to measure (Cox 2003).

Table 18.1 Aspects of methodology of specific research studies using IT

Methods used	Country (Researchers)	Software	Ages	Sample size	Duration of intervention (IT sessions)	Results
Quantitative (ex-con* groups, pre-post tests) & observations	UK (Chera & Wood, 2003)	Multimedia talking books	4	30	4 weeks (10 sessions: 10 mins)	Pre-reading skills
Quantitative (ex-con groups, pre-post tests)	Taiwan (Sung et al., 2008)	Multimedia games	4 and 5	60	60 mins	Taxonomic hierarchical Concepts-relationships
Quantitative (questionnaire), questions	Israel (Passig & Levin, 2000)	Interactive multimedia stories	4–5	90		Gender differences in interface design preferences
Quantitative (pre-post tests), questions	Netherlands (Segers & Verhoeven, 2002)	CD-ROM with multimedia	5	30	3 weeks (6 sessions: 15 mins)	Early literacy skills
Quantitative (ex-con groups, pre-post tests)	USA (Din & Calao, 2001)	Playstation, CDs	5.5 5–6	25 47	(3 sessions: 25 mins) 11 weeks (40 mins daily)	Pre-reading skills, development in spelling
Quantitative (pre-post tests)	Israel (Nir-Gal & Klein, 2004)	Games Logo	5–6	150	17 weeks (51 sessions: 20 mins)	Effect of adult mediation on cognitive gains
Quantitative (ex-con groups, pre-post tests)	USA (Carlson & White, 1998)	CD-ROMs	5.5–6,5	32	2 weeks (10 sessions: 10 mins)	Enhancement of understanding of concepts 'right'/'left'
Observations	Australia (Ellis & Blashki, 2004)	Interactive multimedia	2,5–3	9	60–70 mins	Improvement of mouse control
Case study	USA (Moxley et al., 1997)	Wordprocessing, picture-programs	3 and 4	12	2 academic years (15–30 mins)	Improvement in spelling, story development, pre-writing skills
Qualitative-field notes, observations	UK (Marsh, 2006)	Film-editing software	3 and 4	3	1 academic year	Visual literacy skills

Method	Country (Author)	Technology/Tools	Age	Sample	Duration	Findings
Case study, observations, interviews	UK (Siraj-Blatchford & Siraj-Blatchford 2006)	Programmable toys, digital-cameras	3–5	14 pre-school settings	2 academic years	Collaboration-communication, literacy, numeracy, fine motor skills
Observations, interviews	USA (Liu, 1996)	Interactive-multimedia	3–5	12	10 days (10 sessions: 20–35 mins)	Successful use of input devices
Case studies, observations, interviews	UK (Stephen & Plowman, 2003b)	CD-ROMs audiovisual resources	3–5	7 pre-school settings	7 weeks (1–30 mins)	Lack of teacher training and explicit pedagogy
Observations, interviews, field notes	USA (Hutinger & Johanson, 2000)	KidDesk, switches, adaptive devices	3–5	44	3 year project: children with disabilities	Improvement in language, pre/reading-writing, self-confidence, communication
Observations, field notes, interviews	Australia (Romeo et al., 2003)	Jumpstart, Kidpix, Microworlds	3–4 and 5–6	45 and 24	over 7 weeks	Difficulties in using touch screens
Observations	USA (Jones, 1998)	Wordprocessing	3–6	33	3 weeks	Improvement in grammar, increased word density
Observations, pre-post discussions	Canada (Andrews et al., 2003)	Participant simulation	4,5–5,5	11	2 sessions: 24 mins	Acquisition of pre-mathematical skills
Observations, interviews, field notes	USA (Labbo et al., 2000)	CD-ROM talking books, Kidpix	5–6	21	1 academic year	Literacy skills, different modes of interaction with computers
Observations, discussions	USA (Clements, 2000)	Lego-Logo geometric programs, Logo	6–6,5	18	12 weeks	Problem-solving, critical thinking, enhancement of creativity

* ex-con: experimental and control groups

Cultural-political factors also influence the choice of the research methods. The issues discussed below are not independent, but are interrelated.

The nature of young children's learning and development

Any use of computers should take into account the nature of young children's learning and their age. The methods for researching and 'assessing' young children's learning and development in IT environments should be driven by their cognitive and developmental needs. For example, findings that showed children's performance with Logo-based activities to be limited by the children's age and cognitive development impose the need for researchers to understand how learners think (Cox and Marshall 2007). As the computer is a screen-based medium, computer activities cannot be as effective as the use of objects (Yelland 1999). Studies that administer pre- and post-tests to young children have subjects aged four years old or above, whereas case studies often have as subjects three-year-old children.

The type and quality of the software

As young children are increasingly exposed to various types of programs, software type, quality and appropriateness are essential. Researchers (Haugland and Wright 1997) discuss extensively what constitutes developmentally appropriate educational software. The effectiveness of computer learning depends critically on the type and quality of the software, the amount of time children work with the software and the way they use it (Clements and Sarama 2003). Different types of software (e.g. drill and practice, educational games) need to be addressed separately because their impact is expected to be different, and this should be examined in combination with other factors such as adult mediation and learning activities.

The way IT is used: pedagogic approaches, educational activities, amount of time

Literature on early childhood education and IT has emphasised that computer use can be a valuable learning experience when it is utilised in a pedagogically appropriate manner and integrated into the naturalistic learning environment. There is a strong link between research methods and pedagogic approaches, learning activities etc. Adults (teachers, parents, carers) can play an important role in supporting and extending children's experiences with IT. Haugland (1992) has shown that when computer activities are combined with off-computer activities, the learning outcomes can be better. Researchers recommend that kindergarteners do not use computers for longer than 20–40 minutes at a time.

Conclusion

Although the body of empirical evidence has not been conclusive, research studies and reviews of research concur in that the computer can be used as a tool to support young children's learning and development. Researchers need to be aware of ethical issues when conducting research with young children. As the role of IT in young children's learning and development is still debated, there is a need for more empirical studies. As methods are linked to a variety of factors, there is not a single appropriate practical method for every study. Quantitative approaches that use experimental-control groups and paper and pencil tests are practical for children aged four or above, while qualitative approaches are practical for younger children. Research studies with small samples, though not easily generalisable, are valuable in early childhood education settings. Qualitative approaches can reveal how IT is actually used, while interviews with teachers are useful in assisting understanding their goals and views about IT use with children. The more practical methods seem to be those that use or incorporate approaches adapted to the specific context of the study. Issues that should be taken into account are the nature of young children's learning and development, the type and quality of the software, and the way IT is used.

References

Andrews, G., Woodruff, E., McKinnon, K. and Yoon S. (2003) 'Concept development for kindergarten children through a health simulation', *Journal of Computer Assisted Learning*, 19: 209–219.

Cameron, H. (2005) 'Asking the tough questions: a guide to ethical practices in interviewing young children', *Early Child Development and Care*, 175: 597–610.

Carlson, S. and White, S. (1998) 'The effectiveness of a computer program in helping kindergarten students learn the concepts of left and right', *Journal of Computing in Childhood Education*, 9: 133–147.

Chera, P. and Wood, C. (2003) 'Animated multimedia "talking books" can promote phonological awareness in children beginning to read', *Learning and Instruction*, 13: 33–52.

Clements, D. (2000) 'From exercises and tasks to problems and projects – unique contributions of computers to innovative mathematics education', *The Journal of Mathematical Behaviour*, 19: 9–47.

Clements, D. and Sarama, J. (2003) 'Strip mining for gold: research and policy in educational technology – a response to "Fool's Gold"', *Educational Technology Review*, 11: 7–69.

Cordes, C. and Miller, E. (eds) (2000) *Fool's gold: A critical look at computers in childhood*, College Park, MD: Alliance for Childhood. Online. Available HTTP: <http://www.allianceforchildhood.net/projects/computers/computers_reports.htm> (accessed 19 June 2007).

Cox, M. (2003) 'How do we know that ICT has an impact on children's learning? A review of techniques and methods to measure changes in pupils' learning promoted by the use of ICT', in G. Marshall and Y. Katz (eds) *Learning in School, Home and Community, ICT for early and elementary education*, Boston: Kluwer.

Cox, M. and Marshall, G. (2007) 'Effects of ICT: do we know what we should know?', *Education and Information Technologies*, 12: 59–70.

Din, F. and Calao, J. (2001) 'The effects of playing educational videogames on kindergarten achievement', *Child Study Journal*, 31: 95–102.

Ellis, K. and Blashki, K. (2004) 'Toddler Techies: a study of young children's interaction with computers', *Information Technology in Childhood Education*, 1: 77–96.

Flewitt, R. (2005) 'Conducting research with young children: some ethical considerations', *Early Child Development and Care*, 175: 553–565.

Goodwin, L., Goodwin, W., Nansel, A. and Helm, C. (1986) 'Cognitive and affective effects of various types of microcomputer use by preschoolers', *American Educational Research Journal*, 23: 348–356.

Haugland, S. (1992) 'The effect of computer software on preschool children's developmental gains', *Journal of Computing in Childhood Education*, 3: 15–30.

Haugland, S. and Wright, J. (1997) *Young Children and Technology, a world of discovery*, New York: Allyn & Bacon.

Heath, S., Charles, V., Crow, G. and Wiles, G. (2007) 'Informed consent, gatekeepers and go-betweens: negotiating consent in child-and youth-orientated institutions', *British Educational Research Journal*, 33: 403–417.

Hutinger, P. and Johanson, J. (2000) 'Implementing and maintaining an effective early childhood comprehensive technology system', *Topics in Early Childhood Special Education*, 20: 159–173.

Jones, I. (1998) 'The effect of computer generated spoken feedback on kindergarten students' written narratives', *Journal of Computing in Childhood Education*, 9: 43–56.

Labbo, L., Sprague, L., Montero, M. and Font, G. (2000) 'Connecting a computer center to themes, literature and kindergartners' literacy needs' *Reading Online*, 4. Online. Available HTTP: <http://www.readingonline.org/electronic/labbo> (accessed 10 July 2007).

Liu, M. (1996) 'An exploratory study of how pre-kindergarten children use the interactive multimedia technology: implications for multimedia software design', *Journal of Computing in Childhood Education*, 7: 71–92.

Marsh, J. (2006) 'Emergent media literacy: digital animation in early childhood', *Language and Education*, 20: 493–506.

Moxley, R., Warash, B., Coffman, G., Brinton, K. and Concannon, K. (1997) 'Writing development using computers in a class of three-year-olds', *Journal of Computing in Childhood Education*, 8: 133–164.

Nir-Gal, O. and Klein, P. (2004) 'Computers for cognitive development in early childhood – the teachers' role in the computer learning environment', *Information Technology in Childhood Education*, 1: 97–119.

Passig, D. and Levin, H. (2000) 'Gender preferences for multimedia interfaces', *Journal of Computer Assisted Learning*, 16: 64–71.

Romeo, G., Edwards, S., McNamara, S., Walker, I. and Ziguras, C. (2003) 'Touching the screen: issues related to the use of touchscreen technology in early childhood education', *British Journal of Educational Technology*, 34: 329–339.

Segers, E. and Verhoeven, L. (2002) 'Multimedia support of early literacy learning', *Computers & Education*, 39: 207–221.

Siraj-Blatchford, I. and Siraj-Blatchford, J. (2006) *A guide to developing the ICT curriculum for early childhood education*, Oakhill, Staffordshire, UK: Trentham books.

Stephen, C. and Plowman, L. (2003a) 'Information and Communication Technologies in pre-school settings: a review of the literature', *International Journal of Early Years Education*, 11: 223–234.

—— (2003b) *'Come back in two years!' A study of the use of ICT in preschool settings*, Dundee: Learning and Teaching Scotland. Online. Available HTTP: <http://www.ltscotland.org.uk/earlyyears/resources/publications/ltscotland/ComeBackinTwoYears.asp> (accessed 19 June 2007).

Sung, Y., Chang, K. and Lee, M. (2008) 'Designing multimedia games for young children's taxonomic concept development', *Computers & Education*, 50: 1037–1051.

Yelland, N. (1999) 'Reconceptualizing schooling with technology for the 21st century', *Information Technology in Childhood Education Annual*, 1: 39–59.

Chapter 19

Visualisation, multimodality and learning with information technology

John Vincent and Anne McDougall, University of Melbourne, Australia
Herminia Azinian, formerly of University of Buenos Aires, Argentina

Introduction

This chapter argues for students to be able to work in visual modes in various settings. To support the case it describes, as an example, a research project illustrating roles for IT in both the substance and the methodology of study in this area.

Visual literacy, information literacy, and technological literacy are among the multiple literacies needed in the Information Society. Meanwhile at school, children are still immersed mainly in a world of words, as text-based literacy predominates. However, IT tools can generate diverse representations of concepts and data. For instance, in a genetics simulation it is possible to see the characteristics of a subsequent generation by means of a figurative representation (pictures of each offspring), a pie graph (percentages) and numeric fractions. Statistical data can be manipulated graphically to analyse variables and to explore relationships. Dynamic three-dimensional representations in subjects such as mathematics, geography or chemistry enable rotation, or change of proportions or of variables, so that processes as well as effects can be visualised. In mathematics the role of visualisation is important as graphical representations of structures can allow forms of reasoning other than deductive inference, and can assist comprehension. Another well-known application of visual representations to support general learning processes is mind mapping (Buzan 1995).

Salomon (1997) argues that different representational forms require different symbolic capacities, and that appropriate interaction with technologies helps in the development of a richer set of capacities. The use of abstract, symbolic, graphic and figurative visual images (maps, tables, charts, graphs) is central to representation of problems and communication of information, a crucial aspect of successful problem solving.

Many are calling for schools to redefine literacy in the light of new technologies available to young people, to include the multiple modes of expression that exist in the world around us, and especially the visual. Hill (2007) claims that visual and digital literacies and print-based literacy are not oppositional concepts, but that both are required for effective functioning in the 21st Century. She considers the computer as a 'symbol machine', providing the symbolic raw materials that allow children to negotiate a complex interplay of multiple sign systems. Kress (2003) argues for the inclusion of multimodal expression as part of the curriculum.

Multimodality and learning with IT: computer technologies that transform

Daiute (1992) defined children's early expressive work as multimedia experiences. Children in their first year of school are encouraged to express themselves in pictures, in drama, in sounds as well as in symbols that become writing. As children progress through the grades, written expression is generally expected in verbal text. She went on to show that a computer and multimedia software provide visual and other modes in supporting children's literacy, especially those whose literacy development is weak by fourth grade (ten-year-olds). She demonstrated this through using a multimedia computer software environment with three case studies, all reluctant writers. She reasons that technology is a good replacement for the more concrete multimedia of the infant years.

Beavis (2001) described a student who found writing difficult, and spelling and handwriting considerable obstacles. Yet he produced a remarkable multi-layered and multi-semiotic story based on a Nintendo game. Using the technology to create visual effects, he selected fonts to fit the fantasy and pasted in wordprocessed text, and overlayed drawings he had made. He included a personally invented and profusely illustrated map for his game-story and added a computer disc with a music compilation to accompany the reading of the work.

Sutherland (1995) studied a group of fifteen-year-olds who were not succeeding at school mathematics. She analysed their plight as having very sparse use of language and difficulties in expressing themselves in natural language. Yet many of them could solve mathematical problems visually. She illustrates with the case of one student who could not express his 'seeing' in algebraic language, but who learned to communicate this 'seeing' in spreadsheet language.

> I conjecture that many pupils who are unsuccessful in school mathematics have this potential to work with visual systems and the computer could be one way of helping them communicate their ideas within a sentential system, thus helping them develop a more flexible way of working.
>
> (Sutherland 1995: 74).

It is clear that for some students, working in visual modes is vital for both understanding and communication.

Multimodality and text production

Many people are calling for a new computer multimodal literacy, for various reasons: inclusion of visual literacy in the school curriculum; inclusion of popular culture; response to the multimedia world (and ability to be critical of such literacy); extending multimodal classrooms to enrich the overall curriculum, and to provide equity. Fewer, however, have asked serious questions about the role of the computer's multimodal text tools in supporting and scaffolding those for whom verbal literacies are not performing their communicative function. It is this crucial role that will be examined further in this chapter.

Vincent (2009) studied a class of 26 ten-year-olds for one year to examine the relationships between style and text production. The students began the year writing handwritten texts and moved in turn to word-processed texts, and finally to multimodal texts constructed in *Textease* and *MicroWorlds*. In the class was the usual spread of apparent linguistic capabilities with verbal-only texts; four of the 26 students were receiving compensatory support for language, such as reading or spelling help. These four struggled to cope with verbal expression in any form (although one was fluent orally), yet in every other way appeared to be alert and intelligent students. However, their verbal difficulties condemned them to the danger of failing in school. In statewide language tests (wholly verbal) they scored well below the mean for the state and the school, and thus were considered 'at risk'.

Remarkable observations were made when four of these students met multimodal text agents such as *MicroWorlds*. Vincent (2007) reported on Peter, who previously had never written more than ten words at a time, rarely used syntax that even resembled a sentence, and exhibited severe spelling deficiencies. Yet when he came to compose in the multimedia Logo environment *MicroWorlds*, he created a complex, semiotically integrated five-screen multimodal narrative about being lost in a cave. The impact of *MicroWorlds* on Peter was electrifying. In the research observation log there is a reference to Peter becoming 'totally absorbed with possibilities'. He wanted to know what the application could do. During the development sections of each lesson he constantly assailed the teacher with new features he had discovered. He spent the next three weeks tinkering with the 'Cave' narrative. Time, however, was not an issue. A number of research log entries at this stage indicate that Peter was inventing. He set himself problem after problem and then spent long happy hours solving these problems. He begged to be allowed to stay in the classroom at recess times. At lunch he was always to be found in the library with his notebook computer, usually working alone but sometimes collaborating.

In Peter's narrative a 'mood' is set as the narrative opens, by the flashing of the title and the automatic playing of a rather spooky melody. Screen 2 (Figure 19.1) was a complex page and Peter seems to have set and solved all

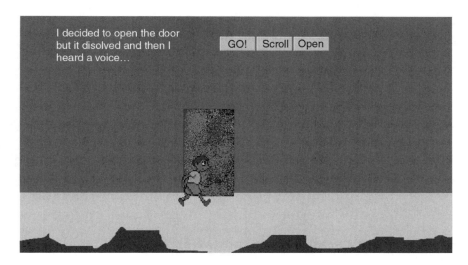

Figure 19.1 'Cave'.

the problems by himself. One problem he worked on for a long time was the animations. A figure walks along near some rocks and approaches a door.

For some reason, probably to do with the spatial balance of the page, Peter did not want the figure to actually move forward, so he devised a way of moving the landscape and giving the illusion of the figure walking, using the 'launch' primitive that he had learned earlier. He wanted more text on the screen than he had room for at the size he had chosen, but he didn't want the text to dominate. The very fact that the problem of needing more text arose is highly significant, because it appears that text was becoming a necessary ingredient for him. Peter's solution to the problem was ingenious. He 'recycled' the text box by adding the text to the programming, so that the text scrolls from a programming command instead of a scroll bar. The text does not stand by itself; it only makes sense when integrated with graphics and sound. The sound is an eerie 'come-in' in a deep voice. A note in the researcher's log records that when asked who recorded it for him, Peter said that it was 'my own voice and I digitally altered it'. However, it is the images, animations and sound that tell the tale. This can be tested by taking out the text, and apart from the fact that the text is needed to link to the voice, and to give instructions ('To see what happens you will have to open it yourself. Click Go!'), meaning is given by the other modes. At the end, the navigation process becomes a semiotic mode itself, carrying meaning by embedding the page change into the opening of the door. The embedded navigation has been programmed with a short 'wait' command. This gives a glimpse of the colourworld that appears later, and activates the bidding voice, before the page changes. On each screen of five, messages are carried by different systems, but each system adds to the whole message.

Peter's work was mirrored by the other three students, all of whom had struggled with words but gloried in multimodal communication. Nina, for instance, created a narrative about a space adventure to a black hole, ending with a screen with no words but a figure getting smaller and smaller and spiralling into a black hole. It is a powerful message, given without words, by a student who practised high-level avoidance of any verbal writing work. One feature of the multimodal material created by these students was the words. Although words never dominated, except for one notable page of typing by Peter, they were used when they were needed. This resulted in far more verbal text than these students normally produced, and it was generally structurally sound. Peter, for instance, prior to this rarely wrote in sentences. In the multimodal text, he always did.

Multimodality scaffolding translation in text production

Csikszentmihalyi (1996) conducted interviews with 91 creative public figures to attempt to find patterns in the origins of their creativity. One pattern that emerged time and again from the respondents was that 'creativity generally involves crossing the boundaries of domains' (Csikszentmihalyi 1996: 9). This represents an idea of translation, of carrying semiotic material over from one semiotic domain to another, and the transformation that occurs when this happens.

However, some evidence suggests that translation and transformation is not an uncommon phenomenon, nor is it restricted to the kinds of exceptionally creative people described by Csikszentmihalyi. There is now a wide range of literature showing that with a computer and its multimodal software, it is possible for creativity to flourish with any individual, not just great creative minds.

Intertextual resonances from a student in Beavis's (2001) study described earlier, who previously found all monomodal (verbal) language difficult, suggest a translation process in which for this student there was a new awakening as he crossed and recrossed modal boundaries carrying semiotic materials. And Sutherland's (1995) study of mathematics students suggests that translation and transformation due to the visual affordances of computer technologies are not restricted to literacy.

Semi-structured interviews were conducted with the students in Vincent's study after they had completed multimodal narratives using *MicroWorlds*. It became clear that students of that age are able to develop deep reflective insights into their semiotic translations. The use of the computer to construct multimedia artefacts has allowed much more fine-grained observations of such translations in progress. Vincent (2007) described how student interviews allowed insights into the semiotic translations that were occurring. In the interviews, Kosta said that because it is faster it helps him not forget what things look like. Both Peter and Kosta claimed they did not carry images in their heads as they wrote. Peter, with the class, had been asked to write a descriptive piece about a candle, and his interview included this exchange:

Interviewer:	And in a description word picture, do you keep a picture in your head?
Peter:	No, not really.
Interviewer:	So how did you do the writing about the candle?
Peter:	Go through words that sound right.

The four students claimed that they could not hold images in their heads, but had to rely on seeing them to use or describe them. They claimed they carried no images, but they were able to use rich imagery, animation, music and sound effects to carry messages when they composed multimodal texts. Crucially, they made the visual, animation and sound messages first, but then used those to provoke and stimulate verbal texts.

It is difficult to escape the notion that the ability to use the computer and its multimedia software to store and move those images is performing a scaffolding function. When Kosta says that 'because of the images, he can see what he's writing about', there is a real sense that he needs the images and animations as concrete means of translating into other message carriers such as words. Vincent (2006) reported that Kosta (student B in that text) later developed this skill (of creating images to translate into words) to create several very substantial multimodal narratives in which verbal text became fluent and accurate, but always subservient to images and animations. A text about an aboriginal tale described in that article was highly accomplished and words began to play an important part.

For such students, computers with multimodal tools became a means of access. They produced multimodal texts that were complex, and utterly integrated. But they also provided an insight to process. They needed the scaffolding of computer-generated imagery and other semiotic modes on the computers in order to translate those into the messages, including words. They were also able to initiate translations across all modes. Their multimodal texts became modally integrated through constant translations.

Different students approach communication in very different ways. In the example from Vincent's study (Vincent 2009) there was a complete range of students in the one class. For some, translation across modes is a mental process, with much of the text-based writing arising from the transmediation, the crossing of semiotic boundaries, for example from images into words. Others struggled with any communication until given the scaffolding of concrete images. The former group far preferred to communicate in verbal modes. The latter group far preferred to work with images, and it was the

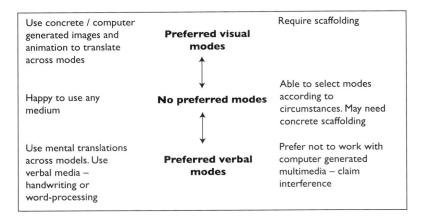

Figure 19.2 Preferred communication modes continuum.

computer that allowed them to construct their multimodal texts. In between were students with many transitional styles, some of whom were able to switch from verbal to visual communication at will. Figure 19.2 summarises this situation.

By exploring the process of literacy expression through multimodal computer tools, there is an unfolding story in which communication styles and text production are intricately woven together as students move from monomodal to multimodal contexts. There is a wide range of changes that take place when the students move from verbal monomodal contexts to multimodal contexts. Here, it is being asserted that there is a very substantial growth in textual complexity and success in message giving for certain students, mainly those who are otherwise struggling in the classroom.

Conclusion

One of the surprises of the twenty-first century has been the impact of computer-generated multimedia in helping language-constrained students to communicate effectively. For many students, those for whom expressing themselves in words is both difficult and intensely disliked, the discovery of a multimodal world in a computer is a blessing of major proportions.

Vincent's work indicates that provision of computer-based multimedia as an option for expressive work could be considered an equity issue, overcoming the unwillingness and inability of some students to work with words, while compulsion to use multimedia may disenfranchise those who normally succeed verbally. The research project we have described concerns the particular area of multimodality and children's expressive writing. Further investigations of these and similar questions in a range of curriculum areas are needed, and much more research is needed into the role of the teacher and teacher communicative style in the complex functioning system that is a classroom.

References

Beavis, C. (2001) 'Digital culture, digital literacies: expanding notions of text', in C. Durrant and C.Beavis (eds) *P(ICT)ures of English: teachers, learners and technology*, Adelaide: Wakefield Press.

Buzan, T. (1995) *The Mind Map Book*, London: BBC Books.

Csikszentmihalyi, M. (1996) *Creativity: flow and the psychology of discovery and invention*, New York: Harper Collins.

Daiute, C. (1992) 'Multimedia composing: extending the resources of the Kindergarten to writers across the grades', *Language Arts*, 69: 250–260.

Hill, S (2007) 'Multiliteracies in early childhood', in R. New and M. Cochran (eds) *Early Childhood Education: an international encyclopedia*, Vol. IV, Westport CT: Praeger.

Kress, G. (2003) *Literacy in the New Media Age*, London: Routledge.

Salomon, G. (1997) 'Of mind and media', *Phi Delta Kappan*, 78: 375–380.

Sutherland, R. (1995) 'Mediating mathematical action', in R. Sutherland and J. Mason (eds) *Exploiting Mental Imagery with Computers in Mathematics Education*, Berlin: Springer.

Vincent, J. (2006) 'Children writing: multimodality and assessment in the writing classroom', *Literacy*, 40: 51–57.

—— (2007) 'Writing and coding: assisting writers to cross the modes', *Language and Education*, 21: 141–157.

—— (2009) *Computer Mediated Multimodal Text Production: ten-year-olds crossing semiotic boundaries*, Cologne: Lambert.

Chapter 20

Research in the field of intelligent computer-aided assessment

*Christine Bescherer and Christian Spannagel,
University of Education Ludwigsburg, Germany
Ulrich Kortenkamp, University of Education
Karlsruhe, Germany
Wolfgang Müller, University of Education
Weingarten, Germany*

Assessment

Assessment is the 'systematic evaluative appraisal of an individual's ability and performance in a particular environment or context' (Payne 1997: 474). In classrooms it usually involves artefacts such as papers, written tests, presentations and portfolios, as well as teacher observations, oral contributions, or learner presentations. Summative assessment is the type used for grading, ranking, or awarding certificates. Assessment may also be used to support validation and improvement of learning and teaching; then it 'becomes formative assessment when the evidence is actually used to adapt the teaching work to meet learning needs' (Black *et al*. 2004: 10).

In many school systems (e.g. in Germany) summative assessment still plays the major role. However, forms of summative assessment have changed during the last ten years, and ideas on new forms of assessment following the use of open-ended problems and collaborative work in classrooms have influenced teaching and assessment practices (cf. Grunder and Bohl 2001). Relevant publications are typically teacher guides and worksheet examples (see for example Race *et al*. 2005). Still, there remains a major question of how to achieve fair grading of students working, for example, on open-ended problems or in collaborative settings.

In other countries the idea of formative assessment is more accepted; e.g. the 'assessment for learning' initiatives in English-speaking countries. Black and Wiliam (1998) advocate formative assessment as essential in classroom work, arguing its potential to raise standards of teaching and learning. Both summative and formative assessment require a variety of approaches and procedures; nevertheless, the general techniques for assessment – collecting and processing information – remain similar.

For formative assessment, students must be assessed individually and continuously or repeatedly to provide the information necessary to adjust teaching and learning. In classes with thirty and more students, teachers don't have the time to observe individual students sufficiently, or to grade daily tests; they often just check parts of the homework, or observe only a few students per day. To include all students permanently in the process of formative assessment, tools are needed to collect data, to pre-select good or bad examples, to identify non-standard solutions, to visualise results, and to show statistics.

IT-based assessment has been proposed as a solution to this problem. Computer Aided Assessment (CAA) refers to approaches to assessing students' performance using a computer. CAA promises that test results can be analysed and compared with minimal effort in minimal time, enabling more regular assessments than is possible otherwise. Thus, teachers could gain more detailed knowledge of students' progress and identify problems earlier. Further, tests could be tailored to match students' abilities.

CAA is widely used in distance learning and in higher education, where the number of students is much larger than in schools, and assessments require even more resources. It is also being used for comparative assessments between schools and institutions. However, CAA has hardly made it into the classroom. There are several reasons for this (Chalmers and McAusland 2002). CAA techniques are usually restricted to assessing factual knowledge using objective tests and multiple-choice questions. The construction of these tests is very time consuming and requires very specific knowledge.

'Intelligent Assessment' refers to another approach to IT-based assessment. It is based on assessment tools that assess and analyse not only students' products, but also the processes of their generation. This semi-automatic approach enables detection and filtering of standard solutions and errors. Unusual and novel solutions that cannot be categorised automatically are forwarded to teachers for 'human' assessment.

A problem with analysing processes for feedback or assessment is the sheer number of potentially correct and incorrect solutions. In many programs for mathematics it is possible for correct answers obtained by alternative solution strategies to be evaluated as incorrect. Possible mistakes are individual in nature and unlimited in number. Consequently, intelligent assessment must not restrict students to the preconceived solution paths of test developers. This requires the integration of expert systems to minimise the number of possibly unrecognised solutions.

Examples of intelligent assessment

Intelligent assessment with the focus on semi-automatic analysis methods is an emerging field of research. To show the viability of this approach, we give three examples in the context of mathematics education, based on prototypical implementations or adaptations of existing software. From these, we develop research questions to encourage educators, researchers, and technologists to engage in intelligent assessment projects and to direct research in this new area.

Saraswati

Saraswati (Bescherer *et al.* 2004) is an example of an intelligent assessment system in the field of algebra, for solving linear systems of equations. The system provides a complete framework for authoring and solving exercises as well as their assessment and analysis.

The *Saraswati* analyser component plays the key role in this system. Its purpose is to grasp the process of reaching a solution, not only its correctness. It checks the correctness of each individual transformation step, and applies heuristics to identify types of errors and possible corrections. It examines transformations in the light of previous errors, and collects and compiles all assessment results to provide statistics and detailed information on both individual students' and class level performances.

Cinderella

Cinderella, an interactive geometry intelligent tutoring system (Richter-Gebert and Kortenkamp 1999) applies an automatic theorem checking technique to support assessment. The *Dynamic Geometry System* (Kortenkamp 1999) acts as an authoring tool for geometric construction exercises. Based on a sample solution, one or several checkpoints in the construction sequence may be defined, together with individual help and comments for students that are stuck. Students can ask for hints. The software recognises geometric elements independently of their formal definition using an automatic theorem proving approach. It then decides which hint is appropriate. Help and hints are provided in text messages, automatically opened web-pages, or by automatically adding missing elements to the construction. The same data is used without explicit request all the time during the solution process to monitor the student's progress, give additional information, and finally to check whether the desired result has been reached.

CleverPHL

CleverPHL is a capture and replay tool that combines screen videos with the analysis of log files (Spannagel *et al.* 2005; Schroeder and Spannagel 2006). *CleverPHL* can be used with learning tools written in Java; thus, it is not restricted to a special subject domain and has wide applicability. In mathematics it can be used to log and analyse solution processes, for example in Java-based interactive geometry systems or spreadsheet calculators.

With *CleverPHL*, user actions such as mouse motion and clicks, or keyboard input can be captured and stored as detailed, chronologically ordered 'interaction records'. Furthermore, *CleverPHL* provides a plug-in mechanism to add modules capturing more expressive actions on the target application (semantic events). *CleverPHL* also offers automatic analysis of interaction records. Sub-sequences of actions can be grouped to build high-level actions (cf. Hilbert and Redmiles 2000). The combination of several semantic events into larger units helps to recognise and describe solution processes of (mathematical) problems. To support the analysis of user behaviour in a specific learning tool, new high-level actions can be added to *CleverPHL's* analysis engine by implementing detection algorithms for specific action sequences.

Research questions

For application of the paradigm shown in the three preceding examples to different subjects and technologies, a number of open research questions arise. These can be roughly organised into two classes: content-specific and technology-specific. This distinction is superficial as content-specific questions must be answered with technological feasibility in mind, and computer-based solutions must relate to content-specific demands. We propose five questions regarding intelligent computer-aided assessment focusing on process knowledge. This is not intended to be exhaustive – a list of research questions never is!

Content-specific research questions

1. *What are the identifiable categories of mistakes in a specific subject area or in a concrete task?*
    This is mainly a task for educators, but the viewpoint is very different when these categories are to be used to describe software behaviour. This problem has to be tackled from two directions: students' solutions have to be collected and categorised in a bottom-up manner, while a theoretical framework of mistakes has to be developed top-down.
2. *How can we measure the distance of two solution processes?*
    Such a measure is important in order to compare students' solution processes to a prototypical one, or two different solutions with each other, and for the detection of plagiarism (cf. Saikkonen *et al.* 2001).

Technology-specific research questions

3. *Which error classes and patterns identified in Question 1 can be described in a way detectable by software?*
    Errors need to be specified formally to enable automatic detection. Means for describing correct and erroneous processes must be developed. It must be possible to describe and evaluate partial solutions (Ashton *et al.* 2006). There are areas where it is not possible to assess

using technology only (Jackson 2000), but better some automatic assessment than none at all.

4. *How can comprehensive process information be retrieved from event recordings and log files?*
   Technologies for process recording need to be developed or improved and applied in different contexts, and interfaces for statistical treatment have to be provided. Yet the recording of the processes alone does not solve the problem. The detection of meaningful events in the recorded process path is still a challenging task, and system events have to be mapped to accomplished steps in solving the problem.

5. *How can intelligent assessment be organised in a normal school situation?*
   Workable solutions have to be found for organisational issues such as whether the assessment task can be done at home or only under supervision. In addition, technological dependability must be ensured, and means of quality assurance must be implemented (cf. Harwood 2005).

Summary

The characteristics of intelligent computer-aided assessment of process knowledge have been described, and three examples used to illustrate the feasibility of technical implementations of intelligent assessment. Open research questions have been formulated for this new field of computer-supported assessment.

Future work should investigate how formative assessment can benefit from methods of intelligent computer-aided assessment. Today we are still far from a broad-based implementation of summative and formative intelligent assessment in our classrooms. Yet we believe that computer-aided semi-automatic intelligent assessment has the power to enhance the acquisition of process skills in primary, secondary, and higher education.

References

Ashton, H.S., Beevers, C.E., Korabinski, A.A. and Youngson, M.A. (2006) 'Incorporating partial credit in computer-aided assessment of mathematics in secondary education', *British Journal of Educational Technology*, 37: 93–119.

Bescherer, C., Müller, W., Heinrich, F. and Mettenheimer, S. (2004) 'Assessment and semi-automatic analysis of test results in mathematical education', in L. Cantoni amd C. McLoughlin (eds) *Proceedings of ED-MEDIA 2004 – World Conference on Educational Multimedia, Hypermedia & Telecommunications*, Chesapeake, VA: AACE.

Black, P. and Wiliam, D. (1998) 'Inside the black box: raising standards through classroom assessment', *Phi Delta Kappan,* 80: 139–148.

Black, P., Harrison, C., Lee, C., Marshall, B. and Wiliam, D. (2004) 'Working inside the black box: assessment for learning in the classroom', *Phi Delta Kappan*, 86: 9–21.

Chalmers, D. and McAusland, W.D.M. (2002) 'Computer-assisted Assessment', in J. Houston and D. Whigham (eds) *The Handbook for Economics Lecturers: assessment*, Bristol: Economics LTSN. Online. Available at HTTP: <http://www.economics.ltsn.ac.uk/handbook/> (accessed 18 February 2009).

Grunder, H-U. and Bohl, T. (eds) (2001) *Neue Formen der Leistungsbeurteilung in den Sekundarstufen I und II*, Baltmannsweiler, Germany: Schneider-Verlag.

Harwood, I. (2005) 'When summative computer-aided assessments go wrong: disaster recovery after a major failure', *British Journal of Educational Technology*, 36: 587–597.

Hilbert, D. M. and Redmiles, D. F. (2000) 'Extracting usability information from user interface events', *ACM Computing Surveys*, 32: 384–421.

Jackson, D. (2000) 'A semi-automated approach to online assessment', in D. Joyce (ed.) *Proceedings of the 5th Annual SIGCSE/SIGCUE Conference on Innovation and Technology in Computer Science Education (ITiCSE2000)*, New York: ACM.

Kortenkamp, U. (1999) 'Foundations of dynamic geometry', unpublished doctoral thesis, Swiss Federal Institute of Technology, Zurich.

Payne, D. (1997) *Applied Educational Assessment*, Belmont, CA: Wadworth Publishing.

Race, P., Brown, S. and Smith, B. (2005) *500 Tips on Assessment*, 2nd edn, London: Routledge Falmer.

Richter-Gebert, J. and Kortenkamp, U. (1999) *The Interactive Geometry Software Cinderella*, Heidelberg: Springer-Verlag. Online. Available HTTP: <http://cinderella.de> (accessed 19 February 2009).

Saikkonen, R., Malmi, L. and Korhonen, A. (2001). 'Fully automatic assessment of programming exercises', in D. Finkel (ed.) *Proceedings of the 6th Annual SIGCSE/ SIGCUE Conference on Innovation and Technology in Computer Science Education (ITiCSE2001)*, New York: ACM.

Schroeder, U. and Spannagel, C. (2006) 'Supporting the active learning process', *International Journal on E-Learning*, 5: 245–264.

Spannagel, C., Gläser-Zikuda, M. and Schroeder, U. (2005) 'Application of qualitative content analysis in user-program interaction research', *Forum Qualitative Sozialforschung / Forum: Qualitative Social Research*, 6. Online. Available at HTTP: <http://www.qualitative-research.net/fqs-texte/2-05/05-2-29-e.htm> (accessed 18 February 2009).

Chapter 21

Information technology learning aids for informatics

Sigrid Schubert, Peer Stechert and Stefan Freischlad
University of Siegen, Germany

Methodology of research in didactics of informatics

IT research deals with two aspects: IT as subject matter, and IT used as learning material. In this chapter we investigate the development of IT learning aids. The contribution of didactics of informatics is the transfer of experiences from the subject Informatics to other subjects. We give criteria for the development and evaluation process from both didactic and informatics perspectives, describe a methodology for development of IT-based learning aids, and reflect on its benefits and drawbacks.

Learners come with intuitions when they use informatics systems or want to explain how they work. If these intuitions do not match the behaviour of the system and result in wrong conclusions, they cause cognitive barriers. Identification of such barriers provided the starting point for the development of learning aids that enable learners to overcome these barriers through experiments.

Generalisation of results is not important here, so we have used a case-based methodology. We choose two case studies in the area of understanding of informatics systems. Informatics systems can be investigated according to their behaviour (A), their internal structure (B), and implementation details (C). Learners have to combine these three views to see the whole picture (Stechert and Schubert 2007). As an example, we will discuss IT-based exercises on observable system behaviour (A) and its combination with its internal structure (AB). Exercises for A comprise investigating, classifying and documenting the behaviour of the system. The aim of these observation activities is to prepare learners to conduct experiments, using a systematic approach to prove a hypothesis. For learners' first experiments, the teacher provides the hypothesis (A). For experiments of type AB, the typical task is conducting an experiment that includes creation of hypotheses by the learner about the internal structure of the system and consequences for its behaviour.

The first learning aid in this case study is a program where different users have different access rights, realised with a proxy design pattern controlling access. Learners can switch the proxy off to observe and document different behaviour. Learning objectives are:

- $S_{A,1}$: Understand the fundamental idea of access control and the need for access control via investigating the behaviour of the program
- $S_{AB,1}$: Understand the fundamental idea of access control via description of objects that participate in the scenario.

The second learning aid contains an animation and two exercises to describe dynamic processes within an automated teller machine, which is also realised with a proxy.

The learning objectives are:

- $S_{A,2}$: Understand the fundamental idea of access control via observation and documentation of an animation
- $S_{AB,2}$: Learners are able to describe the dynamic process of access control via sequence diagrams, and assign activities to the persons and objects involved.

Cognitive barriers and expected misconceptions

Within the case study the educational concept is based on the *Didactic System* (Freischlad and Schubert 2007). This approach has already been applied successfully for object-oriented modelling. The *Didactic System* comprises three components that affect one another:

- exercise classes used to create high-quality exercises for the learning process
- knowledge structures that describe the structure of the learning process with the learning objectives
- learning software, such as exploration modules.

The use of these learning aids leaves the design of the learning process to the teacher. Exercise classes provide data on the activities of the learners within the learning process. In this section we illustrate cognitive barriers to understanding of access control and the consequences for the development of an IT learning aid.

To understand access control it is necessary that normally undisclosed processes are observable by students and that these processes can be manipulated by them. One expected misconception is that an object such as a document itself evaluates a request for accessing it; however, for security and performance reasons, there will actually be a placeholder having the same appearance as the object, and this can evaluate access rights, count the number of access attempts, and redirect the call to the right object. The placeholder can have the same appearance as the original object, and this is a known barrier. The relevant informatics principle is 'inheritance'. If the original object and the placeholder inherit from the same abstract class, both will have the same interface, but they will have distinct specialisations. For example, the original object will permit important data to be obtained through an operation called 'show data'. If a user tries to get access to the object calling its operation 'show data', the placeholder will be activated instead. The placeholder's operation 'show data' consists of confirming access rights, and if successful will call the object's operation.

Furthermore, informatics education aims to enable learners to describe dynamic processes using formal diagrams. Learners should be able to formalise a real-life situation as a first step towards machine processing. Formalisation is also a known cognitive barrier. We need formalisation to permit description of real-life situations, and to identify the abstract concept of a design pattern which can be applied to further situations. The fundamental ideas of informatics, access control and inheritance, are part of a network of fundamental ideas. Here, IT learning aids come into play. Learners need practical approaches to such abstract concepts to avoid misconceptions.

Learners' activities provided by IT learning aids

The development of IT learning aids has to be done in the light of known cognitive barriers and misconceptions. To illustrate the principle of access control it is necessary to observe the processing behind the graphical user interface. To explain how the process can be realised, a design pattern is used as a typical representation in informatics. Its structure describes both a static and a dynamic view of the process. To understand fundamental networked ideas within one design pattern in an information system, an exploratory approach is required. IT learning aids enable interaction with the principles of the informatics system. The combination of learners' different views and, particularly, changes in views caused by experimentation by the learners, is essential for the learning process. The guided use of selected basic functions within a bounded subscenario is typical of IT learning aids.

The module on access control starts with an animation illustrating this process $(S_{A,2})$ via a placeholder. This animation should avoid learners' misconceptions, for instance that an object controls access to itself. Later, learners will start with diagram-based exercises to describe the internal structure during the real-life process of withdrawing money at an automated teller machine $(S_{AB,2})$. This means that informatics notation of design patterns in a static class diagram is combined with a real-world view, overcoming the cognitive barrier associated with inheritance. The user of the program can only decide whether there is a proxy supervising access from the program's behaviour $(S_{AB,1})$.

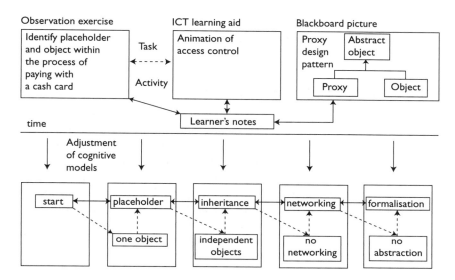

Figure 21.1 Exemplary cognitive development supported by learning aid.

The cognitive barrier of formalisation is difficult to overcome. The given class diagram is another formal representation that assists learners to formalise their concepts. A Help function, that can be called by learners while they are solving the exercise, supports the learner-centred approach by providing a description of how to deal with the type of exercise efficiently and how to construct a formal sequence diagram illustrating the process of access control. Such Help functionality shows another aspect of IT learning aids within the learning process. Students must give time and effort to achieving media competence. Figure 21.1 shows how the IT learning aid can enhance the learning process.

Most software is not designed for educational purposes. Using it in schools is problematic: the application is necessary but there is no opportunity for teachers and learners to investigate its structure. Therefore, we need IT learning aids that enable learners to actively investigate complex informatics artefacts. Theoretical analysis of the learning process must precede the development of learning aids. The process must be described and informatics concepts must be identified. Learning objectives and learner activities are determined. Afterwards the software is trialled using criteria such as the benefit of the digital media, and possibilities for learner interaction and achieving learning objectives. In this case, real-life examples appropriate to exemplify informatics concepts were selected. These scenarios are important for learners' motivation and to bridge the gap between learners' previous knowledge and new abstract concepts. We utilise the efficiency of research methods of informatics and didactics of informatics, that is, modularisation and structuring, to ensure reusability of learning material.

Evaluation of the learning process

In the learning process, access control was introduced via a placeholder, that is, a proxy. Learners have the concept of a placeholder and its substitution from their daily life experience. We started the lesson on access control with an animation showing a cash card as a placeholder for coins ($S_{A,2}$). Learners became aware of different kinds of access control via proxy, for instance, there is a protection functionality, and additional actions such as storing data about the use of the card can be performed. Following this animation, the second learning aid was introduced. This was a program realising different access rights for the roles of administrator, user, and guest. An administrator has read and write access to a file, a user is able to read a file, and a guest is neither allowed to read nor to write while there is a proxy controlling access. The proxy can be switched off by learners and the behaviour of the system can be observed. The learners described the different access rights in a table ($S_{A,1}$) and discovered analogies to real-life situations leading to hypotheses about behaviour; that is, they expected a certain behaviour on a certain input.

The research methodology exemplified in this case study specifically connects methods of empirical research with the procedure model of engineering science informatics. To evaluate the case study we interviewed the teacher, and the learners answered a questionnaire. The teacher gave information about the use of the learning aids within the learning process, whereas the learners meta-cognitively described their own learning process for each learning objective.

This chapter has discussed the development and application of small pieces of learning software for understanding of informatics systems. The automated teller machine example is a module within a more complex learning software product, *Pattern Park* (see http://www.die.informatik.uni-siegen.de/pgpatternpark). For its development an iterative software development process was applied to ensure high quality of the software: correctness, efficiency, portability, robustness, usability, and maintainability. The challenge of the development process was to ensure successful support of the learning process with the learning aid. The development was informed by educational research data from testing in a school. This evaluation focused on acceptance by learners and has led to a refinement of modules. Learning software also supports further exercises on the observable behaviour, internal structure and implementation details of informatics systems as well as the combinations of these views.

References

Freischlad, S. and Schubert, S. (2007) 'Towards high quality exercise classes for internetworking', in D. Benzie and M. Iding (eds) *Proceedings of IFIP-Conference IMICT 2007*, Boston: IFIP. Online. Available HTTP: <www.die.informatik.uni-siegen.de/ifip-wg31/publications.html> (accessed 16 February 2009).

Stechert, P. and Schubert, S. (2007) 'A strategy to structure the learning process towards understanding of informatics systems', in D. Benzie and M. Iding (eds) *Proceedings of IFIP-Conference IMICT 2007*, Boston: IFIP. Online. Available HTTP: <www.die.informatik.uni-siegen.de/ifip-wg31/publications.html> (accessed 16 February 2009).

Index